"Pamela McCarroll makes an eloquent plea for North American Christians to commit a subversive and countercultural act. Her creative application of the theology of the cross effectively reinterprets our primary vocation in terms of waiting in hope, open to a hidden God whom we cannot master. This book is important for all who are caught in systems of modernity that limit hope to what we can imagine."

—SARAH TRAVIS
Adjunct Professor of Homiletics, Knox College, University of Toronto, Canada

"*Waiting at the Foot of the Cross* is a compelling invitation to reconsider the theology of the cross in a North American context through the complementary lenses of George Grant and Douglas John Hall. Far more than simply a recapitulation of Grant and Hall, however, the discussion turns over new theological ground and offers a thick account of hope as 'waiting' that is both prophetic and consoling. McCarroll has written an important and timely book."

—THOMAS E. REYNOLDS
Associate Professor of Theology, Emmanuel College, University of Toronto, Canada

Waiting at the Foot of the Cross

DISTINGUISHED DISSERTATIONS
IN CHRISTIAN THEOLOGY

Series Foreword

We are living in a vibrant season for academic Christian theology. After a hiatus of some decades, a real flowering of excellent systematic and moral theology has emerged. This situation calls for a series that showcases the contributions of newcomers to this ongoing and lively conversation. The journal *Word & World: Theology for Christian Ministry* and the academic society Christian Theological Research Fellowship (CTRF) are happy to cosponsor this series together with our publisher Pickwick Publications (an imprint of Wipf and Stock Publishers). Both the CTRF and *Word & World* are interested in excellence in academics but also in scholarship oriented toward Christ and the Church. The volumes in this series are distinguished for their combination of academic excellence with sensitivity to the primary context of Christian learning. We are happy to present the work of these young scholars to the wider world and are grateful to Luther Seminary for the support that helped make it possible.

Alan G. Padgett
Professor of Systematic Theology
Luther Seminary

Beth Felker Jones
Assistant Professor of Theology
Wheaton College

www.ctrf.info
www.luthersem.edu/word&world

Waiting at the Foot of the Cross

Toward a Theology of Hope for Today

PAMELA R. McCARROLL

FOREWORD BY
DOUGLAS JOHN HALL

PICKWICK *Publications* · Eugene, Oregon

WAITING AT THE FOOT OF THE CROSS
Toward a Theology of Hope for Today

Distinguished Dissertations in Christian Theology 11

Pickwick Publications
An Imprint of Wipf and Stock Publishers
199 W. 8th Ave., Suite 3
Eugene, OR 97401

www.wipfandstock.com

ISBN 13: 978-1-62032-063-1

Cataloguing-in-Publication data:

McCarroll, Pamela R.

Waiting at the foot of the cross : toward a theology of hope for today / Pamela R. McCarroll ; foreword by Douglas John Hall.

Distinguished Dissertations in Christian Theology 11

xxvi + 220 pp. ; 23 cm. Includes bibliographical references.

ISBN 13: 978-1-62032-063-1

1. Jesus Christ—Crucifixion. 2. Grant, George Parkin, 1918–1988. 3. Hall, Douglas John, 1928–. I. Title. II. Series.

BT453 .M32 2014

Manufactured in the U.S.A.

This book is dedicated to my parents
Kathy Smith McCarroll,
who taught me to live the faith as justice, love and radical hospitality,
and
Paul McCarroll,
who taught me to think the faith with my heart, never settling for easy
answers amidst the struggles and messiness of life.

Contents

Foreword

Douglas John Hall

With this book, Pamela McCarroll joins the growing company of younger theologians who are finding in the tradition Martin Luther named "theology of the cross" a *different* way of understanding Christian faith and of being a Christian people. It is not accidental that that company includes several women who, in the attempt to move beyond the triumphalism of the Christian past, with its inevitable patriarchalism, see in the crucified Christ not a valorization of suffering but an affirmation of divine solidarity with all *human and creaturely* pain.

As Jürgen Moltmann so succinctly put it, the *theologia crucis* has never been "much loved."[1] In English-speaking Christianity, however, it has not only been unloved, but (with a few notable exceptions) practically unheard-of. This cannot be separated, I suspect, from the fact that English-speaking Christianity, particularly in the post-Reformation period, has been inextricably bound up with empire—the British Empire and now, even more ubiquitously, the American Empire. Victorious empires are hardly cultural contexts in which Luther's *crux sola nostra theologia*[2] could achieve popular appeal! Ours has been (our churches still love to declare it) "a *resurrection* faith." Ernst Käsemann, who countered that "the resurrection *is a chapter in the theology of the cross,*" also insightfully observed that Anglo-Saxon Christians generally assume that any reference to a "theology of the cross" is a reference to the doctrine of the atonement.[3]

---

1. *Crucified God*, 3.
2. "The cross alone is our theology," drawing from St. Paul in 1 Cor 2.
3. "Pauline Theology of the Cross," 151.

But *theologia crucis* connotes a whole way of "doing" theology; it is a spirit and method of reflection on the core events and texts of the faith that differs markedly from the manner in which the historic Church from Constantine onward represents Christianity. Luther called the latter *theologia gloriae*: "theology of glory." Important and profound exceptions notwithstanding, the Christian Religion, following its Constantinian-Theodosian Establishment, has shown up in human history as a religion of and for "winners." Catholic and Protestant Orthodoxies offered people an *ultimate* victory (heaven, or being numbered among the Elect); humanistic Christian liberalism championed more worldly forms of winning; but either way Christianity appealed to a very human desire to overcome the limits of creaturehood and attain . . . "salvation." Such "salvation" not only implied a subtle rejection of the essential goodness of creation; it also failed notoriously to address the suffering that inheres in creatureliness.[4]

The triumphalism of empirical Christianity has been most blatant, however, in the ecclesiology that it engenders: the *theologia gloriae* quite naturally begets an *ecclesia gloriae*. It is seen to be the duty and destiny of the Christian religion to "win the world for Christ." *Christendom* (that is, the dominion of the Christian religion) is thus not, in this understanding, a novel and biblically questionable development in the evolution of Christianity, occurring under the impact of Christianity's fourth-century radical politicization; rather, it is the logical and even "necessary" flowering of an aggressively missionary faith. Thus, in the "Christian" West, empire after empire has claimed the victorious Christ, crucified by empire, as its spiritual foundation. Ironically, the One who "was despised and rejected" by both secular and religious power became the titular "corner stone" of a faith that has been the great inspirer of successful systems and successful people.

But . . . *"the human story is not a success story"!* These words[5] were written beneath an artist's portrait of Reinhold Niebuhr that appeared on the cover of TIME Magazine's 25th anniversary edition, March 8, 1948; and as such they may be thought to herald the inauguration, on the part of a small but significant minority of Christians in North America, of the need for a new—or perhaps very old—way of thinking about the spirit and meaning of the Christian faith. That need had already become

---

4. See my *God and Human Suffering*.

5. In an earlier, less gender-conscious form, read "Man's story is not a success story."

conspicuous in Europe, where avowedly Christian nations had so recently engaged in slaughtering one another.

What became "Neo-Orthodoxy" but was first called "theology of crisis" and "dialectical theology" was a courageous response to that need. If any justification whatever can be found for considering the Christian thinkers loosely associated with Karl Barth a "new" form of Christian "orthodoxy," it is only because, over against the reigning liberalism *and* the old, moribund orthodoxies of Christendom, Barth and his generation of critical theologians and biblical scholars demanded a return to foundational *biblical* themes—the transcendence ("wholly otherness") of the God of Bethel and of Golgotha, the radicality of evil, the ubiquity and mystery of sin as alienation, the priority of divine grace over human volition, the delicate dialectic of continuity/discontinuity between reason and revelation, etc. The theology of crisis was a renunciation of the modern illusion of human mastery and a poignant testimony to the pathos of the human condition—a condition that requires stronger medicine than rote recitations of the Nicene Creed or moral exhortation with Jesus as the Great Example.

Predictably enough, Barth's theology has been taken up in later decades by many who promote forms of religious certitude and finality that Barth himself would never have condoned. Though he was perhaps a little naïve about the manner in which his ideas could be *used*, Barth had no intention of issuing yet another version of the *theologia gloriae*. While Barth's later works, written in the wake of Europe's degradation and ruin, may tend to accentuate too unguardedly the motif of triumph, those who have followed the evolution of Barth's theology *from its beginnings* understand that the only triumph Karl Barth intends to celebrate is that of Jesus Christ, which is a victory *for* humanity but never *of* humanity. By no stretch of the imagination could it be claimed that Karl Barth trumpets the Christian religion, or the superiority of "the Christian West," or the glories of the Church. At bottom, Karl Barth's theology remains a "theology of the cross"—though he himself, perhaps (as I shall suggest later) with justification, mistrusted that nomenclature because of what it had come to connote in certain "Lutheran" or "Nordic" settings.

If that is understood, it will also be understood that, contrary to much of the discussion of subsequent decades, there was and is a remarkable consonance in the great outpouring of Christian theology that later generations have grouped together under the (highly questionable) label, "Neo-Orthodoxy."[6] Those whose names are usually cited in that classification (Barth, Brunner, Bonhoeffer, the Niebuhrs, Tillich, and others) certainly do not agree easily on many important subjects. It is well known that Brunner accused Barth of denying humanity *any* capacity for revealed truth; that Bonhoeffer lamented Barth's "positivism of revelation"; that Barth and many other Protestant thinkers considered Tillich more a philosopher than a theologian; that Reinhold Niebuhr was uncomfortable with Barth's "Biblicism," and that Niebuhr himself was thought by some nothing but a "reconstructed Liberal," etc., etc. *However,* despite their differences and viewing the whole "Neo-Orthodox" movement from a twenty-first century perspective, it may and should be seen that they are *all* engaged in a critical deconstruction of Christendom's *theologia gloriae* and a search for something like the theology of the cross.[7] They are looking for a way into the future for a faith that can no longer be driven by religious *hubris,* ecclesiastical bravado, and Western imperialism. They are conscious in a new way, not only of the violence inherent in militant Christianity, but also of the enormous discrepancy between the biblical God of justice and compassion and the omnipotent deity of historic Christianity. In a beginning sort of way they are also newly aware of the non-Christian faiths,[8] whose presence and reality they have encountered in the clash of civilizations that had been opened up by two global wars: a faith driven by the need to "win the world for Christ" could only be part of the problem—a very large part of it!—in such a pluralistic world society.

It is surely one of the most unfortunate turns in the evolution of Christian thought that the work of these great exponents of Christian faith who were active in the first six decades of the twentieth century did not filter down into the pews of the churches. While their *names* have been remembered by many, and *aspects* of their thinking still make their way into Christian scholarly discourse (even now and then the secular

---

6. See my *Remembered Voices.*

7. Tillich may have understood this more than most. In a conversation in the late 1960s, Marcus Barth told me that upon his return to America after a final return to Europe and visits with Barth and many other old friends, Paul Tillich had said to him (Marcus Barth) that "Your father and I, despite our earlier differences, have been saying *the same things* really." This can be attributed to Tillich's well-known "inclusiveness," but it should, I feel, be understood as a genuine sense of theological camaraderie.

8. See in particular the works of Hendrik Kraemer.

press), the profoundly radical nature of their vision simply did not penetrate the life of the churches. Perhaps it was too soon: well into the 1960s, the churches, especially in North America, could still be considered "going concerns"; their continuing numerical and economic viability kept them from becoming serious about their *de facto* disestablishment. The challenge of Barth, Tillich, the Niebuhrs, and others was simply too consummate a "shaking of the foundations" (Tillich).

Then, with the countercultural movements of "the sixties," there came to be—especially in North America, though also in Western Europe—a whole spate of theological agendas that by their immediacy effectively displaced the earlier, comprehensive theologies of the first part of the twentieth century. These "new" theologies, which for the most part grew out of the experiences of marginalized and neglected elements within and around the churches, and which in their own right were absolutely timely and necessary, nevertheless had the effect of throwing into question the critique of theological triumphalism that was so deeply ingrained in "Neo-Orthodoxy." For these theologies concerned the plight of persons, races, sexual and other minorities that positively *needed* to accentuate triumph and victory and hope and all things positive. They needed to assert their rights and their possibilities both as humans and as Christians. They needed to achieve mastery over the classes and systems that oppressed them. In short, they needed to "overcome."

The problem, which can be seen at least in retrospect, is that the enthusiasm, activism, and positivism inherent in these new identity- and issue-driven theologies was co-opted by the so-called mainline churches, *as if it were their own*! Everyone wanted to talk about "liberation" and "hope." White Anglo-Saxon Protestant congregations, peopled largely by the economically and personally secure, mimicked Black and other minorities in loud choruses of "We shall overcome . . . ," when they should have been singing "We *did* overcome . . . and in the process we've likely lost our souls!" (Matthew 16:26!)

I have begun with this brief survey of recent theology because, being one of the two whose works are treated in Professor McCarroll's important study, I felt that I should locate myself within this historical framework. It was certainly the *theologia crucis* that prompted me to begin, in my twenties, to take Christianity very seriously—at a time, indeed, before I'd have been able even minimally to use or explain the meaning of a term like *theologia crucis*! For a host of historical, biographical, psychological, and other reasons that are far too complex to decipher, I could never embrace a faith that answered all the questions. The Christian narrative as a success story struck me even in my adolescence as being exaggerated and premature. Like most Canadians—indeed like most northern peoples, I think—success stories, which have provided the mythic foundations of the United States of America, crumble and break apart on the harsh realities of nature and history. Christianity only began to make sense to me when, with the help of St. Paul and Luther, I began to see that the Bible was not talking about a God who wanted us all to be good little boys and girls with bright, happy futures, but to become serious and mature human beings who could face the incongruities and incompleteness of existence honestly and (as McCarroll expresses it) "wait for hope at the foot of the cross." It was this strange biblical admixture of rigorous truth and persistent hope that gave me the audacity to consider Christian ministry as my vocation.

Through my early reading of Dietrich Bonhoeffer and Karl Barth, I began to understand that these adolescent stirrings, prompted by the Bible and Luther, were by no means mine alone, but were, indeed, part of a great post-War human longing that could no longer be satisfied with "happy endings," religious or secular. Throughout the 1950s, at Union Seminary in New York City, I encountered some of the most articulate Christian representatives of that longing—not only Paul Tillich and Reinhold Niebuhr, but scholars in every theological discipline who were in one way or another exploring the possibilities of a Christian future beyond the horrors of war and the demise of shallow humanistic idealism. After seven years of intensive study under these unforgettable teachers, I emerged from Seminary as one who not only knew the term *theologia crucis*, but had contemplated and been profoundly moved by the great exemplars of that "thin tradition," as I called it in my first longer book.[9] I began my ministry in a congregation of my denomination located in a small town at the top of Lake Huron in the autumn of 1960. My sermons were undoubtedly heavily theological and even, on occasion, offensive to some; but on the whole their reception confirmed me in the belief that "ordinary Christians" are quite capable of "thinking theologically"—if they are given half a chance! I also began to realize, of course, that my theology was still too theoretical—or better, too "universal." It had to be particularized, "brought down to earth"—even this rock-hard Canadian earth of North America's near-north.

---

9. *Lighten Our Darkness*; later published in a revised and enlarged edition under the editorship of David Monge by the Academic Renewal Press of Lima, Ohio, 2001.

And just here is where George Parkin Grant enters my story. By great good fortune, the woman I married was not only a better student than I; she was also a good friend of George and Sheila Grant. My wife introduced me to the Grants during the first months of our marriage, but it was not until I tried to write three lectures for the 50th Anniversary of the Student Christian Movement of Canada[10] that I began to be excited about Grant's work. I remember well the very first of George's many memorable sentences that struck an important chord with me:

> In a field as un-American as theology, the continually changing ripples of thought, by which the professionals hope to revive a dying faith, originate from some stone dropped by a European thinker.[11]

The sentence was, to me, like a clarion call to become what I was: a Canadian, a North American, a twentieth-century Christian living on the edge of empire![12] So much of our theology in North America, I realized, was exactly what George said it was: warmed-over, second-hand ideas borrowed from our parental culture. We took the results of other peoples' struggles (and from the 1960s onwards this included Latin Americans, African Americans, gays and lesbians, et al.) and lightly claimed them for ourselves. Without entering our own "darkness," we snatched bits of a light that was kindled in the gross darkness of war-torn Europe—light that had been seen by the few who courageously and thoughtfully entered that darkness. Was it because, intuitively, subconsciously, we were

---

10. This event was held in 1968, and the lectures were later published by the World Student Christian Federation under the title, *Hope Against Hope: Towards an Indigenous Theology of the Cross*. As such, they became the "program," so to speak, for most of my work that was to follow, beginning with *Lighten Our Darkness*.

Readers may notice that the concept of *contextuality*, which came to be associated with my work, first appeared in written material under the nomenclature, 'indigenous.' The latter, in subsequent decades, acquired a quite different connotation because of its associated with the "indigenous peoples" of North America and elsewhere; but in the subtitles of both *Hope Against Hope*, and *Lighten Our Darkness*, I use "indigenous" as a synonym for "contextual," the term I later adopted as a methodologically central concept of my thinking about the faith.

11. George Grant, *Technology and Empire*.

12. Living "on the edge of empire," a phrase that I invented in the wake of my introduction to Grant, is a metaphor for the Christian life that is lived seriously today no matter *where* it is lived. Conscientious and thoughtful US-American Christians are in some ways more nearly "on the edge of empire" than are Canadians, who may live there literally without much reflective awareness of the fact!

afraid of facing the contradictions and deceits of our own subtle night, lit up as it was by the imported lamps that we stole from others?

Grant's social and cultural analysis became, then, the best guide I could find for the exploration of my own time and place—my own context. Not all by itself, of course; Canadian and American literature, especially novels, plays and films, also gave me the entrée that I needed, as a theologian, to comprehend the *Zeitgeist* with which I had to wrestle. But George Grant, more than anyone apart from his friend, my wife, helped me to decipher "the little point where the battle rages."[13] It is, as George knew very well, an extremely subtle and evasive "little point," for it is all "sicklied o'er" with highly positive and even revered assumptions about ourselves and our "noble experiment."

> On this continent [Grant wrote] the modern mass age has arrived as to no other people in the world. North America is the only society that has no history of its own before the age of progress, and we have built here the society which incarnates more than any other the values and principles of the age of progress . . . Ours is the world of mass production and its techniques, of standardized consumption and standardize education, of wholesale entertainment and almost wholesale medicine. We are formed by this new environment at all the moments of our work and leisure—that is, in our total lives.[14]

Though George Grant knew himself to be a child of this same "mass culture" (he was in fact a member of a prominent English-Canadian family), his innate discomfort with the pale Canadian version of "the American dream" led him to embrace critical ideas that his illustrious Canadian forebears would have found shocking. Through his studies at Oxford and his own intuitive reflections as a conscientious objector during World War II, he gained a profound knowledge of the Western philosophic

13. This is a reference to a quotation attributed to Luther that has functioned, for me, as the most succinct statement of my understanding of my calling as a theologian—and the irony of this is that this statement in Luther's works cannot be decisively located, though I know perfectly well that I copied it from one of Luther's writings early in my career as a teacher. The full quotation runs,

> If I profess with the loudest voice and clearest exposition every portion of the truth of God except precisely that little point where the world and the devil are *at that moment* attacking, I am not confessing Christ, however boldly I may be professing him. Where the battle rages, there the loyalty of the soldier is proved, and to be steady on all the battlefield besides is mere flight and disgrace if he flinches at that point.

14. *Philosophy in the Mass Age*, 2–3.

traditions from Plato to Nietzsche; and this, in addition to his theological acquaintance with British thinkers like John Oman, Austin Farrar, and C. S. Lewis, in time provided a vantage-point from which to assess the reality of "the West":

> Like all civilisations the West is based on a great religion—the religion of progress. This is the belief that the conquest of human and non-human nature will give existence meaning. Western civilization is now universal so that this religion is nearly everywhere dominant. To question the dominant world religion is indeed to invite an alienation far greater than the simply political.[15]

Mastery over "human and non-human nature" and "the elimination of chance" in human affairs would be achieved, according to this "religion," by technology. But for Grant, as for Jacques Ellul,[16] technology is much more than sophisticated machinery! "I consider technique to be 'the totality of methods rationally arrived at and having absolute efficiency (for a given stage of development) in every field of human activity.'"[17] The usual mantra of the policy making classes is of course that technological systems may be used for good or bad purposes; but Grant, like Ellul, knew that the mechanics of technology were nothing more nor less than the objectification of a cultural mindset. "We *are* technique," Grant finally concluded. Long before environmentalists complained that human arrogance lay behind the degradation of nature, Grant was proclaiming that the heroic anthropocentrism of modernity had expressed itself, finally and quite logically, in a conception of the human species as destined for the control, not only of the natural order but also of its own species as part of the natural order.

The "un-American activity" of theology, as popularly expressed in the churches, was of little help against this false *imago hominis*:

> I hoped for years that our ecclesiastical organizations (being the guardians of the beauty of the gospel) might continue to be able to permeate this society with something nobler than the barrenness of technical dynamism. I hoped for this when every piece of evidence before me was saying that it was not true. I could not believe that the only interpretation of Christianity that technological

---

15. *Technology and Empire*, 77.

16. George once told me that he regarded Ellul's book, *The Technological Society*, as the most important book of its decade.

17. *Philosophy in the Mass Age*, iii (the quotation is from Ellul's *Technological Society*, xxxiii).

liberalism would allow to survive publically would be that part of it . . . which played the role of flatterer to modernity.[18]

Harris Athanasiadis, in his *George Grant and the Theology of the Cross: The Christian Foundations of His Thought,* has ably demonstrated that in the theology of the cross George Grant found a form of Christian theology and faith upon with which he could ground his own quest for hope. It is, however, as Athanasiadis rightly claims, largely an implicit rather than an explicit foundation for Grant's thought.[19] In any case, as I wrote in my essay for the symposium held in George's honour at Erindale College in the spring of 1977, it was not George Grant's specifically theological thought but his cultural analysis that evoked my keen interest in his writings. What I needed was a satisfying description of the socio-historical *context* in which I felt called to teach and write as a Christian; for the theological tradition to which I had been led, the "thin" or minority tradition called by Luther *theologia crucis,* positively demands of its exponents that they acquire the deepest, most concrete understanding of their own time and place. The gospel is indeed for *all*; but it can only be received by human beings in all the particularity and specificity of their socio-historic condition. That condition is never static. Gospel for sixteenth-century Germans, Scots, or Swiss is not necessarily gospel for twentieth-century Canadians; gospel may indeed be, primarily, a matter of *liberation* for African-Americans and the desperate poor of Latin American cities, but when white, Protestant, middle-class North Americans pick that message up as if it were intended precisely for them, they are using religion exactly as Karl Marx pronounced: as a drug to help them repress their own actual condition. The most demanding aspect of Christian theological thought is—not the comprehension of the inherited doctrinal traditions of the faith, but the discernment of the *Zeitgeist* in which the Good News is to be preached. That discernment is extremely difficult, because one is oneself part of it. There is no high ground from which to observe the "little point where the battle rages." One needs a good deal of help from one's fellows who perhaps are a little taller than oneself![20]

18. *Technology and Empire,* 44.

19. Ibid., 48.

20. That is why theology has always turned to philosophy and other human disciplines for help. It is the reason why Augustine turned to Plato and Thomas Aquinas to Aristotle and Paul Tillich to the existentialists. Faith, to be sure, has its own windows onto the world, but in some real sense faith's assumptions and "answers" always cloud

George Grant, a decade my senior and a thinker far more steeped than I in the philosophic traditions of the West became that "taller" contemporary for me, or at least chief among such.

> [H]e has thought through the meaning of our identity as North Americans in general and Canadians in particular, in a way that is both profound and unique. I believe that Christian theology, to be faithful to its roots, must always be *contextual,* and my thesis here, to state it very broadly, is that Grant's analysis of our culture can contribute to the contextualization of theology on this Continent—a quality which it has consistently lacked.[21]

It is unfortunate, I think, that Grant's work did not receive a wider notice in the United States. Robert Bellah is among the few Americans who have cited Grant. Yet Grant's cultural analysis plumbs depths never reached by the popular sociological analyses by which Americans (and Canadians too) have been excited, decade after decade. In my opinion, only Ernest Becker, among American commentators on our North American condition, achieves something like George Grant's cultural wisdom, though of course Becker uses other lenses to view our reality.[22]

Although it was Grant's cultural analysis, not his theology, that first caused me to listen more attentively to a thinker who had become a friend, I was always aware of the fact that Grant's philosophic approach was what it was, in great measure, because of his Christian faith. It was therefore no surprise to me when, in working with Harris Athanasiadis on his graduate research,[23] I realized how truly Grant's Christianity had been shaped by the same questions and intuitions that had led me to find in "the theology of the cross" a compelling alternative to the "official optimism" in which our "officially Christian" culture had been immersed. It is personally gratifying, therefore, that Pamela McCarroll has written so insightfully about the link not only of friendship but of faith between George Grant and myself.

The "theology of the cross" was well and truly named by Luther, and I know of no other nomenclature by which to designate this "thin

its vision of the realities and the questions with which the world itself is living. Theology that does not listen to the stories the world tells of itself tend to view the world too pessimistically or too optimistically. Christian Realism, as exemplified by Reinhold Niebuhr, presupposes a faith that is always in open dialogue with the world it wants to address.

21. "The Significance of Grant's Cultural Analysis," in *George Grant in Process,* 120.

22. I refer especially to Becker's *Denial of Death.*

23. See Athanasiadis, *George Grant and the Theology of the Cross.*

tradition"; yet I have never been entirely happy about the term. It lends itself much too easily to that contemporary habit of identifying theological positions by this or that central metaphor, emphasis or "concern." The *theologia crucis* should not become yet another "theology *of*"! If and when that happens, the whole spirit and method of this theological approach is reduced to a caricature of itself. It becomes, indeed, a pious or theoretical fixation on the cross of Calvary; moreover, as noted earlier, given the proclivities of Christianity in the West, this quite naturally leads to the assumption that *theologia crucis* is a synonym for the doctrine of the atonement—explicitly, to the *Latin* doctrine of atonement. For so powerfully has the Anselmic conception of the meaning of Christ's death dominated Western Christian thought that a term like "theology of the cross" reinforces, for many, not only an unhealthy and unbiblical fixation on human guilt but also a Christology that must needs posit God as the great Opponent of humanity, One whose wrath against the creature can only be assuaged by the blood of His Son. The Jews have been right, I believe, in seeing this informing concept of Latin Christianity as something entirely discontinuous with the faith that remembers how father Abraham, unlike Anselm's holy and righteous deity, was relieved by grace of the awesome burden of infanticide!

The theology of the cross is grounded, not in a tribal religion of retribution, revenge, and blood sacrifice but in the faith of prophets of Israel, who were deeply persuaded of the pathos of God, that is, God's unrelenting compassion for the creature.[24] The incarnation of the divine Word is nothing more nor less than the historical enactment of that "suffering love" (*agape*); and the crucifixion at Golgotha is nothing more nor less than the completion of the painful trajectory of that divine compassion—God's full and final act of solidarity with the beloved creature. It was our cross, the cross of humanity—the cross of creatures whose existence in the first place is perhaps impossible, creatures who move inevitably towards extinction, and who know this: it was our cross that Jesus "took up." Only from within the "body of death" (Romans 7:24) that is our life, individually and corporately, could the love that is stronger than death begin its long, arduous labour of rebirth.

---

24. The central thesis of Abraham Heschel in his magisterial book *The Prophets*.

Standing in the shadow of that cross, where "the dark is light enough," we who are dying men and women, members of dispirited churches, citizens of tumultuous states and tragic, failing empires[25] do not lose hope.

25. See Hedges, "What if America Fails?" (The concluding paragraph of this important essay should be contemplated by all Christians. Hedges writes that the most pathetic aspect of the "fall of the American Empire," of which many have spoken, is that "[w]e are not psychologically, emotionally or intellectually prepared. *We lack the self-reflective mechanisms to understand*" [33, my italics].) What does such an assessment say about *the churches* in North America?

Acknowledgments

How do I begin to acknowledge and thank those many people who have supported and been a part of the writing of this book? I am grateful to the Knox College community and especially to Principal Dorcas Gordon for the incredible support and encouragement for this project by providing a sabbatical leave and by offering engaged leadership, ongoing interest, and dedicated mentoring. I offer a heartfelt thank you to Harold Wells whose enthusiasm, keen theological sensibility, and commitment have guided and encouraged me enormously; to Iain Nicol, a mentor and friend whose contemplative ways, humour, and gentle theological proddings have borne much fruit in my life and thought; to the late Arthur Van Seters, whose support and effusive encouragement of my work gave me the inspiration to transform the dissertation into a book; to Thomas St. James O'Connor, whose early support convinced me that I could complete the task set out before me; to Kay Diviney, whose detailed editing, thoughtful questioning, and heartfelt engagement have been central to transforming the manuscript into the form we now have before us.

I am grateful to my colleagues at Knox College, who, each in different ways, has given me vision and strength for the journey. It is a privilege to work among you. I am grateful also to my colleagues at the Toronto School of Theology, the CPE Teaching Supervisors in Toronto and Hamilton, and to my friends and colleagues in ministry in the church, whose struggle to live faithfully amidst these changing times is both a challenge and an inspiration. I am grateful also to my students, many of whom have taught me much about life, faith, and ministry.

I especially wish to acknowledge and express my deepest thanks to Douglas and Rhoda Hall, whose encouragement, attentiveness, generosity, and openness to me and my work have given me a sense of grateful accountability and gracious hope. For the life-changing influence of your lives and work upon me, I raise humble thanks. It is an honour that you have contributed the Foreword to this book, which itself makes the book worth buying! I also wish to acknowledge the late Sheila Grant for her incredible hospitality and spirited enthusiasm for this project.

Thank you to the bodies that have contributed financially to the coming-to-be of this book: the Knox College Faculty Support Fund; The Louisville Institute's Dissertation Fellowship Program; the Ontario Graduate Scholarship Fund; and the Cameron Doctoral Bursary fund of the Presbyterian Church in Canada.

Finally, I wish to express my gratitude to my friends and family: To my life partner Harris whose willingness to read through every draft, to talk out all the glitches, to join with me in expanding our theological imagination gives me hope. Your eye for seeing invisible possibilities has been an inspiration and a promise that has accompanied me through some dark nights. I am delighted also to take a moment to sing out a huge thank you to my children, Ben and Caleb. Thank you for cheering me on and for the many ways you and your step-siblings, Hannah and Mark, continue to teach and challenge me to further think through what it means to be human in this beloved and bedraggled world. To my sister Wendy, your faith and humour always energize and buoy me up. And to my parents, Paul and Kath, to whom this book is dedicated and around whose table I was nourished in all manner of things theological, I clamour out blessed gratitude. Your wrestling and active faith challenges me to live authentically and to never cease in the struggle to discern what it means to love in each moment of every day.

And to you, dedicated reader, thank you for your interest and your willingness to explore together the character of hope for the living of these days.

Pamela McCarroll

December 10, 2012

I

Hope at the End of Hope?

The Crisis of Hope, North American Style

NORTH AMERICA FACES MANY crises. We need only turn on the daily news to glimpse the layers of global crisis in which our continent is embedded. There is no way to enumerate these crises exhaustively for they pile upon each other and our very existing with a weight that smothers. What is central, however, is that the extremity of contemporary crises has brought us to a place that is truly novel in the history of humanity, and indeed, in the history of the planet. Never before has the destruction of much of creation been as possible as it is now, with our high-tech weapons of mass destruction, with our dependence upon ecologically devastating practices, and with the global-scale systemic injustice of which we are all a part.

Unlike any previous generation, the generations of English-speaking North Americans raised in the sixties and after have never known a time when nuclear annihilation was not a possibility on any given day.[1] Nor have they known a time when the effects of ecological devastation were not experienced, with disease in the very air they breathe, food they eat, and water they drink. These generations have never known a time when

1. My reference to North America and North Americans throughout this section refers primarily to the English-speaking, historically dominating peoples of North America who share a certain history and experience with the land and their sense of identity and purpose in this land (which will be discussed at length later in the book). It does not presume to include the French, Spanish, or Aboriginal-speaking peoples who have often had uneasy relations with the English-speaking majority. Further, although I am included in these generations, in the forthcoming appeal to experience I use the third person plural throughout.

the staggering effects of systemic injustice—of starvation, genocide, poverty, disease, torture, and refugee camps—were not a part of their daily consciousness. They have been raised with a shadowy awareness of the malevolence of which humanity is capable (particularly the white middle class educated parts of humanity), for which the poignant names of Auschwitz and Dachau, Hiroshima and Nagasaki are but shorthand. Perceptions of humanity's inhumanity have only been reinforced in these generations by the wars in Vietnam and Iraq and by the clandestine participation of the American Empire in the torture chambers and army camps of Central and South America, Africa, Asia, and the Middle East. Indeed, as never before in the history of the planet, these generations have been raised on daily injections of the destructive end to which human beings seem bound as we brazenly leap toward the *nihil* through the threat of nuclear annihilation, ecological devastation, and global-scale systemic injustice. More than anything else, what sets these generations apart from previous generations is that they have no memory of life before the possibility of massive scale destruction at any moment, on any day.

Even worse, as these generations have become increasingly conscious of the massive layers of global crisis, they have also recognized the extent to which they are on the one hand implicated in the mechanisms of global crisis and on the other powerless to do anything meaningful about it. Even the many who opt to repress, escape, or plead indifference to the realities of contemporary life cannot escape the sense of dread about the reality of things as they are in the world.[2] There is an overwhelming sense of powerlessness in the face of the massive scale of the global crises.[3] Sadly, the once-effective rallying cries to "change the world" ring hollow; they no longer inspire action. The scale of the crises and sense of powerlessness in the public realm are some of the dynamics that have pressed in upon the horizon of meaning for these generations.

These are generations that have been raised in the dominant North American way, wherein meaning and purpose are derived from one's ability to make a difference in the world, to change the world, to make one's mark on the world. In this context, to be confronted with one's own powerlessness to make a difference in the world for good is to be confronted with meaninglessness. Given recent protest movements

2. See Hall, *Lighten our Darkness*, 27–43.

3. See McQuaig, *Cult of Impotence*. McQuaig identifies a dominant and rampant sense of powerlessness within the public sphere, although she does counter the assumption that powerlessness is an economic necessity.

regarding economics and democracy,[4] it remains to be seen how these actions will have an impact. While these protests stand as signs of hope, meaning, and investment in public life, the general trend over the last several decades has been a withdrawal from participation and lack of investment in public life. Paradoxically, over recent decades we have seen that meaninglessness has itself become a horizon of meaning.

In the public realms of civic and church life in North America, this nihilistic horizon of meaning has manifested itself in a cynicism toward both church and polis, as well as to the very idea that human institutions might serve the good. These generations have been raised within a "once-mainline church" that seems (at best) inconsequential to life or (at worst) malignant toward life.[5] Is it a surprise that they rarely darken the entrance to any sanctuary? In the civic realm, too, they are increasingly opting out of the electoral process.[6] They are beginning to die of inactivity[7] as they sit in their cars and bow interminably before the thrones of their computer and TV screens—their self-enclosed lenses into the world.

Indeed, this all sounds rather dire and to some this appeal to experience will sound lopsided. However, what I am seeking to get at is the fact that over the last fifty years massive shifts have taken place in the public realms of civic and church life of North America, and these shifts reflect a deeper spiritual crisis of meaning and purpose—a crisis about what it means to be human. In public and religious life, the pervasive cynicism and despair over human purpose and meaning are manifested as a crisis of hope. The institutions of civil society and the church no longer earn our loyalty, nor can they any longer carry the burden of our hope.

4. I am thinking here of recent protests against the G8 and G20 meetings and the so-called Occupy Movement that has emerged across North America (and elsewhere) in recent months.

5. The term "once-mainline church" is Douglas John Hall's, used throughout his corpus. From the perspective of the margins of power, the once-mainline church has been malignant toward life in the oppressive ways it has functioned since its arrival on the shores of North America—for instance in its oppressive relationship with First Peoples and African Americans, with women, and with LBGT communities; in its silence about the internment of Japanese *Canadians* during World War II; and in its ongoing temptation toward anti-Semitism. Many once-mainline churches have repented and sought forgiveness and reconciliation on a number of these issues, yet the history of oppression remains what it is.

6. "National Voter Turnout in Federal Elections: 1960–2012," infoplease, http://www.infoplease.com/ipa/A0781453.html.

7. I am thinking here of the massive increase in obesity rates and in illnesses caused by obesity in recent decades.

The experience of despair that now marks North American life is manifest variously in cynicism, hopelessness, and indifference. Etymologically, despair (Latin *desperare*, from *de-* + *sperare*, "to hope") means "without hope": "No way out into the future appears."[8] It is expressed in a retreat from the public into the private sphere that involves a numbness to and disengagement from organized institutional public life. Given the particular quality of North American history and culture, despair as a pervasive experience in the North American context is truly novel.[9]

Like no other place on earth, North America came into being as the embodiment of the modern liberal dream. The public life of North America was built with the very materials of modernity—with foundations of freedom, walls of progressivism, and windows of optimism. In this modern experiment, the human was imaged as one who in freedom creates her own reality and who works with purpose to bring forth a better future based on freedom, equality, and justice for all. It is precisely this modern liberal image of the human as free and self-creating potentiality, innately directed toward the good, that, except in superficial terms, has been darkened in our current context. Its meaning and truth have been distorted beyond recognition. Where we once placed our hope in the potential of human will, reason, imagination, and ability as that which would actualize a future society with justice and freedom for all, now we are cynical about the potentialities of the human. Our North American understanding of hope as a collective vision for the future towards which we must move has become increasingly emptied as daily crises fragment our imaginations with uncertainty and fear. We have glimpsed the heart of the liberal modern dream and have found illusion. Images of future potentiality that used to kindle our hope and draw us together in worship and action now only rarely call us beyond the walls of our private lives. The collective horizon of meaning for the North American church and civic life, based as it was in modern liberalism, is fragmenting, and there seems to be nothing to replace it but the relentlessness of its negation, the *nihil*. It is no wonder that hopelessness abounds.

We live in or on the periphery of what continues to be the most powerful Empire in history. Cynicism and indifference in the public realm are frightful at the best of times. However, to find such a numbing dynamic in the very heart of the American Empire is frightful beyond measure.

8. *Shorter Oxford English Dictionary* and Tillich, *Courage to Be*, 54.

9. Among others, see Lasch, *True and Only Heaven*.

Indeed, the power of the Empire in the world is increasingly detached from any sense of accountability beyond its own fearful self-protection. Furthermore, since the destruction of the Twin Towers, the American Empire has been thrust deeper into its reactive fear.[10] While the Empire has fearfully attacked the enemy "out there" who lurks everywhere, we who live within and on its fringes increasingly express our hopelessness and fear by retreating away from the public realm into the safety of our own self-made security, which now is even less secure than it used to be.

Hopelessness abounds and so it must, for in the public realms of church and state, it is a fearful and overwhelming time. To pretend that it is otherwise is to live in denial or to lie: it is to call "evil good and good evil."[11] However, the fact that we experience the hopelessness of life today in North America paradoxically reflects the possibility for authentic hope. Our hopelessness reflects the cracking of the foundations of the modern project as it has been gloriously manifested in North America. Our despair in the modern liberal image of the human and our cynicism toward civic and church life based on such an image marks the destruction of a false reality. This is a good thing. Such destruction of falsity contains within it a possibility—a possibility that might just open our hearts and minds to see anew the truth of things. Today only a hope that emerges from the midst of the hopelessness of the North American dream and dares to face our contemporary meaninglessness and fear head-on, only this kind of hope holds within it the possibility for a renewal of spirit and thought about our life together as church, continent, and globe.

A Theological Response to the Crisis of Hope

The extremity of the global and spiritual crises of these times demands response, evokes contemplation, and calls for a re-thinking of who we are, where we have come from, and where we are going. This is the most urgent task for theology in North America for the living of these days. By contemplating the character of authentic Christian hope through the work of George Grant and Douglas John Hall, this book engages the

10. See Rohr, "Fear Itself," and Polter, "Politics of Fear" and "Not a Happy Nation." "Although this culture [of fear] has been most palpable during the last couple of years, it did not . . . emerge from the rubble of Ground Zero. In fact my research shows that . . . America has demonstrated growing levels of technological anxiety, fear of complexity, fear of the "other" (in the form of sexism and xenophobia), and fear of violence at least since the early nineties"; Adams, "Continental Divide," 63.

11. Luther, *Heidelberg Disputation*, 40.

crises of these times through the most compelling and challenging of all traditions in Christianity—*theologia crucis*, the theology of the cross. The theology of the cross, over and against the theology of glory, provides both Grant and Hall with a Christian foundation for recognizing the particularities of our context, for naming the temptations toward which we are drawn, and for beginning to point to the character of authentic hope. This book examines Grant's and Hall's distinctive and complementary understanding of the theology of glory and the theology of the cross in the traditions of Athens (Grant) and Jerusalem (Hall), which enables each of them to engage the North American context critically. It shows how both the methods and content of their work embody a posture of hope as waiting at the foot of the cross. These theologians of the cross[12] have faced, known, and named the origins and manifestations of North American hopelessness with depth and insight through incisive analyses of this context. As we shall see, their work, when considered together, provides a solid basis for further development of a theology of hope in the North American context. Finally, through contextual theological reflection on hope as "waiting at the foot of the cross," this project builds constructively upon their work so as to further outline a theology of hope for our time and place.

Why a Theology of the Cross?

I concur with many others[13] that the theology of the cross, rooted in the writings of the apostle Paul and most elementally expressed in Martin Luther's *Heidelberg Disputation*,[14] is one of the most prophetic and provocative critiques of power throughout the Christian tradition. We Christians who live within and on the fringe of the most powerful Empire ever to have existed in history are challenged to wrestle with the ethos of power

---

12. Hall identifies himself as a theologian of the cross and his theology as theology of the cross. See, among others, Hall, *Lighten Our Darkness* and *Cross in Our Context*. Grant does not use the term about himself. However, Grant's orientation to the theology of the cross is becoming increasingly appreciated in Grantian scholarship. See Athanasiadis, *George Grant and the Theology of the Cross*, and Sheila Grant, "George Grant and the Theology of the Cross." See also Wells, *Christic Centre*, 7.

13. Including Jürgen Moltmann, Sharon G. Thornton, and Douglas John Hall.

14. Forde, *On Being a Theologian of the Cross*. I stand in agreement with the many scholars who consider the theology of the cross to embody the essential character of Luther's entire theological thought. See Althaus, *Theology of Martin Luther*, von Loewenich, *Luther's Theology of the Cross*, and McGrath, *Luther's Theology of the Cross*.

of which we are a part and with the way in which this ethos impacts our spirits and our experience of hope. We cannot rest easily and uncritically in our context. The theology of the cross enables a Christian critique of power as it has been manifested in North American public religious and civic life through an incisive undercutting of the image of the human as master that lies at the root of the modern experiment. This theology continually strips away the adornments of power, status, and prestige, so that we know and are known in our honest vulnerability before God and in relationship. The theology of the cross reveals worldly power to be an illusion hiding the truth of things. We are all exposed as beggars before God and each other. The walls that divide and protect us one from another are radically deconstructed. The possibilities for the hidden hope of resurrection love come into focus, most visibly on the cross of Christ.

In retrieving the richness of the theology of the cross through Grant and Hall as a foundation for theological reflection in contemporary North America, this book explores how modern notions of human mastery and power have dominated North American thinking about what it means to be human and what it means to think critically—and how such notions have located hope within a particular understanding of history. The theology of the cross provides Grant and Hall with a critical perspective—a *via negativa*—that enables them to explore what the human *is not*, what hope *is not*, and thereby to engage the nihilistic horizon of meaning that looms among us. They do this by naming and analyzing the various manifestations of the theology of glory that shape North American self-understanding in public and church life.

In different ways, Grant and Hall both challenge modernist notions of thought as "technical reason," which they interpret to be the theology of glory. Technical reason, in the guise of true thought, shuts down possibilities and imprisons thought into falsity in what it presumes to know and control, holding thought captive unable to think beyond the framework of technical reason. In their methods of the cross, Grant and Hall explore alternatives that unhinge the theology of glory as it has dominated modern forms of thought. In clarifying the extent to which the "glorious" false visions of reality have been a driving force in North America, these thinkers urge us to claim the object of our despair as the failure of the North American dream and the falsity of its means. In clearing the way by the *via negativa*, they invite us to be open to new possibilities about what it means to be human, to think, and to hope in our context. In contrast to the theology of glory, the theology of the cross is a "broken" theology, unwilling to engage easily in constructive speculation on the things of God that are unknowable to experience. In general, the theology of the cross is hesitant toward constructive (or positive) moves in theology because it recognizes the propensity for humans to assert their wills in speculative thought about God, which ultimately leads to false understandings of God and the human. To be a "broken" theology means that there comes a point where human language about the mystery of God cannot speak, where the human will cannot go, where the gap (or brokenness) in meaning held within the paradox of the cross can only be uttered as silence.[15] Despite this reticence, however, the theology of the cross can provide pointers as to what it means to be human and what it means to hope in this suffering and beloved world, as reflection on Grant's and Hall's work shows. In proposing the image of "waiting at the foot of the cross" as a picture of hope for the living of these days, I seek to integrate, respond to, and build upon Grant's and Hall's work—their method and content, as well as their critical analyses and their constructive intimations.

The despair, nihilism, and false optimism that characterize our age represent three quite different responses to the falsity of liberalism. Where despair recognizes the unrequited desire for something other than what is, nihilism lashes out in resentment at what is. In other quarters, false optimism continues to masquerade in the guise of hope. It is over and against these temptations of our times—despair, nihilism, and false optimism—grounded in the demise of liberalism, that the character of authentic Christian hope becomes visible. Authentic Christian hope emerges from a different narrative than that of modern liberalism. It is not based on images of human mastery and power nor upon understandings of thought and hope that are dependent upon the active agency of the human will and imagination.

The theology of the cross is instructive in drawing forth the Christian narrative that most challenges the falsity of our North American ways, including the idolatry of power in which we participate. Not only does it point to the hidden ways of God; it also suggests a posture of "waiting" as the most authentic expression of Christian hope. Over and against images of human and divine power and glory, God comes unexpectedly, paradoxically revealing the hidden power of resurrection love in the weakness of the cross. In the cross of Christ, the hidden ways of God

---

15. In the theology of the cross, paradoxically, the glory of God is to be found on the cross of Christ. See Althaus, *Theology of Martin Luther*, 25–34.

are revealed. God is present on the cross in the place least expected—not gloriously and self-evidently, but tragically and unexpectedly. The cross disturbs the securities within which we live—undermining our illusions of human grandeur and pretensions to mastery, calling us to the truth of our limitations and finitude, our neediness and dependence—upon each other and upon all of creation. Furthermore, the unexpected ways of God are revealed in the hiddenness of the resurrection, recognized only to the eyes of faith, and not victoriously and plainly to the eyes of all. There is a double movement that undermines all expectations of glory and victory in both the tragic reality of the cross and in the hidden revelation of the resurrection. Recognition of the unexpected and hidden character of God is key for critical Christian analysis of our context. We cannot think or plan our way to God to figure out God's ways. Rather, God comes as one who disrupts our sense of what God is supposed to be, both in the acute drama of the cross and in the quiet breath of the resurrection.[16]

When we belong to God who is revealed in the crucified and risen One, we wait for and upon God's hidden revealing in the world and know ourselves in the light of such revealing. This is our hope. As Christians we claim our belonging to One who challenges the world in its self-made security, self assurance, and desperation for power. We belong to the One hidden in unexpected places and people, the One who seeks to draw us to the truth of our creaturehood—dependent, limited, fragile; a truth that becomes visible only in the waters of love, compassion, and relationship with "other" human and non-human creation.

Hope as Waiting

Over and against modern liberalism's "outcomes orientation" of technical reason and of hope driven by the mastery of the human will, the biblical tradition, through the prophets and Psalms, through the whole newer testament and the theology of the cross, reflects a vision of hope as "waiting"—the people of God waiting for God's revealing. Similarly, over and against Christendom's outcomes orientation wherein the cross is understood primarily as the means to resurrection, the theology of the cross places us in a posture of waiting for God's revelation on the cross and in the real and historical details of life. The revelation on the cross is completely dependent upon resurrection faith. Were there no experience of resurrection, there could be no recognition of divine love on the cross.

16. See Wells, *Christic Centre*, 52–53, 67–79.

Ultimately it is the hidden experience of resurrection faith, glimpsed quietly only by a few, that re-orients us to glimpse the truth of the cross in all its tragic and breath-taking reality.

A posture of waiting as hope is particularly subversive in the North American context. Waiting challenges all the ways that the modern image of the human as creative agent and master has shaped our self-understanding as a people and a continent. We use our knowledge and science to change and control the world, to make it into what we want it to be. In North America, we are "doers." We *make* history. We do not wait upon or for it. To wait means we are at the mercy of some o/Other.[17] Waiting challenges our compulsion for fix-it solutions and our sense that we can create the world as we desire it to be. Furthermore, in our consumer culture the call to wait flies in the face of the dominant and flimsy metaphors of meaning rampant in the broader society: "Buy more!" "Make more!" "Get more!" "Do more!" "Be more!"

The waiting implicit in the hope of the cross is not, however, a passive or blind waiting. Rather, it is waiting that is alert, engaged in the world—recognizing the concrete day-to-day-ness of life as the arena of God's hidden ways. God does not and will not come as one from on high in glory. Authentic Christian hope must be rid of such triumphalist imagery. It is a waiting that challenges the idea that God comes as a guest—obvious and visible—and not as one hidden. When we wait for the hidden God, we critique all theology, political dogma, and churchtalk that presumes God's self-evident visibility in the world. Recognizing the one for whom we wait means recognizing God as One who is powerless in force, powerful only in love. Indeed, the fact of suffering and affliction in the world are the most obvious signs of God's powerlessness in force. As those who wait upon and for God's hidden revealing, Christians must name the absence of God's control over the world, counter all that says otherwise, and attend to the hidden revelation of God's true power of love, grace, and beauty in unexpected places and people—even in the midst of weakness and vulnerability. Over and against mastery, control,

17. Throughout this book, the terms "other" and "Other" are used frequently. Lower-case "other" is a noun referring to that which is other to the one/self/community/species/creation—the relationship with which is of utmost concern. Thus, "the other" may be another person, creature, or group, or creation as a whole. Upper-case "Other" refers to God, the One who transcends creation yet stands in relationship with creation as "other." Throughout the body of this book I include "other" and "Other" in the text without highlighting the term in quotation marks. When it is used as a noun, it refers to the aforementioned definition.

and power, as followers of the crucified one we are called to postures of being that are ready and waiting to recognize God's hidden revelation. Attentiveness, openness, receptivity: these are the postures of waiting in thought and action before God's hidden presence in the world; these are the postures of hoping that manifest the truth of who and whose we are—creatures fitted for love and for relationship.

Authentic Christian waiting embraces the past, the present, and the future. We wait for the coming of the hidden presence of God, *who came* on the cross and came quietly in the resurrection. We wait for God *who comes* unexpectedly each day to open up possibilities for love to reveal itself in redemptive and life-giving ways. We wait for God *who will come* unexpectedly to creation, breaking in upon us to loose the chains that bind us to false ways of thinking and living. We wait for and upon the advent of God, who reveals in the very stuff of life the inextinguishable power of love in relationship with all that is—in the history of our lives, in the history of the world—past, present, and future. This is an eschatological hope that is lived each day through the posture of waiting.

Theology of the Cross and Theologies of Liberation

Because a contextual theology of the cross engages, disputes, and intersects with the presuppositions implicit in the best theologies of liberation, the relation between the two theological perspectives constitutes a background interest of this book. Indeed, there are a number of theologians who successfully integrate theologies of liberation with the theology of the cross.[18] While there is much room for dialogue and discussion around questions of power and powerlessness, the meaning and possibilities in history, the suffering of God, and so on,[19] the most essential areas of dialogue between the theology of the cross and theologies of liberation concerns what it means to be human and what constitutes true human freedom. Both theologies are rooted in the idea that freedom is the essence of the human, yet they have very different understandings of the freedom that they presuppose as the goal and purpose of human life.

18. Including Moltmann, *Crucified God*; Sobrino, *Christology at the Crossroads*; Wells, *Christic Centre*; and Thompson, *Crossing the Divide*.

19. See Wells, "Theology of the Cross." In this article Wells fleshes out a number of areas for intersection and discussion between the two traditions: the suffering of God; justification; hermeneutical suspicion; oppression; option for the poor; incarnation; the cost of discipleship; and the priesthood of all believers.

Liberation theology privileges the external systemic conditions of freedom and equality and often presupposes (and, in its worst forms, ignores) the internal coherence of freedom in persons.[20] The theology of the cross, on the other hand, privileges the internal dimensions of freedom and presupposes (or, in its worst forms, ignores) the external expressions of freedom in the signs of justice-making and investment in life. Liberation theologies have been critical of the possibility of the theology of the cross being too inward, too focused on individualistic renderings of themes like forgiveness, justification, grace, and atonement. Reminding us of Luther's lack of support for the peasants in the Peasants' War and of his doctrine of the Two Kingdoms, some liberationists contend that the theology of the cross can lead to quietism, passivity, and non-engagement in politics and worldly power.[21] I agree with the liberationists' contention that, unless the internal human yearning for freedom and wholeness is manifest in the world, including through political and social action—unless it bears fruit—it is meaningless. However, I do not agree that the external dimensions of human freedom should be given priority over the internal dimensions. In saying this I do not mean to suggest that the external conditions people experience do not affect their internal being—or that the external conditions of fighting for freedom do not affect the internal struggle for freedom.

In fact the theology of the cross pushes theologies of liberation to be far more radical and subversive than they might otherwise be. In emphasizing freedom as the internal essence of the human that is intended to be externally realized and ordered in creation, the theology of the cross offers three insights into the relationship between inner freedom and its outer manifestation: (1) Internal freedom means that humans are ultimately free only in their "bondage" to God—humble, open, and trusting before God. Contrary to worldly (and "external") notions of freedom, this is not a freedom of the will to do as one wants. It is a freedom of essence *to be who one is* in the Creator's unique design, while at the same time recognizing the constant human compulsion to separate from God and be our own creators and masters.[22] (2) Such "bound freedom" means that humans are free from the tyranny of worldly power to oppress their

---

20. Hall, *Confessing the Faith*, 176–77.

21. See Wells, "Theology of the Cross," 160–61.

22. This is classically expressed by Luther: "A Christian is a perfectly free lord of all, subject to none. A Christian is a perfectly dutiful servant of all, subject to all" (*Freedom of a Christian*, 344).

souls and imprison them in dynamics intended to diminish their possibilities to love, to care, and to be fully alive. (3) The outward sign of inward "bound freedom" (to God) is lived each day in every interaction, in the ways we organize ourselves and seek to disempower the tyrannical power that inhibits and distorts the possibilities for creaturely flourishing. Who could be more threatening to the powers of the world than those for whom worldly power is internally impotent? Who could be freer to act against the power of tyranny in the world than those whose soul is not possessed by it?

In the theology of the cross, indifference and quietism are not options. Rather, the theology of the cross plunges us into deeper contemplation of the human condition, compelling us to re-image the nature of power and love and how their dynamics are played out in the world in the way we think, in the relationships between humans, and within creation in general. This is indeed a political theology, but it is also more than that. In the theology of the cross, the truth of things is hidden beneath its opposite. Thus the only true power is that of love—unquantifiable and limitless; the only true understanding of freedom is found in obedience to God and is lived out in relationship to others and to creation. Because our North American understanding of hope and liberation through modernity has depended on an image of the human rooted in mastery and power, the radical critique and reconstruction of power offered by the theology of the cross opens up new possibilities for understanding what it means to hope and to be free in the public spheres of contemporary North America.

Why George Grant and Douglas Hall?

George Grant (1918–1988), outspoken political philosopher, Christian, and public intellectual, wrote and spoke extensively in the Canadian public realm regarding the experience of living in the West at the end of the modern era. Douglas John Hall (b. 1928), prolific Protestant theologian, writes and speaks primarily to the North American "once-mainline" churches regarding what it means to be church in North America in the era of post-Christendom. Both Grant and Hall locate themselves as Canadians on the periphery of the American Empire—politically, intellectually, economically, geographically, and spiritually defined.[23] They speak

23. Some theologians would critique Grant and Hall for the way they can tend to generalize a whole culture and civilization in a particular age. They acknowledge the

with distinctively Canadian voices on the edge of the Empire. As such, both have been the foremost thinkers in their fields in Canada and, in the case of Hall, in the United States as well. Most importantly, they speak as ones whose thought has been formed by the theology of the cross.

Given that Grant was Hall's senior, the thought of the former had a greater influence on the latter than visa versa. The two developed a warm acquaintance with each other in the 1950s, through Rhoda Hall, Hall's wife, who worked with Grant at Dalhousie University prior to her studies at Union Theological Seminary. Hall acknowledges Grant's great influence on him for his own cultural analysis and more widely cites Grant's unique theological import for doing theology in the North American context:

> My reason for pursuing this topic [developing a Canadian con-
> textual theology] . . . stems . . . from the conviction that [Grant]
> has thought through the meaning of our identity as North
> Americans in general, and Canadians in particular, in a way that
> is both profound and unique. I believe that Christian theology,
> to be faithful to its roots, must always be contextual, and my
> thesis here, to state it very broadly, is that Grant's analysis of
> our culture can contribute to the contextualization of theology
> on this Continent—a quality which it has consistently lacked.
> Beyond that, I think it is equally possible that a theology which
> had sufficiently immersed itself in its own milieu might serve,
> in turn, to provide some incentive and direction for the very
> "search" Grant believes necessary for us as a people to under-
> take: the search for "new meaning" and a way into the future.[24]

In 1989, Douglas and Rhoda Hall tracked some of Grant's key insights and the extent of the impact of these insights upon their own development as theologians of the cross. For example, after reading *Technology and Empire*, the Halls testify that Grant's devastating critique of technology, modernism, theology, and Christendom hung over them like a summons.[25]

---

power of "the" modern western meta-narrative and seek to engage it in its dominant manifestations in society at large. In taking seriously their analysis of the North American context, I recognize the import of their over-arching analysis without denying the fact that it is shaped by the particularity of their social-economic-cultural-gender-racial locations. See Wells, *Christic Centre*, 241.

24. Hall, "Significance of Grant's Cultural Analysis," 120–29.

25. See Hall and Hall, "George Grant (1918–1988), A Tribute," 73, 76.

Was it possible for Protestants to discover in their origins a pre-modern stand, a vantage point from which, here and there in this most problematic of societies, they might find the courage and the intellectual honesty to enter the darkness of our epoch without succumbing to ultimate anxiety and despair? That sabbatical leave was to become, in response to this question and summons, the beginning of our own modest effort to rethink the received tradition of Protestantism from a more ancient vantage point—that of Luther's pre-modern *theologia crucis* ("theology of the cross"). We felt it might be possible from such a frame of reference to recover authentic Christian hope without equating it with the official philosophy of optimism and what Grant called the "religion of progress."[26]

Later in this same article, the Halls suggest that in the early years Grant too was preoccupied with the concern that has inspired their own theological vocation to rethink theology in the Reformed tradition so as to contribute "to the formation of an indigenous Protestant theology in North America."[27] It was a rethinking, Hall laments, that Grant had little time to pursue. Indeed, it is this rethinking to which Hall has given himself. Hall recognizes the extent to which Grant's analyses have provided the content to the negating task of his theology. He distinguishes between himself and Grant, however, in that his own call as a theologian has taken him also to the positive and constructive task of theology.

Others have also noted the relationship between the thinking of Grant and Hall. In "George Grant and the Theology of the Cross," Sheila Grant draws parallels between Grant and Hall regarding their understanding of the import of the theology of the cross for speaking truth in this context.[28] Further, in conversation with Harris Athanasiadis after her reading of Hall's *Lighten Our Darkness* (a book which as far as she knows her husband never read), she noted further resonance between the thought of her late husband and Hall.[29]

In his own book, *George Grant and the Theology of the Cross*, Athanasiadis briefly points to some important links between Grant and Hall,

---

26. Ibid., 77.

27. Ibid., 78.

28. Sheila Grant, "George Grant and the Theology of the Cross," 243–62.

29. The conversation between Sheila Grant and Harris Athanasiadis took place during a May, 1996 visit. The last section of Hall's *Lighten Our Darkness* includes extensive references to Grant's work.

including their shared frame of reference as theologians of the cross and their understanding of hope.

> In explicit dialogue with Grant, [Hall] writes about the possibilities for an alternative vision of faith and life in the technological era. First, he speaks of the possibility of an "indigenous theology of the cross" for North America which would offer a . . . "frame of reference" for "the prolonged and intense experience of negation." Second, such a theology would develop "foundations for raising and meeting the question of limits and an ethical sensitivity for the limits within which human beings should live." Finally, such a theology would "call into being a community whose most conspicuous mark would be the frustration of its every attempt to have a theology of glory" and one which is prepared to suffer . . . For all his brilliant insight and penetrating analysis of technological civilization under the critical scrutiny of a theology of the cross, Grant could only have been further enriched by dialogue with contemporary theologians of the cross . . . Grant could have found support among those theologians who struggle to express a theology of the cross which names things as they are and as they ought to be in the world without calling good evil and evil good, and who speak of a hope that does not ignore the reality of despair.[30]

Other than these works, nothing of significance has been published relating the thought of Grant and Hall. As Canadian thinkers concerned with the particularities of their context on the edge of the American Empire in late modernity and as theologians of the cross, Grant and Hall should be studied and thought together. This book is an attempt do so, and in this way represents a further step in claiming a distinctive theological voice that grows out of North American soil and is consciously located on the northern fringe of the Empire. Reflections from Canada are essential for a theology of the cross in North America at this time. As Canadians, Grant and Hall are part of a people who are deeply invested in the destiny of the American Empire, for better and for worse. They are part of a people who simultaneously are and are not a part of the Empire and who recognize the glory of the United States and are at once drawn and repulsed. In the public sphere, Canadians have grown up with an acute suspicion and self-disdaining admiration of the American Empire, whose colonizing impulse constantly calls Canadian identity to the fore. Indeed, the identity of Canada as a distinctive country carries with it a

---

30. Athanasiadis, *George Grant and the Theology of the Cross*, 248–49.

history of critique of the United States and its origins in the violence of revolution and unilateral action.[31] Canadians live with the globalizing impulses of the American Empire on a daily basis and know yearning, complacency, and resistance to it. "Is it time to play victim, jester, or pawn to the powerful neighbour?" Canadian thought on the dynamics of power and powerlessness grows out of a distinctly different context of power than that of the United States. The location of Grant and Hall as Canadian theologians of the cross living on the periphery of power equips them with a unique perspective for theology that seeks to speak to the crises of our times in North America.

Both of these thinkers articulate the reality of North American hopelessness and point to the possibility of hope with profound insight. Through their respective disciplines they have given their hearts and minds to thinking through the crises of hope that exist in North America through the latter part of the twentieth century, and in Hall's case the early twenty-first century. Both have been inspired by a call to enter into their context—its historical, political, spiritual, and economic underpinnings and realities—so as to bring the riches of their respective disciplines and of their faith to bear upon their understanding. As white Euro-Canadian males attuned to the dynamics of power, vulnerability, and identity; as Christians attentive to the voices of the afflicted and their import as a starting point for thought upon truth; as thinkers toward the end of the modern era in the West, critical of the legacies of liberalism, George Grant and Douglas John Hall have tapped into the soul of North America and glimpsed the insidious darkness of this time and place.

Though Grant and Hall have different audiences and methods, the spiritual and intellectual foundations of each lie in the theology of the cross. Their primal commitment to this theological perspective has guided them within their separate disciplines and methodologies to enter the darkness of hopelessness and stay there awaiting the emergence of hope. Both Grant and Hall recognize that at the very heart of the meaninglessness and despair that abound in North America is a crisis about what it means to be human. They critique the image of the human (and of God) as master presupposed by modern liberalism and recognize that the disappearance of the transcendent moorings of liberalism in North America has occasioned a general sense of hopelessness. Both speak to those within and on the periphery of power in the most powerful Empire

---

31. Indeed it was to Canada that United Empire Loyalists, African American slaves, and Vietnam draft dodgers fled, and it was Canada where they were welcomed.

of history and seek to understand more profoundly the affliction of the powerful and how this precipitates the affliction of the powerless. In resisting liberalism's legacies of Marxist and capitalist analyses of power, their analyses of power are based on the more ancient traditions of Athens and Jerusalem as these are mediated through the theology of the cross.

The hope out of which they speak stands as a critique of the empty optimism of liberalism and of the despair of relativist nihilism, both of which, they recognize, are being powerfully manifested in North American society. The hope out of which they speak is given unexpectedly as the intrusion of grace. It is hope that speaks in and to the real anxieties of this age, shedding the illusions of optimism and walking into the heart of our darkness to await the coming of impossible possibilities. It is hope that is not confined within the vicissitudes of history—eschatologically, technologically, or economically defined—but rather is hope that meets history open to its alterity, and waits upon the surprise of grace, whose source transcends, in-breaks upon, and enfolds history as "other." Such hope manifests a way of *thinking* about life as much as it manifests a way of *being* and *acting* in life.

The Book in Outline

I believe this book will be an important step in further articulating a contextually engaged theology of hope that, though sharing much with each, stands in distinction from post-liberal and liberation schools of theology in North America.[32] In contextually reflecting on the theology of the cross through Grant and Hall, this book seeks to retrieve some of the treasures of the Christian tradition and bring them to bear on contemporary religious and public life. It focuses on both the method of the cross and

---

32. Certainly some theologians in both the post-liberal and liberationist schools of theology claim the theology of the cross as essential to their method and point of departure. Some have noted Karl Barth (generally considered to be the inspiration for the post-liberal school) to be grounded in the theology of the cross. See Wells, "Theology of the Cross and Theologies of Liberation"; Hall, *Lighten Our Darkness*, 130–35, and *Remembered Voices*, 11–26; Lewis, *Between Cross and Resurrection*, 197–214; and Jüngel, *Karl Barth: A Theological Legacy*, 127–38. Jüngel is himself another important mentor of the post-liberal school for whom the theology of the cross is central. See Jüngel, *God as the Mystery of the World*, and Lewis, *Between Cross and Resurrection*, 234–55. On the other hand, political/liberation theologians such as Jürgen Moltmann and Jon Sobrino consider the theology of the cross to be intrinsic to liberation theology. Douglas Hall also considers that there is a deep and abiding resonance between the theology of the cross and theologies of liberation.

contextual critique of the cross and in so doing demonstrates how form manifests content, inviting readers to embrace theological thinking as spiritual practice. It is a perspective that resists modernist temptations to envision hope as progressivist futurity. In doing so, it challenges the contemporary church's self-understanding both as it stands before God and within North American society and as it constructs the image of "waiting at the foot of the cross" as an embodiment of hope in our context.

This first chapter has introduced the primary themes and focus of the book, both in its critical and constructive moves. In naming the import of this work both in global terms that respond to the malaise of the age and in narrow terms that identify the novelty and necessity for thinking Grant and Hall together in response to the contemporary crisis of hope, this chapter carves out a distinctive public and academic space for the presentation of the ideas contained in this book.

Part One of this book, entitled "The Method of the Cross as Waiting," explores a theological method of the cross that challenges the dominance of "mastery" in modern thought. Through a discussion of the method of the cross in Luther, Grant, and Hall (chapters 2, 3, and 4 respectively), ways of thinking about reality are presented as spiritual practices of waiting at the foot of the cross. The method of the cross mirrors the theological content of the cross. Over against theologies of glory that emphasize human mastery of thought and the domination of scientific reason, the theological method of the cross emphasizes the incompleteness of all human knowing and waits upon the impossible possibility of God's revelation in the midst of our fractured ways of human knowing.

Chapter 2 discusses Luther's theology of the cross as a method for theology through a brief analysis of his *Heidelberg Disputation*, drawing on the work of key Luther scholars. The distinctive place of epistemology in the theology of the cross is the methodological focus for this chapter.

In chapters 3 and 4 respectively, Grant's and Hall's methods of the cross are studied through their epistemologies, in the categories of revelation and reason and the relationships thereof. The theology of the cross provides the Christian foundation for the thought of both Grant and Hall, as evident in their respective articulations of the relationships between revelation and reason in the tradition of Athens and of Jerusalem. Because the dichotomies between the traditions of Athens and Jerusalem reflect most acutely the central area of tension and mutual critique between these two thinkers, these chapters also explore how their respective moorings in these ancient traditions provide each with distinctive languages and distinctive emphases in their conceptualizations of reality. Yet Grant and Hall both seek to explore "negatively" the apologetic intersection between God and the human, the gospel and the world, and faith and unfaith so as to enable a glimpse of a deeper (and "positive") meaning of life. Grant's philosophy and Hall's theology manifest two different but complementary entry points into the question of hope in contemporary North America. I will show how Grant's philosophy represents the side of "unfaith seeking faith" in the public sphere and Hall's theology represents the side of "faith seeking unfaith" in the ecclesial sphere. Overall, Part One will show how the image of "waiting at the foot of the cross" reflects a method of thought that manifests a theology of hope, the content of which will be further explored in Part Two.

Part Two, entitled "Deconstructing Modern Mastery: Waiting on Hope," is introduced by a brief exploration of the relationship between contextuality and the theology of the cross, by means of a discussion of the intersection between the particular and the universal and of the hermeneutic of the cross (chapter 5). This sets the stage for a focus on mastery and hope in the North American context in the work of Grant and Hall (chapters 6 and 7 respectively). Through their complementary critiques, we recognize that it is the relationship between mastery and hope that represents their shared understanding of the central *problematique* of the North American contemporary context through the lens of the cross. Where Grant explores the relationship of human mastery and hope in the public realm of civic life and thought (chapter 6), Hall explores the relationship of human mastery and hope in the practice and doctrine of Christendom (chapter 7).

In the second chapter of Part Two, I discuss Grant's analysis of mastery, its intersection with false conceptions of hope throughout modernity, and the extent to which this falsity is causing tyranny and moral blindness to rule under the guise of freedom and goodness in the public sphere of North American life (chapter 6). Grant's retrieval of the ancient wisdom of Plato and Christ, through the lens of the cross, provides him with a critical distance for naming the falseness of "glory" in the North American context. Grant argues that the essential contemporary crisis consists in the phrase, "we have been mastered by mastery." Further, he argues, we have been so completely mastered by a false vision of reality that we cannot see beyond the dynamism of its falsity—modern technological liberalism. According to Grant, the modern West (especially North America) has lost all sense of the transcendent and true ordering of reality. In contemplating what this means for the possibility of authentic Christian hope, I draw upon Grant's descriptions of different human responses to the crisis he sees reflected in contemporary North American society: the happy indifference of the "last people,"[33] the fearful mastery of the nihilists[34] and the "hopeful" despair of the honest. It is in his dialogue with Nietzsche that Grant most fully articulates what hope is not. Over against this analysis we can begin to discern the shades of authentic hope as waiting.

In the third chapter of Part Two, I discuss Douglas Hall's contextual critique and his explication of the metaphor of mastery as that which encapsulates the manifestations of the theology of glory in North America particularly in the practice and doctrine of Christendom (chapter 7). Hall draws heavily upon Grant's cultural critique. Without repeating these aspects of his critique, I discuss the intersection of the motif of mastery in his theological analysis of the doctrine and practices of Christendom and the extent to which as church we are living in falsity. In discussing Hall's understanding of the present crises, I consider his categories of "expectancy" and "experience," as well as "overt" and "covert" despair. On the one hand, we live in a context where "official optimism" regarding the possibilities for human mastery has reigned for many decades, particularly in the once mainline church. Hall deconstructs the grounds for optimism and faith in human mastery in our "officially optimistic society." In so doing, by way of the *via negativa*, he, like Grant, clarifies what hope *is not* in contemporary North America. On the other hand, we live in a context where we have seen the failure of human mastery and the possibility for goodness in the face of the horrific realities of the last century. For Hall, the failure of the human will to bring goodness into being represents the failure of the theology of glory (of mastery) in North America. With its failure many fear that there is no meaning to life beyond the parameters of the modern dream—only an abyss, the *nihil*. The problem is, however, that the confusion between hope and optimism in our society runs so deep that, for many, to cease to be optimistic means to cease to hope, to fall into despair, to be utterly hopeless. Such despair has real ramifications in daily life as we struggle to live together in our communities, as nations, and in the world. In exploring the guises of despair

33. Throughout the body of the book I will use the term "last people" as an inclusive alternative to Nietzsche's "last men."

34. For an instance of Nietzsche's discussion of the last people and the nihilists, see Nietzsche, *On the Genealogy of Morals*, 96, 163.

in the North American context, by way of the *via negativa*, Hall points to the possibilities for true hope only as we are enabled to wait in the darkness of our despair and the failure of the modern dream.

In Part Three, entitled "Waiting at the Foot of the Cross: Toward a Theology and Practice of Hope," I elaborate upon the image of "waiting at the foot of the cross" referred to throughout the book (chapter 8). This image provides a means to highlight Grant's and Hall's understandings of hope that emerge from their cultural critique through the *via negativa* of the theology of glory. In this chapter a case is made for "waiting" as an integrative theme that enables contemplation of both the methods and the substance of their perspectives. The "theology of hope as waiting" is not an indifferent waiting of passivity. Rather, as noted above, it is waiting that is attentive and alert to all the "data of despair" (Hall) and reflects the absent presence and present absence of God. Indeed, as Part One demonstrates, Grant's and Hall's methodologies and practices of thought themselves represent a waiting upon God. Not only do their ways of thought and being challenge modernist images of human mastery, potentiality, and faith in the human will; they also reflect a distinctly trust-centered posture in the face of the ambiguities and darkness of life. Such waiting is embodied in receptivity, attentiveness, openness to the o/Other—indeed the opposite postures of being to that presupposed in the modernist image of the human of mastery and power. This final chapter argues that the image of waiting at the foot of the cross is a framework for a theology of hope in our contemporary context. It will show how this image suggests concrete ways of being, thinking, and acting in the world that open us to the possibility of authentic hope in our context.

This project is located within the life of North America at the beginning of the second decade of the twenty-first century. I speak as a North American who has been raised on modern liberal understandings of the world—about what it means to be human and what it means to live together with others. I speak from the midst of those in and on the periphery of the once-mainline Protestant churches in North America for whom modern liberalism was formative and for whom Christian fundamentalism is not an option. This is my assumed audience and conversation partner. However, since the ideas of modern liberalism have shaped the self-understanding of North America in the public sphere, both civic and religious, my reflections on the character of hope and hopelessness in North America have ramifications for the very substance of our life together as church, continent, and globe. This project is driven by a desire, on my part, to speak to the heart of our darkness in North America and, within this darkness alongside George Grant and Douglas John Hall, to contemplate the One who meets us there. I give it as an offering, to God and to God's beloved humanity. I offer it in humility and hope, as a response of faith, as a "kick at the darkness" (Bruce Cockburn).[35]

35. Bruce Cockburn, *Lovers in a Dangerous Time*, True North Records TND318, 1984, compact disc and vinyl.

PART 1

The Method of the Cross as Waiting

2

Luther's Theology of the Cross and Theological Method

THEOLOGIA CRUCIS IS A tradition in theology extending from the apostle Paul to the present day that reflects a way of thinking about reality centered in the hidden revelation of the cross of Christ. Some of the key exemplars of this tradition include the apostle Paul,[1] Martin Luther,[2] Søren Kierkegaard,[3] Dietrich Bonhoeffer,[4] Simone Weil,[5] Karl Barth,[6] Reinhold Niebuhr,[7] and our contemporaries Eberhard Jüngel,[8] Jon Sobrino,[9] and Jürgen Moltmann.[10] For all of these thinkers, the paradoxical reality of suffering and sin in the world and the power and character

1. The key Pauline passages quoted in discussions of the theology of the cross include Rom 1:20, 1 Cor 1:18–25, and Gal 2:19–20.

2. Martin Luther claimed the apostle Paul and Augustine as the primary informers of his thought. See, for example, Luther's *Heidelberg Disputation*, 39–70.

3. See Kierkegaard, *Attack upon Christendom* and *The Present Age*.

4. Bonhoeffer, *Letters and Papers from Prison*, 122.

5. Cayley, *George Grant in Conversation*, 176.

6. In *The Crucified God*, Moltmann refers to several sections of Barth's *Church Dogmatics* that deal with the theology of the cross. See also Jüngel, *Karl Barth: A Theological Legacy*.

7. Hall's *Remembered Voices* includes an essay on Niebuhr, "Reinhold Niebuhr: An American Theology," 47–62. See also "The Cross and Contemporary Culture," and the first two chapters of Niebuhr's *The Nature and Destiny of Man*.

8. Jüngel, *God as the Mystery of the World*.

9. Sobrino, *Christology at the Crossroads*.

10. Moltmann, *Crucified God*. Among the many others who can and should be added to this list are, of course, George Grant and Douglas Hall.

of God's love are revealed in the mystery of the cross as nowhere else. The cross and suffering of Christ are the lens through which these theologians think about and experience the world in their distinctive times and places. Martin Luther is the theologian who coined the term 'the theology of the cross' and who most succinctly summarized the methodological grounding of this theology. The theology of the cross is not a doctrinal theme in theology, but a way of doing theology—a theological method—that establishes the parameters within which doctrinal reflections are considered to point toward truth or untruth.[11] I stand alongside those scholars who consider the theology of the cross to be the key signature in all of Luther's thought,[12] first recognizable in his writings of the mid-teens of the 16th century.[13] Luther's writings give evidence of the extent to which he internalized the theology of the cross throughout his lifetime as a way to think about existence and doctrine.[14] In this chapter, with reference to his *Heidelberg Disputation*, I will briefly present Luther's method for theology and examine the understanding and place of suffering in his method. Further, I will explore the utility of distinguishing between an epistemology and a hermeneutic of the cross within his method. Luther's method will be shown to point to the priority of waiting as a faithful posture for thought about reality. Such waiting resists all attempts to master reality by the power of the will and speculative reason.

11. Cousar, *Theology of the Cross*, 8. Cousar holds that the method of the cross establishes what can be "considered true or untrue." I have substituted "considered to point toward truth or untruth" to highlight the provisional nature of all human knowledge of God.

12. Von Loewenich, *Luther's Theology of the Cross*; Althaus, *The Theology of Martin Luther*; McGrath, *Luther's Theology of the Cross*; Cousar, *A Theology of the Cross*; Käsemann, "The Pauline Theology of the Cross"; Mannermaa, *Two Kinds of Love*. Luther scholars continue to discuss whether the theology of the cross was the essence and core of Luther's thought throughout his life (see Von Loewenich, *Luther's Theology of the Cross*, 13) or whether it represents the "early Luther" that later developed into a more sacramental understanding of reality and the relationship between God and the human.

13. Generally it is agreed that the great shift in Luther's theology is reflected in his *Lectures on the Psalms* (1513–1515) and *Lectures on Romans* (1515–1516); *Disputation Against Scholastic Theology* (1517); *The Ninety-Five Theses* (1517); and the *Heidelberg Disputation* (1518).

14. Von Loewenich's classic work, *Luther's Theology of the Cross*, tracks Luther's theology of the cross from his early writings through his middle and later writings. See also Althaus, *Theology of Martin Luther*; McGrath, *Luther's Theology of the Cross*; Cousar, *Theology of the Cross*.

Luther's Theology as Method

Luther's clearest articulation of the form and content of the theology of the cross as it pertains to human knowledge of God is found in forty theses Luther wrote for a theological disputation held at Heidelberg in 1518. These theses represent the classical expression of the theology of cross as it is defined over and against the theology of glory. Luther succinctly posits the character of human knowledge of God and its consequences for reality as a whole in such a way that a distinctive method of the cross emerges. Contemporary discussions of the theology of the cross continue to point to the *Heidelberg Disputation* as the key to Luther's theological method.[15] Furthermore, both George Grant (implicitly) and Douglas Hall (explicitly) refer to this work throughout the corpus of their writings as central to their own method. While Luther is best known for his radical insight into the grace of God through the doctrine of justification by grace through faith, the theology of the cross provides the methodological foundation for this doctrine.

Although I agree with many scholars who argue that theses 19 to 21 contain the core of Luther's insights in this work,[16] Gerhard Forde argues persuasively that these theses must be read within the context of the wider text of the *Heidelberg Disputation*—its movement from a critique of human attempts to master reality through will and works, to its rethinking of the place of the law of God and its reflections on grace, justification, and the fullness of the love of God.[17] Within this wider reading, however, theses 19 to 21 stand out:

> Thesis 19: That person does not deserve to be called a theologian who looks upon the invisible things of God as though they were clearly perceptible in those things which have actually happened [Rom 1:20].

> Thesis 20: He (sic) deserves to be called a theologian, however, who comprehends the visible and manifest (*posteriora*) things of God seen through suffering and the cross.

> Thesis 21: A theology of glory calls evil good and good evil. A theology of the cross calls the thing what it actually is (*quod res est*).[18]

15. See notes 12 and 14 above.

16. Althaus, *Theology of Martin Luther*; McGrath, *Luther's Theology of the Cross*; Von Loewenich, *Luther's Theology of the Cross*; Moltmann, *Crucified God*.

17. Forde, *On Being a Theologian of the Cross*. The book follows this pattern of argument.

18. Luther, *Heidelberg Disputation*, 52–54.

These three theses function as a turning point in the *Disputation* between discussions of the law of God and the love of God and between discussions on works of the will and on the place of grace, all of which provide the ground for Luther's philosophical theses, which emphasize the right relationship between faith and philosophy (theses 29–40). The turning point (theses 19–21) redirects the reader's focus from critiques regarding knowledge of God and humanity by way of works righteousness and speculative reason (both acts of the human will that grow out of the prideful desire to be as God) to the possibilities for genuine knowledge of God through faith in the crucified Christ.

There has been some disagreement concerning the propriety of contemplating Luther's discussions of the theology/theologian of the cross in terms of theological method. Gerhard Forde, for example, argues that to talk of Luther's understanding of the theology of the cross as if it revolved around a "theological principle"[19] is to miss the fact that Luther is fundamentally concerned with how to be a theologian, rather than with establishing a method for theology. According to Forde, Luther is more concerned with a spirituality of the cross than a method of the cross.[20] Although I have great admiration for Forde's work and appreciate his focus on the spiritual dimension of Luther's thought and its relationship to the life of faith, my reading of Luther and the tradition suggests that, precisely because it articulates the way of being a theologian, the theology of the cross provides both content and form for a distinctive theological method.[21] Theological method "refers to explorations of the conditions under which theological claims may be true."[22] With the method of the cross

19. Von Loewenich considers the theology of the cross to be a theological principle of sorts—that which orders all theological knowledge. "It follows then that in Luther's theology of the cross we are not dealing with paraphrases of the monkish ideal of humility, but with a distinctive principle of theological knowledge that corresponds exactly to the Apostle Paul's theology of the cross" (*Luther's Theology of the Cross*, 13). See also Mannermaa, *Two Kinds of Love*, 27.

20. Forde, *On Being a Theologian of the Cross*, 4–5. Though Forde does not use the phrase "spirituality of the cross," his emphasis on being a theologian of the cross prioritizes lived experience of the cross over a methodological approach. Living the reality of the cross means living the event of the cross in our inner experience of death to self and new life in God. As such it reflects an internal posture of being, a spirituality.

21. According to Moltmann, "The cross is the key signature for all Christian theology" (*Crucified God*, 72). Hall quotes this passage approvingly in numerous places throughout his work.

22. Kelsey, "Method, Theological," 363–68. Kelsey's work on theological method stands in the background of my thought on the theology of the cross as method in theology.

in mind, I will rephrase this definition to say that theological method refers to explorations of the conditions under which theological claims may be understood to *point to truth*. Indeed, Luther's entire description of what it means to be a theologian of the cross refers to such explorations. The priority of faith in the crucified Christ and the implications thereof establish the conditions under which theological claims may be considered to be true. Furthermore, Luther's discussions of the theology of glory—with its emphasis on the power of the will to act morally and its trust in speculative reason to discover the pathway to God—establish the conditions under which theological claims are considered untrue.

As a method, the *theologia crucis* stands against the theology of glory. For Luther, theologies of glory ignore the suffering and the cross of Christ that stand at the very centre of the Christian story, and they displace the living relationship of faith in the crucified Christ, substituting more secure and safe ways of thinking and existing. The theology of glory is recognized in human attempts at mastery through the will and speculative reason. For Luther, the essence of the fallen human condition is found in a constant attempt to be as God, manifested most acutely in the temptation to mastery in the power of the will and speculative reason. On the one hand, the will attempts to act morally so as to gain God's favour in works righteousness that ultimately eclipses God's graciousness. On the other hand, speculative reason seeks to "think its way" to God's glory.[23] Both these attempts assume the possibility of continuity in relations between humans and God,[24] and as such, enable human will to replace God's will, and ideas about God to replace faith in God.

Over against the theology of glory, the theology of the cross posits the impotence of the work of the human will and the limit of human reason as the cornerstones for Christian existence and thought. The theology of the cross is suspicious of all forms of thinking that attempt to understand God in terms that ignore the essential disjunction between God and creation, which includes the disjunction between human knowing and God as it is articulated in theological discourse. Theologies of glory, whatever their context, are thus understood to be manifestations of the temptations of the human condition to mastery in theological form. For

23. "Religious speculation and sanctification by works are only two manifestations of the same desire in [humans], the desire for unbroken direct dealings with God" (Von Loewenich, quoted in Moltmann, *Crucified God*, 71).

24. Or, in Luther's vocabulary, humans assume that we can see through the visible things of the world into the invisible things of God (God's glory).

Luther, the fallenness of humanity is evidenced in a false reliance on and trust in the essential goodness of the human will, works, and reason (as opposed to recognizing them as gifts of grace requiring constant renewal). Furthermore, Luther recognizes that the primal compulsion of the human will and reason is to serve human ends (not divine ends), which inevitably results in the human attempt to master, manage, or masquerade as God, so that humans are blinded to "things as they are," both in terms of the world and of God's revelation. Thus, theology undertaken by the guidance of human will and reason can function only to turn people away from the truth of things—to "call evil good and good evil."

All of this raises questions about how theology can even be undertaken by humans, given the reality of sin, evil, and suffering that distances the world from God. In his context, Luther recognized the extent to which theologies of glory claimed things about God that grew out of an assumed "peaceful" proximity between God and creation and not out of the disjointed and broken truth of things revealed in the cross of Christ. A theology that does not, in its very method, consider the reality of human finitude and fallenness (particularly in terms of its manifestation in the human will and speculative reason) cannot be true theology, for its essential point of departure is flawed. Such a theology of glory serves to placate and spiritually numb people by insisting that there is "Peace, Peace" in and between heaven and earth, when indeed there is no peace.[25] On the other hand, a theology that grows out of the constant challenge of the cross, at the core of which stands the reality of creaturely fragility, vulnerability, and dependence on God, is a theology that can venture to point toward the truth of things because its essential method is honest to faith in the crucified Christ and the revelation on the cross of the human condition. Such a theology resists the temptations to mastery and instead, in humility, acknowledges the brokenness of human knowing and aspirations.

It is understandable that many scholars are critical of considering the theology of the cross as a method for theology. They are critical with right intention. The theology of the cross resists being a "method" per se precisely because the language of method in scholarship suggests the imposition of human mastery, will, and speculation on the interpretation of reality. Consequently, methods seem bound to serve the fallen notions

---

25. Jer 6:14, 8:11. See also Luther, Thesis 92, *Explanation of the Ninety-Five Theses*, 251: "Away then with all those prophets who say to the people of Christ, 'Peace, peace,' and there is no peace!"

of the self, reality, and God that cannot but end in a positive theology that ultimately lies about reality.

How, then, does the theology of the cross address this essential conflict with the power of the will and speculative reason to master thought? It does so by the *via negativa*—the way of negation—wherein the cross imposes itself on the form and content of theology. By engaging reality and our understanding of God critically by the *via negativa*, the theology of the cross draws us into speaking about God and reality itself in a way that rigorously rejects and intentionally disarms the myriad ways human mastery, will, and reason desire their own ends. In terms of the form of the theology of the cross, the *via negativa* provides a pathway by which the efforts of human mastery, will, and reason to insulate and secure itself from the assaults of life and faith are cleared and stripped away. In the theology of the cross the *via negativa* functions much like confession in worship—a stripping naked of the self before God. It is only in moving through the "confessional" of the *via negativa* that the theologian may be open to glimpse and to say "what the thing actually is." The reality of the cross in the heart of the Christian faith relativizes and extinguishes all attempts for human mastery, will, and reason to have their way.[26]

In terms of the content of the theology of the cross, one must engage the negative on two more fronts. Firstly, by the *via negativa* the theologian of the cross must say what a thing is *not* and what is *not* the thing (over and against the theology of glory). This is the critical move in the theology of the cross. Secondly, the theologian of the cross must say "what the thing is" only through the "negating" elements of suffering and the cross. This is the constructive move in the theology of the cross wherein all attempts by the human mastery, will, and reason to speculate upon the things of God are consumed by the *via negativa* of the cross and suffering. When we are drawn to glory in the works of God or of humans, the cross stands (often unnoticed) in our midst, extinguishing our shouts of triumph by the truth of its powerful weakness and challenging us "to call the thing what it actually is."

Related to this is the import of human historical experience as a touchstone for the task of theology. The concrete day-to-day-ness of life grounds our spirituality and thought about God. Indeed, not only must concrete historical experience be recognized for what it is, but also how

26. "The thirst for glory is not ended by satisfying it but by extinguishing it" (Luther, Thesis 22 [Explanation], *Heidelberg Disputation*, quoted in Forde, *On Being a Theologian of the Cross*, i).

one recognizes and thinks about "what it is" has concrete effects in one's relationships with oneself, others, and God. For example, humanity cannot look around and, by reason, recognize God's presence, handiwork, or providence in the world. God is not self-evident in existence. The Creator is not self-evident in creation in terms of a discernable moral structure or unambiguous benevolence. Providence is not self-evident in history in terms of fitting into a definable pattern with a progressive or clearly discernable outcome. This is the truth of things that is given to reason. To speculate upon, to will, and prescribe it to be otherwise is to concoct an illusion that obscures "the thing" to the naked eye of reason and nature. Luther's epistemology emphasizes the importance of reason and thought as the means to be honest about visible things. This is the right purpose of reason—to contemplate the visible world honestly. Thus, "to call a thing what it actually is" is part of what we do when we accept the parameters and limits within which reason and nature are given to function.

With the experience of faith in the crucified Christ, reason is called to serve and engage faith such that the cross is constantly held before us as the boundary which reason must contemplate but behind which reason cannot go. Human reason cannot master the cross of Christ. Knowledge of God is given only to faith and such knowing circumscribes all other knowing of the world, though it must also be engaged by it. Luther challenges people to be rigorously honest about inner experience (as the invisible part of the human, hidden in God—the domain of faith) and outer experience (as the visible part of the human and creation—the domain of reason and the will). It is our inner experience of conviction in the truth of the crucified Christ that he prioritizes and about which we can do nothing, except to wait for God. To lie about inner experience leads to lies about outer experience. Furthermore, to lie about outer experience (for example, to see through the visible to the invisible things of God)[27] establishes blocks to inner experience of faith. It is only the inner experience of faith in the crucified Christ (given in justification, over and over again) that enables one to speak about reality through the lens of the cross and opposed to the mastery of speculative reason. To assume a body of knowledge based upon the content of faith, without knowing the experience of faith as gift from outside oneself, leads to lying. It is only to faith that the hiddenness of God's presence and love is revealed. However,

27. "Thesis 19: That person is not a theologian who looks upon the invisible things of God as though they were clearly perceptible in those things which have actually happened [Rom 1:20]" (*Heidelberg Disputation*, 52; brackets original).

what this revelation reveals is the "negating" side of God known in suffering and the cross—the clothing or backside of God—that hides God from being known in the glory of divinity, and reveals God in the suffering of the human. For Luther, the essence of what is revealed in God's suffering is God's abiding and passionate love. Human speech about the works of God or humanity in terms of glory reveals false faith, for it does not reflect the form or content of faith in the crucified and suffering Christ of love. The theology of the cross always seeks the wholeness and integration of the inner and the outer, of faith and reason, of grace and the will. However, the theologian of the cross knows that the brokenness of life and of the relationship between God and creation makes this an impossibility. Therein lies the tension from which we theologians of the cross must not flee. It is in the event of the cross that the paradoxes exist in the fullness of their tension. The highest thought pushes us to the limits of our finitude and reason, such that at its limit thought, itself, might become an act of worship, an act of waiting upon and for God.

Suffering, Mastery, and Thought in Luther's Method of the Cross

Before turning to more specific discussions of epistemology and hermeneutics, I want to say something about the suffering or waiting of thought that is an essential posture for theologians of the cross.[28] Luther's understanding of suffering functions on a few levels that overlap. He considers that humans suffer because they are constantly forced to reckon with the fact that they are not the masters of their own lives or of creation. Suffering and death constitute that against which humans "naturally" toil—the enemy.[29] Consequently, the fact of suffering in all its forms manifests on one level the reality that we are incomplete: we are not our own masters or the masters of anything else in creation. To live means to suffer the fact that we are not our own masters, that we are not self-sufficient. It is false to say, however, that our finitude is equivalent to our fallenness. Rather, fear of finitude or lack of acceptance of finitude is understood to be that which "triggers" actions of fallenness in which humans seek to be as God.

---

28. For an excellent discussion of the place of suffering in Luther's theology, see Wengert, "Peace, Peace . . . Cross, Cross."

29. "Suffering occurs in the depths of the human spirit and is infinitely more subtle than physical pain . . . [It] has to do with the discovery of death" (Hall, *Lighten our Darkness*, x).

Suffering, in body, soul, and mind, is a mirror that reflects the fact that all our yearnings for perfection and finality, for comfort and safety, cannot in the end be secured by us.[30] In some sense our lives consist entirely of suffering the distinctiveness of our creaturely being—being apart from God, being separated from wholeness and fulfillment in this world. By natural human means, we can never reach the finality and fullness of God.[31]

We also suffer in our thought.[32] For Luther the suffering of thought primarily has to do with the struggle for meaning. He uses the term *Anfechtungen* to include the terrible suffering that comes upon humans in the process of their search for meaning. Our minds seek to know and to understand reality. Our yearning for a comprehensible reality at the deepest level reflects our yearning for God's fullness and completion. This yearning for meaning is a type of waiting for completion through thought. However, most often this yearning for meaning turns in on itself and seeks to master its own ends, unable to live within the incompleteness of created being. Thus, our thought about God naturally rejects the suffering and waiting implicit in such thought and seeks, instead, to posit speculatively prescriptive doctrines of God and creation that fulfill our human need for finality, mastery, and security and that can only end in calling "evil good and good evil." Indeed, at some level in thought, mind,

30. "No one wants to suffer—nor should one want to. But spiritual and cerebral—as well as on occasion, physical—suffering belongs to the life of 'the people of the cross'" (Hall, *Thinking the Faith*, 19).

31. Grant and Hall (as well as other theologians of the cross, especially liberation theologians) emphasize the importance of Christ's suffering as the suffering of God in solidarity with creaturely suffering. Their reflections focus on the incarnational essence of the cross such that all suffering of human (and creaturely) life is held within the event of the cross. Luther's understanding of suffering clearly focuses on the struggle for meaning and understanding as the essential component of suffering that could be (but is not necessarily) precipitated by external trials of life. While bodily/physical suffering is not specifically a focus for Luther, it is a focus for the apostle Paul. Throughout this book it will become clear the extent to which physical/ "outer"/ social suffering is presupposed in all discussions of suffering and how it is related to spiritual/"inner"/personal suffering.

32. Both Grant's and Hall's contemporary accounts of the relationship between suffering and thought take Luther one step further. They both show how untrue thought about the reality of things (i.e. thought that does not suffer) has real-life ethical consequences in the world. When one avoids the suffering of thought, one cannot but end in calling "evil good and good evil." In doing this, one perpetuates evil in the world and puts stumbling blocks in the way of the good. Thus Grant and Hall consider the dynamics of systemic suffering, sin, and evil in the world in light of a primal rejection of suffering from thought and the consequent disconnect from the truth of things.

and spirit we are restlessly suffering or waiting for our restful fulfill-ment in God. For Luther, it is only humility that enables the possibility of thinking about the meaning of things with any measure of truth. It is only in humility that we are open to wait upon and to receive God's visitation to our thought. Yet, even when we are in a posture of humility, truly thinking about the meaning of reality, we must be prepared to suffer the assaults of *Anfechtungen*. A spirit of humility will not protect us from such suffering but only enable us to wait and to receive hidden abundance through it. For Luther the suffering of thought, as I have intimated, is an experience of waiting, constantly preparing ourselves for God's visitation to thought, which is always incomplete when we attempt to master it in language or reason. The moment we think we have mastered the hidden revelation of God to thought, we must be brought again to a place of waiting that reflects trust and humility in the face of our human finitude and incompletion.

In terms of the form of the theology of the cross, Luther recognizes that we suffer when we engage in true thought because of our "fallen" human condition and the constancy of our human yearning for mastery, comfort, and security on our own terms. To think about the truth of things means that we are constantly challenged to let go of all within our thought that cushions us from thinking "the thing as it is." This is the suffering (the stripping, or laying bare) of thought, which is an endless and agonizing process. In the moment one is moved by the *via negativa* and opened to sense the mystery of the whole, one cannot begin to speak positively about it without finding oneself falling back on comfortable ways of thinking about God and reality and, therefore, needing to be stripped again. As theologians we are incapable of seeing the glory of God in nakedness, unable by nature to speak positively about who God is and how God acts without falling into a certain falsity. We always await completion. Yet at the same time, by faith we are given glimpses of the truth of things that can never be spoken in fullness without experienc-ing the desire for mastery and for comfortable ways of speaking about it. We glimpse "fragments" of the beauty of God that illuminate reality. However, the fragments always include that which is beyond them, that within which they (and we) are held, that which exists in the wholeness of God's communion. The fragments themselves cannot be gathered up and pieced together as the utterance of truth in its entirety. This is the most harrowing challenge to human reason and its yearning for mastery and finality. There is suffering that is manifested in our very thought about reality. The *via negativa* is always uncomfortable and continually acts to strip us of our pretences and comfort in thought. As a theologian of the cross one is continually faced with suffering the limit of one's will and reason and the temptation to use them in the service of human comfort, security, and mastery. We are constantly wrestling to let go of all the compulsions that drive us to master life through thought and to wait upon fullness and completion in a posture of receptivity.

On the other hand, in terms of the content of the theology of the cross, Luther recognizes that there is constancy in the suffering of thought for the theologian of the cross because of the contradictory subject matter of theological discourse and the condition of those who think it. The focus of this theology, within which all of reality finds its truth, is the cross and its revelation of the extremity both of God's love and of the suffering of creation. To think through the truth of these two claims (as they are variously manifested and hidden in the world as it is) is to wrestle without ceasing. In the theology of the cross such wrestling is what thought is intended for. Indeed, in pushing the contradiction as far as one is able, the thought of the theologian of the cross reaches its limit; there is nothing then to do but to wait upon God's revealing.[33] In the *theologia crucis*, then, as part of the suffering and acceptance of human limit, thought participates in the soul's waiting upon God—a waiting that is never quiet or easy. As theologians of the cross we are constantly called back to wait at the agonizing place at the foot of the cross—to wait for the in-breaking of revelation by which our souls and hearts are renewed in faithful thanksgiving.[34]

The Epistemology and Hermeneutic of the Cross

In order to discern the critical relevance of a theology of the cross for the contemporary North American context, we must begin by making a distinction between an epistemology of the cross and a hermeneutic of the cross. First and foremost, as I have already mentioned, Luther's

33. This description of Luther's thought draws upon terms used by Simone Weil to interpret what he is saying for a contemporary reading.

34. "The cross of Christ makes plain that there is no direct knowledge of God for [the human]. Christian thinking must come to a halt before the fact of the cross. The cross makes demands on Christian thought—demands which must either be acted on or ignored. If Christian thought ignores the demands of the cross it becomes a theology of glory. If the cross becomes the foundation of thought, a theology of the cross results" (Von Loewenich, *Luther's Theology of the Cross*, 27).

theology of the cross is an epistemology because it revolves around questions about human knowledge of God given the human condition. The priority Luther places on proper knowing of God shapes how all else is known in life. In faith, the knowledge of God and of the creature are intimately related. However, faith reveals that they are related not firstly by continuity but by discontinuity; not firstly by similarity but by otherness between God and the creature. Luther's epistemology of the cross reflects an inward movement, a spirituality of thought, wherein the inner life of the believer awaits the address of that which is other to it and outside it.

In our modern and post-modern western context, where questions of epistemology have become a central concern in most disciplines and where the historicist relativizing of human ways of knowing are celebrated, the epistemology of the cross stands out in critical resistance against all efforts to tame theology into conformity with any ideology or ecclesial-socio-economic-political program. Indeed, no matter where one aligns oneself in the political sphere; no matter what one's social, cultural, or sexual identity, the theology of the cross critiques, challenges, and seeks to cleanse us of our human propensity to usurp the place of God, to defy our limits and creaturely dependence and thereby to shield ourselves from "falling into the hands of the living God" (Heb 10:31).

As a hermeneutic of the cross, the *theologia crucis* posits the cross as the only lens by which to read and interpret the world as it actually is. Just as thought inwardly awaits the clearing and cleansing of revelation given in an epistemology of the cross, outward perception wrestles with and awaits the clearing and cleansing of the hermeneutic of the cross. For example, when we find ourselves noticing the beauty of the world and spontaneously presuming that this is an obvious sign of God's presence and work, the hermeneutic of the cross (given in faith) challenges us to expand our view. The cross is placed in the very foreground of all images of beauty, bringing the tragic dimension to bear upon all that is. The world is that for which, by which, and in which Christ died. To say "what a thing actually is" in this world means that we cannot at once think and know the beautiful without at once thinking and knowing the tragic loss and woundedness of that which is beautiful. In this realm of creation the beautiful and tragic dimensions of reality cannot be separated without venturing to call "good evil and evil good." At the same time, however, the tragic and beautiful dimensions of life cannot, by any efforts of reason, be considered to be mutually descriptive or interactive. It is only by means of a hermeneutic of the cross that the world can be interpreted as it actually is, in a way that includes the gaps that exist within the contra-diction—between beauty and tragedy, between God's love and the reality of suffering. Ultimately the contradiction of faith that always confronts and shapes reason is the reality of the love of God and the suffering of creation, revealed at once on the cross of Christ.

In making the distinction between epistemology and hermeneutics, I do not intend to suggest that these two do not interpenetrate and af-fect one another in the life of faith. Indeed, there is a dynamic interplay between the two wherein the cross dislocates and relocates tidy ways of thinking. Further, by making such a distinction I do not seek to obscure the cross from view but rather to make it more recognizable in the ex-ercise of human thought. The distinction between epistemology and hermeneutics highlights two insights that relate, again, to the dynamic interplay of form and content in the theology of the cross: (1) the priority placed on suffering and the cross in the interior life of faith—a waiting that characterizes the relationship between the believer and God—is reflected in the world in recognizable ways, though ultimately hidden in God; and (2) the priority placed on the knowledge of God through faith in the crucified Christ and the way this knowledge is manifested in our thought shapes our perspectives on all else in life. To read the world through the lens of suffering and the cross signifies a commitment to faith in the crucified One and to waiting upon this revelation in life. Thus, when I speak of the theology of the cross in terms of epistemology and hermeneutics, I am really speaking of how it is that theologians give their whole selves to the task of theology in a faith that seeks understanding. Some contend that this understanding of faith and the whole person does not include the ethical and active dimension of being (the focus of much critique toward Luther and Lutheran theology). However, in the theology of the cross it is clear that there is a dynamic interplay between thought and active engagement in the world. Thinking is rooted in existence. Though some might argue that thought is prioritized in the theology of the cross, it is only prioritized as that which grows out of existence and as that which is intended to serve "cruciform" engagement and living in the world. "A [person] becomes a theologian by living, by dying and being damned, not by understanding, reading and speculation."[35]

In the following two chapters I explore Grant's and Hall's theologi-cal methods of the cross. The majority of the discussion revolves around

35. Luther as quoted in Hall, *Lighten Our Darkness*, 110. "Doctrine incarnates itself in ethics and life" (Hall, *Professing the Faith*, 63).

their epistemologies of the cross (with reference to their hermeneutics of the cross, which will be further elaborated upon in chapters six and seven), as well as the way in which faith in the crucified Christ provides the form and content of human knowledge about God and reality. We will begin to see how thought as waiting at the foot of the cross emerges as both a critical response of resistance to the forms of thought available in modernity and as a constructive spiritual practice grounded in trust.

3

Grant's Method of the Cross

Grant and Hall: Athens and Jerusalem

THE FACT THAT GRANT and Hall speak from within different disciplines and to different audiences shapes the language that they use and the perceived differences between them. As a political philosopher and a public intellectual, Grant speaks with the language of philosophy out of the tradition of Athens (Plato) to the Canadian public. As a Christian theologian, Hall speaks with the language of theology out of the tradition of Jerusalem to those within and on the periphery of the once-mainline churches in North America. Beneath the differences in language, discipline, and audience, however, Grant and Hall speak from the same essential doctrinal foundation or "grammar" of the theology of the cross.[1]

---

1. The latter way of expressing this is influenced by the work of Lindbeck, *Nature of Doctrine*. Lindbeck distinguishes between an "abiding doctrinal grammar" and a "variable theological vocabulary" or language (ibid., 173). Accordingly, I am arguing that Grant and Hall think out of similar grammatical or narrative structures: the biblical narrative is centered and interpreted through Christ, reaching its climax in his crucifixion. The vocabulary they use to communicate this story, however, is different. Where they would differ from Lindbeck (and the "post-liberals" who build on Lindbeck) is that they understand that the relationship between the human experience of the world and the biblical narrative is not uni-directional in terms of one shaping the other. Both Grant and Hall highlight particular kinds of experience (i.e., suffering and brokenness) as that which illumines biblical revelation and is centered on the cross as its deepest reality. They would, however, agree with Lindbeck that the biblical story centered on the cross shapes human experience in the world in that suffering now has the possibility to become "cruciform" and, hence, redemptive rather than destructive. See ibid., 178.

Considering the method of the cross through the relationship between reason and revelation in the thought of Grant and Hall inevitably means considering the relationship and the age-old tensions between Athens (philosophy/reason) and Jerusalem (theology/revelation) as well. The ancient question—What has Athens to do with Jerusalem? (Tertullian)— greets us here in a new context. The fact that we come at this question through the work of a philosopher who speaks with the language of Athens and a theologian who speaks with the language of Jerusalem has implications for a fundamental re-thinking of this question. To assume that a philosopher and a theologian can share the same essential thought foundations, yet express these within different language systems, suggests important things regarding the relationship between thought and language. Priority is placed on inner experience shaped by faith's vision of the cross as that which provides a "framework"[2] for thought that can be engaged, expressed, clarified, and expanded using different vocabularies.[3] In the work of Grant and Hall, we see this possibility. For though they are each sceptical of the other's tradition and the possibility of the "other" language speaking the truth of things and the relationships between things, they are each convicted that truth resides in the cross of Christ. Further, they each believe that, as thinkers of this time and place, it is contingent upon them to think through the meaning of such a claim.

In this chapter and the next, I do not seek to establish that both thinkers are theologians of the cross. This has already been established for each of them in compelling ways. I seek to show *how it is* that each of them is a theologian of the cross and how it is that their differences in language, discipline, and audience provide complementarity in their thought and invite further efforts to think them together. To this end, I will explore Grant and Hall respectively in terms of their epistemologies of the cross as this is reflected in their various discussions regarding the relationship between revelation and reason. The extent to which faith in the crucified Christ shapes the central aspects of their epistemology and distinguishes their thought from that of dominant modern epistemological trends will be apparent. Furthermore, a background theme of the discussion is the dynamic interplay of form and content in the theology of the cross. As we have seen, Luther's theses 19–21 on the knowledge of God presuppose the content of faith in the crucified Christ and the

---

2. Lindbeck, *Church in a Post-Liberal Age*, 33.

3. For a discussion on distinctions between inner and outer experience in the theology of the cross, see Von Loewenich, *Luther's Theology of the Cross*, 77ff; 93ff.

priority of the revelation of the cross as that which forms and directs thought (and the theologian herself). The relationship between form and content in the theology of the cross is dynamic and dialogical. Where priority is placed upon form, form is recognized and discerned by the content of the cross; where priority is placed upon content, content is purged and purified by the form of the cross. In contemplating what it means to think through faith in the crucified Christ, there is a certain disruptive fluidity wherein all thought is weighed in the balance and found wanting and waiting. "I do not know it and I do not understand it, but sounding from above and ringing in my ears I hear what is beyond the thoughts of [the human]."[4] In exploring Grant and Hall's methods of the cross in this chapter and the next it will become evident the extent to which their disciplines of thought reflect a spiritual practice of waiting at the foot of the cross.

Grant's Method: An Introduction

Throughout the corpus of his published and unpublished work, Grant writes a great deal about the relationship between revelation and reason.[5] As we shall see, all of his reflections on revelation and reason are manifested in his oft-cited Weilian understanding of faith: "Faith is the experience that the intelligence is enlightened by love."[6] Grant discusses the relationship between revelation and reason using many terms: revelation and reason; Jerusalem and Athens; theology and philosophy; faith/belief and understanding; charity and contemplation; loving and knowing. As one who "believes so that he may know,"[7] for him each of these couplets reflects different dimensions of and implications for thought. In general, Grant's understanding of the relationship between revelation and reason has four distinct, paradoxical, and inter-related manifestations within which the couplets can be understood in their depth and complexity: Revelation and reason exist in tension and paradox; Revelation serves reason; Reason serves revelation; Revelation and reason are

---

4. Luther as quoted in Hall, *Lighten Our Darkness*, 135.

5. See, for example, Grant, "George Grant and Religion," 47.

6. See, for example, Grant's essay, "Faith and the Multiversity," in *Technology and Justice*.

7. "*Credo ut intelligam*" (Anselm of Canterbury, "Proslogion," 69–70). Grant uses this phrase a number of times throughout his corpus to propose a challenging reordering of thought for modern liberalism.

one. The fact that, for Grant, no single understanding of the relationship between revelation and reason in and of itself speaks the truth of things reflects his grounding in the theology of the cross and his resistance to mastery of thought, both of which are manifested in the complexity of waiting. There is a brokenness and discontinuity between human apprehensions of truth and truth itself (between creation and God, in other words) that foreclose the possibility of speaking in positive and singular terms about the truth of things. The four different and paradoxical understandings of the relationships between revelation and reason speak at different levels and in different ways to the truth of things. They stand in dynamic tension with one another, which in turn points to the fullness of Grant's method of the cross, wherein thought is a means of waiting in receptivity for completion while never possessing it.

Revelation and Reason in Tension

Grant's epistemology of the cross presupposes that revelation and reason are of completely different orders. There is a disjunction or discontinuity between revelation and reason that can never be overcome from the human side. When considering this in terms of Grant's Weilian description of faith,[8] we see that love and the intellect (which for Grant correspond with revelation and reason) are distinctly separate categories. In form, reason cannot think its way to revelation. Revelation has an "otherness" from which reason only receives and towards which it cannot reach. Reason exists within limits. When reason presumes to reach heavenly conclusions, it has gone beyond its limit and therefore cannot see "the thing as it is." Reason is earthbound. Revelation is heaven bound. Or, in Grant's terminology, reason is of "necessity" and revelation is of the "Good." In content, the data of revelation cannot be known through reason. The content given in revelation is, globally speaking, the love and "perfection" of God recognized on the cross of Christ. Such data confounds reason. The content given to reason is only that of the visible world within which the love of God is hidden and within which suffering and evil hold sway. The paradox of the different aspects of truth given to reason (the suffering of creation) and to revelation (the love of God through suffering) reflect the

---

8. See note 6 above. "Faith is the experience that the intelligence is enlightened by love." Grant describes the import of this phrase in Cayley, *George Grant in Conversation*, 172–88.

distance, discontinuity, or division between the Creator and creature that cannot be leapt over from the human side by reason.

Grant's work reflects this understanding of the contradiction between reason and revelation in a number of ways. His own primal experience of faith in Britain during World War II manifested the discontinuity between reason and revelation. The experience of faith, marked by a "religious conversion," combined with his reflections on this experience through his doctoral studies, continued to hold a regulative place in his thought and experience throughout his lifetime.[9] Prior to this experience, Grant had grown up steeped in traditions of liberal Protestantism wherein the goals of liberalism and Christianity were considered to be one and the same. However, even in the early years, it is clear that questions had begun to emerge that challenged the optimism implicit in liberalism. He describes his father, William, as having been "ruined" by WWI.[10] William's ruin in no way confirmed the optimistic progressivism of liberalism, despite the fact that, according to his son, he continued to hold to these ideas. Following William's lead and the conscience of his faith, Grant turned to pacifism as a teen at Upper Canada College. But it was his devastating experience of war in London working in emergency services that threw him into crisis and caused him to question more

---

9. Grant's transfer out of law and history and into theology in his doctoral studies at Oxford reflected his continuing need to think through the meaning of his primal faith experience. He describes that it is Luther who grips him most and has his "most overwhelming admiration. That peasant with his feet set on the ground seeking with all his heart and soul and need a gracious God, and at last out of great rough tribulation finding him, is the noblest of the lot" (Grant, *George Grant: Selected Letters*, 121).

Grant's dissertation on the work of Scottish theologian John Oman gave him the opportunity to think through Oman's philosophy of religion which, much like Grant's own philosophy, "meets the cry of men bewildered by their period" ("Abstract of Thesis," *Collected Works of George Grant*, 1:167). Grant argues here that Oman must be "read within the context of his *theologia crucis*, which is given in his earlier theological writings. Oman's faith is that our Lord on the Cross reveals the Father as Love, who demands from men [*sic*] that they take up their crosses of forgiveness. The Father's Love and man's [*sic*] freedom to partake of it are the essence of Christianity. All else is but relative and unchanging. In so embarking on a philosophy of religion that is regulated by faith, Oman is attempting to reconcile the challenge of the Gospel with its rationality" (ibid., 1:168). In "The Concept of Nature and Supernature in the Theology of John Oman," Grant argues that the content of Oman's faith regulates his philosophy of religion: "Oman's faith centers on his vision of the Cross . . . the agony of Gethsemane and Golgotha . . . the supremacy of charity . . . and forgiveness . . . ." (ibid., 174). Hall describes Grant's primal conversion experience in *Confessing the Faith*, 345.

10. Christian, *George Grant: A Biography*, ix.

deeply the human condition and the foundational claims of liberalism.[11] In an interview during his mid-life Grant reflects:

> The great experience for me was the war of 1939. The liberalism of my youth simply could not come to terms with it. At the worst stage of the war for me in 1942, I found myself ill, and deserted from the merchant navy, and went into the English countryside to work on a farm.[12]

It was at this time when he was in a very dark place that Grant experienced the conversion, being "born again,"[13] which was to be the central turning point of his life. This revelation experience was to transform him in spirit and thought.

> I went to work at five o'clock in the morning on a bicycle. I got off my bicycle to open a gate and when I got back on I accepted God. Obviously there is much to think about in such experiences . . . But I have never finally doubted the truth of that experience since that moment thirty-six years ago. If I try to put it into words, I would say it was the recognition that I am not my own. In more academic terms, if modern liberalism is the affirmation that our essence is our freedom, then this experience was the denial of that definition, before the fact that we are not our own . . . The war of 1939–1945 was the great primal experience for me.[14]

Later in life Grant describes this experience again: "I think it was a kind of affirmation that beyond time and space there is order . . . And

11. See, for example, "To Maude Grant, 3 January 1942," *George Grant: Selected Letters*, 95.

12. Schmidt, ed., *George Grant in Process*, 62.

13. Ibid.

14. Ibid., 62–63. Elsewhere Grant notes that "conversion came to me at the worst stage of the war . . . It happened from then really, I just wanted to think out [the consequences of this conversion]. When I came back to Canada . . . I lived with people all of whom were deeply held in progressive liberalism. And therefore I had to spend my life thinking out what were the consequences of not thinking progressive liberalism. I think that is the basis of why I became [a philosopher]. It just seemed to me an overriding necessity to understand what were the consequences of thinking that there was an eternal order by which we are measured and defined. That's why I have spent so much of my life doing this . . . It was a great turn around for me, the last big war, a terrific turn around of a kind that drove me to thought" ("George Grant and Religion," 52).

that is what one means by God, isn't it? That ultimately the world is not maniacal chaos."[15]

Grant's sense of the gift of this revelatory experience marks it as distinctive from that at which his mind could arrive by reason. Internally, Grant was at a place where all had given way and his thinking through of life and the misery of suffering led him into deep despair. In a journal entry he describes how, having seen the darkness of the world so vividly through the war, he contemplated suicide.[16] Yet, in a moment, there was a cataclysmic shift within him, precipitated not by his thought, nor by his despair, but given to him in his place of utter wretchedness and vulnerability. It was a gift of revelation—a glimpse of eternity—whereby his own suffering and torment and that of all creation were known to be held within a larger and mysterious whole. The distinction between revelation and reason came to be known by Grant in a life-altering way.[17]

Grant's understanding of the tensions between Athens and Jerusalem—philosophy/reason and theology/revelation—vary somewhat throughout his thought which he notes in an interview later in his life.[18] In spite of his change in perspective, however, the distinction between what is given in the two traditions remains clear.[19] Though he sometimes uses the term "Athens" to refer to rational thought, he more often uses the general term "philosophy" to denote such thought. He regards the content of the Gospels to be that which is "other" to philosophy—something that can be thought about by philosophy but that is not itself a work of philosophy. "It has been my life," says Grant late in life,

> to ask about the best way to think the truth of the gospels . . . Obviously, we don't know what the life Christ may have had that we

15. Cayley, *George Grant in Conversation*, 49.

16. Christian, *George Grant: A Biography*, 69–112.

17. This is in no way intended to suggest that Grant stopped struggling or facing the darkness of being with a terrible ferocity. Indeed, as a theologian of the cross he always found himself struggling with the realities of suffering in the world and his experience that "beyond time and space there is order" (see Cayley, *George Grant in Conversation*, 45–62).

18. Ibid., 59–60.

19. Regarding the difference between philosophy and theology, Grant states. "Philosophy above all means openness to the whole . . . . Theology is taking the tradition of Christianity as a given. It avoids the uncertainty and wonder that is present in philosophy. This has its killing side among philosophers as the practicality can have its killing side among theologians. Theology is a much more immediate, practical science" ("George Grant and Religion," 47).

are not given in the gospels, but going to the cross is not an act of philosophy quite, is it? There doesn't seem to be much philosophy in the gospels; and if you want to think of the gospels in relation to the rest of the world, you at least need some coherent discourse with which to think about it. This is why theologians have used philosophy isn't it?[20]

Though Grant prefers the ancient synthesis of philosophy and theology wherein the eternal order is considered to be an integral part of thinking about reality and truth, he is clear that philosophy does not necessarily require a specified tradition of revelation in order to participate in thought about the whole.[21]

Philosophy can be an end in itself quite apart from the gospels. There are lots of wonderful philosophers who are not members of Christianity, Judaism, or Islam, who are open to the whole without accepting one form of revelation or another . . . Philosophy, it seems to me, is something that belongs to human beings as human beings.[22]

With this statement, clearly Grant is suggesting that with philosophy one can think about the whole (including the content of revelation) without doing theology. To do theology implies that faith plays a primary part in thought, and when faith plays such a role, thought functions as a sort of spiritual discipline.

Grant considers that the tradition of Athens reaches its height in Plato. This is a central distinction in understanding his use of the term "Athens." Where many (including Hall) consider the tradition of Athens to include all the ancient Greek philosophers and thinkers, Grant is increasingly clear that it is Plato (over and against Aristotle in particular) who represents the apex of the tradition of Athens. In Athens he recognizes that Plato and Aristotle manifest two opposing visions of reality, the content of which continues to have relevance today. Where Plato holds that the highest source of enlightenment is the Good Beyond Being—transcending the realm of necessity—Aristotle holds that reason is the ideal

20. Ibid, 60–61.

21. Grant uses the term "the whole" to include God, humanity, and the world. He is commonly considered to have received the term from the work of Leo Strauss. However, this is questionable since he uses the term in 1959 prior to his encounter with the works of Strauss. Grant, *Philosophy in the Mass Age*, 28. See also McCarroll, "Whole as Love: George Grant's Theological Vision."

22. Cayley, *George Grant in Conversation*, 62.

and human reason the means to enlightenment. Grant, along with many others in the history of Christianity, sees a resonance or complementarity between the philosophy of Plato and the Gospels. "At the heart of the Platonic language is the affirmation—so incredible to nearly everyone at one time or another—that the ultimate cause of being is beneficence."[23] This is also the central affirmation of Christianity mediated in the person of Jesus. However, for Grant the distinction between even the best of the traditions of Athens and Jerusalem is also important. This distinction is clearly reflected in the contrast between the death of Socrates and the death of Jesus, which reveal quite different perspectives on suffering and the Good.[24] "When we look . . . at what we are as Western people the central task of thought requires us to be aware of some tension between what comes to us from Athens and what from Jerusalem . . . I prefer to say . . . Socrates and Christ."[25] The distinctiveness of the deaths of Socrates and Christ acts as a kind of metaphorical imaging of the difference in the content of the two traditions. Where Socrates died gently and relatively painlessly, administering a cup of poison hemlock to himself, with the love and support of his followers, Christ was tortured and scourged, experiencing agony, abandonment, despair. Indeed, Grant is always clear that the death of Christ in the tradition of Jerusalem holds within it a mystery that challenges and confronts Athens. More than anywhere else, Grant holds this to be true in his understanding of the Incarnation and the reality of God's love revealed in the external and internal suffering of the Christ. Referring to Simone Weil, he affirms

> "Human nature is so constituted that any desire of the soul insofar as it has not passed through the flesh by means of actions and attitudes which correspond to it has no reality in the soul. It is only a phantom." That is the supreme truth of Christianity—the Incarnation—everything divine has come to us by passing through our flesh.[26]

While Grant's thinking about Jerusalem (that is, revelation) changed over the years, in using the term "Jerusalem" Grant always means the Gospels—the stories of Jesus culminating in the Passion. The fact that

---

23. Grant, "Faith and the Multiversity," in *Technology and Justice*, 42.

24. For discussion on this, see "Appendix, Faith and the Multiversity," in ibid., 71–77.

25. Grant, "Addendum," 18.

26. Quoted in Christian's "Introduction" to Grant, *Time As History*, xxxv.

the revelation given in the narratives of the Gospels "is not an act of philosophy" yet cannot be thought through without philosophy is an essential point for him in discerning the distinctiveness between traditions of reason and revelation. Some who have noted that Grant has little appreciation for the Older Testament question the extent to which he truly received the tradition of Jerusalem in his thought.[27] Grant's resistance to the Older Testament grows out of his concern about the portrayal of God as a god of power and coercion. In the Gospels, through the revelation of Christ on the cross, Grant sees God as one who is wounded and broken, one who suffers and speaks words of love and forgiveness—the image of God's divine love. Because the vulnerability and weakness of the cross are so powerfully imprinted as God's revealing presence, the cross critiques and relativizes all other images of God—even and especially those of the Older Testament. On the other hand, Grant would say that all representations of God that reflect the truth of God revealed on the cross of Christ (in the Old Testament or elsewhere) are in accord with the truth of things. In this sense Grant's understanding of the tradition of Jerusalem, and of truth in general, is specifically Christocentric. Even in doctrinal perspectives on Christ, Grant functions with a "canon within the canon" centered on the crucifixion of Christ. Indeed, it is Christ's crucifixion that defines the rest of the narrative, including the resurrection.

In terms of Grant's contextual analysis, the tension between revelation and reason functions critically in two ways. On the one hand, Grant criticizes theology within which God and providence are assumed to be "scrutable" and therefore recognizable by reason, so that reason is eclipsed by revelation under the pretence of serving it. On the other hand, he criticizes thought about reality that excludes God, the Good[28]— the eternal dimension—wherein revelation is eclipsed by reason.

In the former case, Grant critiques liberal theology, which tends to highlight the "love of God" as the content of revelation. Such content seems reasonable enough. However, the problem arises when liberal theologians neglect the distinction and tension between the content of revelation and reason, as is evident in articulations of the doctrine of providence. "As a believer," Grant says, "I must reject these Western interpretations of providence. Belief is blasphemy if it rests on any easy

27. See Schmidt, *George Grant In Process*, 102ff.

28. For Grant the terms God and the Good mean the same thing.

identification of necessity and good."[29] This kind of identification is the mark of the theology of glory. Related to this temptation is the tendency in North America to undermine thought in favour of a faith of easy answers. "The North American Protestant temptation," Grant argues, "is to rely on faith and forget the duty to seek understanding."[30] In such theology the "Love of God" is posited as the end point (revealed truth) to which reason must think its way so as to bridge the gap between heaven and earth. This expectation of ease and continuity between the two realms simultaneously elevates reason to speak falsely of things invisible and deflects it from its true purpose, thereby reflecting the ignorance and arrogance of the modern age. Grant's criticism of modern theology in general stems from this sense that the content of revelation is such a given to reason—so "scrutable" to thought—that theologians too easily leap from the darkness of the world to the love of God. They ignore the limits and parameters of reason and provide pat answers that are not rigorous about the truth of things, which can only lead to calling "evil good and good evil." Furthermore, without the disruptive truth-revealing cross, the love of God becomes scrutable in a platitudinous and innocuous version of love.

In the latter case, Grant criticizes modern liberal epistemology in general—especially in history, politics, philosophy, and education—for the extent to which the eternal dimension (that which is glimpsed in moments of revelation) ceases to function in thought. He describes ours as "an age when the paradigm of knowledge has no place for our partaking of eternity,"[31] and he calls forth the pre-modern language of Plato to help bring to awareness the dire consequences of sheer historicism and the need for the re-emergence of concepts of the Good.

In both cases Grant recognizes the functioning of the most blasphemous lie of modernity—the conceptual collapse of the distinctions between the realms of revelation (eternity) and reason (history) implied both in thought that assumes the "scrutability" of God in history (providence) and thought that discounts the "God factor" completely. He recognizes the ethical consequences of the eclipse of the eternal order by the order of necessity and the blasphemy that results in the trivialization and rationalization of suffering. Grant sees the domination of reason (and

---

29. Grant, *Lament for a Nation*, 89.

30. Grant, "Two Theological Languages," 6.

31. Grant, "Faith and the Multiversity," in *Technology and Justice*, 51.

thus the human creature) in full sway in the collapse of the distinctions between revelation and reason, such that even God is considered to be at the mercy of reason, to be understood or dismissed at will. When God can be "understood" or dismissed by reason, God ceases to be God. Without the horizon of eternity that marks the limit of and circumscribes creaturely being—including history and reason—all is reduced to relativistic subjectivity, and authentic morality is impossible.

Revelation Serves Reason

In considering how revelation serves reason in Grant's epistemology of the cross, we are really exploring how it is that he prioritizes revelation over reason. It is revelation, in this case, that provides the foundation for the proper functioning and content of reason. When we consider this in terms of his Weilian understanding of faith—"faith is the experience that the intellect is enlightened by love"—we can see that it is "love" that illuminates the intellect and not the other way around. For Grant, the truth of love in the face of its opposite in the world is the essence of revelation as it is given on the cross of Christ. In claiming the priority of love for the illumination of the mind, Grant emphasizes revelation over reason: revelation serves the illumination of reason in the recognition of truth. In considering his task as a thinker within Christianity late in life, Grant remarks, "however difficult it is to affirm that life is a gift, it is an assertion primal to Christianity . . . To be a Christian is to attempt to learn the substance of that assertion."[32]

Grant recognizes that the content of revelation is that which may be received by faith and engaged by reason. The content of revelation marks the limit of reason, though it can be given over to reason in trust. In the practice of theology, the primal experience of faith is given priority, and the content thereof is taken seriously by reason. The experience of faith/revelation thereby enables the discipline of theology. In a very real sense, Grant holds that without an experience of God, one cannot do theology (though presumably, one can do philosophy), for the content of revelation has not been received in lived experience. Theology implies the priority of faith experience and therefore has a deeply spiritual dimension to it.

Needless to say, Grant's own primal faith experience or conversion was essential to his apprehension of the priority of revelation

---

32. Grant, "Addendum, Two Theological Languages," quoted in Whillier, Introduction, to Whillier, ed., *Two Theological Languages*, 2.

and its service to reason. At the point of Grant's conversion, Anselm's challenge—"Believe so that you may know"—took on its deep and life-long significance. Indeed, the priority of faith in thought revealed in his experience, and contemplating the meaning and truths therein, became that to which Grant gave himself for the rest of his life.[33] It is clear that in many ways his philosophy manifests theology as "faith seeking understanding." The language of philosophy, through Plato, enabled him to think through his faith and do theology in the public realm. The priority of faith and the purpose of thought to articulate, discern, and "purify" this faith[34] marks what is essential in understanding Grant's writings in terms of reason and revelation/ philosophy and theology/ Athens and Jerusalem. At the deepest level it is Grant's inner experience of faith in God as ultimate "beneficence,"[35] his thinking through of this and the implications thereof, that provides the critical edge for his political philosophy and cultural critique. It is the reality of Grant's Christian faith that shapes and integrates his thought and distinguishes his philosophical discourse as theological discourse.

In an interview with David Cayley late in life, Grant reflected on questions pertaining to the relationship between revelation and reason in terms of his experience as a Christian philosopher:

> Cayley: When you ask, How can one be a philosopher within Christianity?, do you mean how can one be a philosopher when the answer to one's questions has already been definitively revealed?
>
> Grant: Revelation doesn't teach you many things, but it teaches you the end for man.
>
> Cayley: And in a sense forecloses certain questions?
>
> Grant: Yes, and it also puts something higher than philosophy: it puts charity higher than contemplation. I think there's no

33. In a 1942 letter, Grant wrote, "Of course, the approach to God . . . for me must always be *Credo ut intelligam*; the opposite of that is incomprehensible" (see Christian, *George Grant: A Biography*, xxii, and *George Grant: Selected Letters*, ed., Christian, 104–5).

34. Grant, "Two Theological Languages," quoted in Whillier, 2.

35. Grant, "Faith and the Multiversity," in *Technology and Justice*, 42. Late in life, Grant describes the content given in revelation in a description of grace: "Grace simply means that the great things of our existing are given us, not made by us and finally not to be understood as arbitrary accidents. Our making takes place within ultimate goodness" (Grant, "Addendum (1988)," 2).

getting away from this, that Christianity is in some sense a break from Plato. Now there are all kinds of ways of uniting them, and this is what western society at its height has been; but it does seem to me that on the question of the place of charity and contemplation in life and their respective importance, there is a break between Christianity and philosophy (i.e. Plato).[36]

In this "break between Christianity and philosophy" (reflected also in the categories of revelation and reason; Jerusalem and Athens; charity and contemplation), Grant places priority on the former (Christianity, revelation, Jerusalem, charity) as that which establishes the parameters and feeds the content of the latter in each case. The revelation of Christ on the cross cuts to the very heart of existence and truth.

> The fact that what is given us in Socrates and Christ leaves us in tension does not say anything as to the primacy between the two. But revelation is, after all, revelation. And we may say again what has been said so often: Either Christ is what he claims to be or misguided to the point of lunacy . . . Whatever may be said . . . of Socrates at his execution, that scene is not as comprehensively close to the very heart of being as are Gethsemane and Golgotha. The appalling admonition "Take up your cross and follow me" cuts to the heart of our existing and indeed to the heart of both being and goodness.[37]

And in another place he confesses, "Doesn't [Christ's] account of death go more to what life is than Socrates'—the fear, his sweat was like great drops of blood falling to the ground. All this is what convinces me of Christianity; it seems to me important. This is more what life is like."[38]

Grant's thinking regarding the priority of revelation and its service to reason[39] shapes his critical and constructive reflections on the North

---

36. Cayley, *George Grant in Conversation*, 62.

37. Grant, "Addendum," 19. See also "Appendix, Faith and the Multiversity," in *Technology and Justice*, 71–77.

38. Grant, "George Grant and Religion," 58.

39. Following Weil, Grant would argue that the best philosophy, that of Plato, recognizes the place of revelation. See Plato, "Allegory of the Cave" (*Republic*, Book 7), in *Great Dialogues of Plato*, 312–20. Plato argues that love is something given from above and not made by humans. "Now take the making of all things, who will dispute that they are the clever work of Love, by which all living things are made and begotten" (*Symposium*, in *Great Dialogues of Plato*, 92). Grant recognizes that in both Plato and the Gospels, love is the content of revelation. However, Grant would say that Christ crucified, as no other, reveals the cost of love in a broken and crucified world in that it

American context. Grant integrates the content of revelation—the love of God on the cross of Christ—both critically and constructively into his reflections on modern epistemology. Critically, much of what Grant sees as wrong with modern liberalism is the eclipsing of the Good by necessity—the realm of revelation by the realm of reason. As discussed earlier, he sees Nietzsche's historicist trajectory being lived out in North America, with sheer relativism holding sway. The retrieval of the pre-modern priority of God/ the Good (the content of revelation) in Grant's thought relativizes the narrow perspective of modernity and enables clarity in response to the contextual question, "what's wrong?" In reclaiming the priority of the transcendent, eternal order as glimpsed in revelation, Grant is able to critique scientific/ historicist epistemologies effectively from a conceptual location that rejects relativistic nihilism at its core. Furthermore, in constructive and positive ways he integrates the content of revelation such that "what's wrong" might be set right.

For Grant another manifestation of the relationship between revelation and reason comes in his discussions about the relationship between love and knowledge, charity, and contemplation. For example, in his essay "Faith and the Multiversity," Grant considers the relationship between revelation and reason under the terms "loving and knowing," "faith and the intellect."[40] The problem with modern epistemology, he argues, is that it has lost this foundational footing in love. "Suffice it to say that what is given in the modern paradigm is the project of reason to gain objective knowledge."[41] "To reason" in modern method is to "objectify" a thing—hold a thing up—such that it is required to provide reasons for its being.[42] This is contrasted with the ancient understanding of knowledge (and the

---

reveals love shining through the very face of affliction. Revelation comes in two parts, for Grant: the truth of love and the reality of affliction. In the cross the contradictory truth of these disparate realities is held together in such unutterable tension. In the cross of Christ the revelation of love is unparalleled and reflects the centre and core of all other love.

40. An example of Grant's thought in action can be seen in his vision for the Department of Religious Studies at McMaster University in Hamilton where he worked from 1960 to 1980. Each member of the teaching faculty was expected to be a believer in the tradition of faith in which he or she was teaching. The importance of "faith" for true and authentic knowledge of religion was central. Related to this was Grant's condemnation of the "Multiversity" for its unacknowledged faith in secularism (and consequent silencing of faith within institutions of higher learning).

41. Grant, "Faith and the Multiversity," *Technology and Justice*, 36.

42. Ibid.

Weilian understanding of faith) which considers that true knowledge of a thing can only be received by love. When one loves, Grant affirms, one consents to the being of the other. Knowing and loving, he argues, must be held together. For a thing to be really known, its beauty and otherness must be apprehended. Over and against modern paradigms of knowing that presuppose distance and a certain tyranny/mastery over the other, leading to the utilitarian purposing of the other, ancient paradigms of knowledge integrate love into knowledge such that the utilitarian purposing of an "other" is foreclosed. The apprehension of beauty and the soul's opening to otherness is the height of knowledge. Grant appeals to experience or, perhaps more accurately, intuition throughout this essay to draw people to recognize the problem and the possibility. In "Faith and the Multiversity," the priority given to love (revelation) in the service of knowledge (reason) enables him to engage modern paradigms of knowledge critically to discern "what's wrong" and to elaborate constructively on how "what's wrong" could be "set right."

Finally, Grant's emphasis on the content of revelation over reason is also manifest in his discussions about the relationship between charity and contemplation. For Grant, it is charity that rightly orders contemplation.[43] For instance, in contrast with the political philosopher Leo Strauss, who argues that it is contemplation that leads the soul to the heights of being, Grant argues that it is through charity that the soul is brought to the heights of existence and truth.[44] He notes that valuing contemplation over charity can lead to social and political elitism, which is at odds with the truth of things. Charity—and the possibility of all people acting in charity—is of a higher order than contemplation: "The village idiot who lives the good knows more than Aristotle."[45]

Reason Serves Revelation

Grant's exploration of the way in which reason serves revelation exposes perhaps the most mystical side of Grant's thought, inspired as it was by Simone Weil's theology of the cross.[46] Weil's formula for faith—"Faith is

43. For a discussion of his distinction from Strauss in this way, see Athanasiadis, "Political Philosophy and Theology, 23–32.

44. See Grant, "Tyranny and Wisdom," in *Technology and Empire*, 103ff.

45. Cayley, *George Grant in Conversation*, 175.

46. "She is essentially a theologian of the cross" (Cayley, *George Grant in Conversation*, 176). See also Athanasiadis, *George Grant and the Theology of the Cross*, 61–66,

the experience that the intelligence is enlightened by love"—highlights experiences of faith that begin in the intellect's waiting to be illuminated by the revelation of love. Such faith experiences confirm the primal reality within which the categories of reason and revelation are grounded. The content of revelation—broadly speaking, the love of God on the cross—is a paradox that reason cannot reach, although reason can engage it within the parameters of its own limits.

The task of reason, then, is to think through the contradiction inherent in the content of revelation. The soul waits upon the visitation of love when it "thinks" the content of the contradiction between the perfection of God and the "misery" of humanity—between the love of God and suffering and evil in the world—and when it considers how this contradiction is manifested with particularity in the world and in the cross of Christ. This aspect of the relationship between revelation and reason is that which most reflects the suffering of thought and the mystical and cruciform dimension of the spiritual life in thought. Reason in service of revelation is called to think through the contradiction without the content of revelation and reason collapsing each into the other. Thought of this kind requires the spiritual discipline of waiting upon God, and it entails the agony of being unable to resolve the tension by thinking it through. Such unresolved tension brings one to the foot of the cross of Christ, in its agony and mystery. It is in such waiting upon the experience of revelation that thought participates most fully in the life of the Spirit.

A certain agnosticism is central to this understanding of the relationship between revelation and reason such that God cannot be posited as the end result of thought, nor anticipated, nor presupposed. As we have seen, Grant consistently stands against theology that posits God as an outcome of human thought rather than a contradiction to human thought. Reason can only engage the idea of God in a posture of attentiveness, awaiting God's self-revelation to faith. Indeed, Grant's choice of philosophy (over theology) as a means to think through the extremes of being (given to reason and revelation) may be understood to reflect the rigor of his faith and his engagement in the real world. Reading Plato, he says, "taught me how it was possible to think rationally about God and about justice and about things that concern us here below . . . To think about God coherently."[47] In privileging philosophy over theology as the

84–120, 226–33.

47. Cayley, *George Grant in Conversation*, 56.

best means of thinking about the whole, Grant emphasizes the importance of reason being experientially engaged. Also, within the framework of philosophy, reason can be pushed toward and thus meet its end. In this way—reason meeting its end, conceding its finitude—the human being is opened to receive that which comes from outside its limits, that which is of God. The cost of thinking things through coherently is summarized by Weil and often quoted by Grant—"I am ceaselessly torn between the perfection of God and the misery of man [*sic*]."[48] The tension of these two sides of the contradiction always puts the idea of God in question. Grant quotes and comments on Weil regarding the import of thinking the contradiction.

> "I am ceaselessly and increasingly torn both in my intelligence and in the depth of my heart through my inability to conceive simultaneously and in truth, the affliction of men [*sic*], the perfection of God and the link between the two." Or in other of her words, "As Plato said, an infinite distance separates the good from necessity—the essential contradiction in human life is that man [*sic*], with a straining after the good constituting his [*sic*] very being, is at the same time subject in his [*sic*] entire being, both in mind and in flesh, to a blind force, to a necessity completely indifferent to the good." This contradiction above any other is for her the means by which the mind is led to truth.[49]

Revelation and Reason Are One

Paradoxically, for Grant a hidden unity of truth is the true ground of both reason and revelation. Some of his earliest writings and some of his latest point to this unity.[50] Despite the fact that there are many tensions between them, for Grant, Athens/philosophy and Jerusalem/theology are finally one in their desire to seek truth and their yearning to glimpse the unity of the whole. "Anyone who wishes to partake in philosophy, and also hopes that he or she is made with the sign of Christ, must be aware of some tension in the relation between thought and revelation, though

---

48. Weil, "Letter to Maurice Schumann," in *Seventy Letters*, 178.

49. George Grant, "Introduction to Simone Weil (1970)," in *George Grant Reader*, 248.

50. Grant is later critical of his essay "Two Theological Languages"; nevertheless, he states a sentiment in it that stays with him throughout his career: "Clearly we can all agree that philosophy and theology are both faith seeking understanding" (ibid., 6).

at the same time knowing that finally they must be as one."[51] In his descriptions of philosophy, we see that he seeks to reclaim its revelatory essence,[52] which in the modern era would more commonly be associated with theology: "Astonishment about being itself, about what is, is philosophy."[53] Furthermore, his discussions on the place of Plato's writings in his own spiritual integration point to the overlapping character of theology and philosophy for Grant: "What Plato enabled me to do was to see some unity between thinking about ordinary things and my belief in God."[54] Later he describes: "The word *good* for me is just a synonym for the word God. As Plato said, the idea of the good is just the idea of final purpose. The whole is opened to one when one asks questions of final purpose." In terms of epistemology, Grant considers that there is a close proximity between Socrates and Christ:

> The close connection between Socrates and Christ lies in the fact that Socrates is the primal philosophic teacher of the dependence of what we know on what we love . . . Our various journeys out of the shadows and the imaginings of opinion into the truth depend on the movement of our minds through love into the lovable.[55]

It is false, however, to think of the unity of philosophy and theology, of Athens and Jerusalem, of revelation and reason in a way that effaces the distinctions between them. They are one (on the human side) in that as human disciplines of thought, the traditions of Athens and Jerusalem manifest the same yearning for the eternal in the face of the limits of the temporal that is implicit in the human condition. They are one, finally, in their seeking for truth. However, it is to faith only that the possibility of revelation and reason being one is intimated. The unity of truth that is sought by reason is hidden in and to the world; it can be glimpsed only in moments of illumination that reveal a deeper mystery pointing to a unity of truth.

51. Grant, "Addendum," 18.

52. "I wouldn't take the Thomistic-Aristotelian account of reason and revelation as held apart . . . but I would certainly take the position that reason at its best is a kind of illumination" (Grant, "George Grant and Religion," 44). Grant understands the content of revelation to be love. Thus philosophy, the love of wisdom, is illuminated by the revelation of love.

53. Cayley, *George Grant in Conversation*, 56.

54. Ibid, 57.

55. Grant, "Appendix, Faith and the Multiversity," in *Technology and Justice*, 72–73.

Simone Weil's understanding of faith—"Faith is the experience that the intellect is enlightened by love"—helps us to see that love is both the essence of faith and the content of the unity of truth. This unity is hidden from the world and from the mind of reason. The unity of truth is tasted in moments of love when the soul opens to otherness, consents to otherness, and recognizes the beauty of the other known in the illumination of love. For Grant, the unity of truth that we seek we can never find in ideas about things, but only in the thing itself as it grasps us from beyond and tears away all false barriers, revealing the hidden presence of the All in All: Love.

Grant's Paradoxical Method in Conclusion

Grant identifies himself in the tradition of negative theology wherein the distance between God and the world—between perfection and misery—structures his thought.[56] Indeed, all four aspects of his understanding of the relationship between revelation and reason can be considered in light of the *via negativa*. Recognizing the distance between the suffering of creation and the love of God presupposes belief in God as transcendent to and absent in the world.[57] Thus, faith in God (given in revelation) provides the foundation for thought in a hidden way such that "the unity which we seek we can neither know in principle or in detail."[58] Unity is known primarily by its absence—an absence that transcends this earthly realm. Reason is given in order that this absence might be recognized in the distance and contradiction between the realms of necessity and the Good. Indeed, for Grant, following Weil, it is in recognizing the distance between the realms that thought (reason) is attentive to and waits upon the disruptive enfolding of love (revelation). In the cataclysmic experience of the mind's illumination by love, the whole is glimpsed, within which all is one.

For Grant, it is on the cross of Christ that the contradictions between suffering and love, between reason and revelation, emerge with an unrelenting ferocity in the "absent presence" and "present absence" of God. The contradiction (or distance) between God and the world with

---

56. "Simone Weil," Grant says, "is the being who expresses most deeply, as far as I'm concerned, the moment of God's absence from the world. In Christian theology there have been two traditions: the positive tradition and the negative tradition. The positive tradition [Aristotelianism] moves to God through the world; the negative tradition moves to God by negating the world" (Cayley, *George Grant in Conversation*, 177).

57. Grant, "Beautiful and the Good."

58. Ibid.

all its tension and agony must remain a contradiction to human thought, without scrutable unity. This is the task to which the theologian and philosopher are called: to bring to light the thing as it is—the contradiction between the love of God and the affliction of the world in all its vast particularity; to think through the contradiction with rigorous trust and courage; and to await the illumination of the mind by love. "Faith is the experience that the intelligence is enlightened by love"—love that *unreasonably* holds together from above that which cannot be held together from below. Indeed, love is the essence of the Whole—the oneness of the all in all. Grant's philosophical thinking through of the relationality within the Whole—between God, humanity, and creation—is based on his primal faith in God as One of beneficence. In the priority of faith in his thought, Grant is a theologian who challenges us to rightly order our knowing such that it is open to the deepest truth of being, the truth of love. Grant's philosophy calls us to the task of theology: "Believe so that you may know."

In exploring the four different ways that reason and revelation are distinct and related, we recognize the extent to which Grant's thought and method are grounded in a practice of waiting upon finality and completion. The diverse and intersecting complexity demonstrated here resists the temptation for thought to be an act of mastery or tyranny over that which is beyond it. Instead, through the dynamic interplay of revelation and reason, thought participates in waiting at the foot of the cross, wherein the mystery of the paradox between suffering and love points beyond itself to God's hidden possibility.

4

Hall's Method of the Cross

DOUGLAS HALL IS A theologian of the cross who addresses members of the once-mainline churches and those on the periphery of faith in contemporary North America. In locating himself within the "thin tradition" of the cross, he claims the theology of the cross as the "key signature" and "informing perspective"[1] for all his theological discourse. From his very earliest works and throughout the corpus of his publications, Hall is intent on thinking through the content of the theology of the cross in a North American context and fleshing this out in terms of Christian doctrine, the Christian life, and the mission of the church. For Hall the theology of the cross enables both critical and constructive theological moves shaped by a deeply contextual sensibility. Though Hall would not consider himself to be a scholar of Luther, his engagement with Luther's theology of the cross is profound, and in continuity and dialogue with some of the best scholarship on Luther and the theology of the cross.[2] Unlike Grant, whose cruciform thought implicitly underlies all he writes, as a theologian Hall gives himself explicitly to contemplating the concrete particularities of the theology of the cross in a contemporary North American context. Before considering Hall's epistemology of the cross through the categories of "revelation" and "reason," I will first clarify Hall's understanding of the traditions of Athens and Jerusalem. These

1. Hall, *Thinking the Faith*, 24–25; *Cross in Our Context*, 7; *Waiting for Gospel*, 76–92.

2. See the section on Luther in Hall's *Lighten Our Darkness*, 108–17, as well as discussion throughout his other books, especially *Thinking the Faith* and *Cross in Our Context*.

traditions are central to the interplay between reason and revelation in the thought of both Grant and Hall, although in different ways.

Thinking about Athens and Jerusalem

Hall uses the terms "the tradition of Athens" and "the tradition of Jerusalem" regularly throughout his work.[3] For the most part, Hall identifies himself with the tradition of Jerusalem over and against the tradition of Athens. In a rare example of a positive and parallel assessment of the two traditions,[4] Hall draws on Grant's analysis of the bankruptcy of the modern image of the human in comparison with these two ancient traditions. "Both Athens and Jerusalem, as George Grant has shown in his book *Time as History*, depict the human being as one whose fundamental posture is that of the recipient."[5] Hall considers the complementarity of the two traditions in theology as "the meeting of two stories"—the conceptual and universal of Athens and the narrative and particular of Jerusalem.[6] He goes on to acknowledge that the two traditions understand "human being and calling" in fundamentally different ways and points out that, although they meet in the New Testament, they are in no way reconciled there. "However," he states,

> when the two ancient foundational traditions of Western civilization are compared with the modern view of human nature (human mastery reflected in "having" and "doing"), which borrowed elements from both of them, their differences pale in relation to their common divergence from the latter . . . Neither Greek nor Jew is able to claim human mastery. Both, indeed,

---

3. The terms, "the tradition of Athens and Jerusalem," Hall borrows from Grant. Hall, *The Future of the Church*, 33n8.

4. See Hall, *Lighten Our Darkness*, 202–3ff.

5. Ibid. See also Hall, *Thinking the Faith*, 238n2: "Referring to a sentence of Mozart, in which the composer describes the way that musical compositions come to him ('I understand them altogether in one moment'), George Grant points out that "it is worth remembering when Mozart speaks of understanding . . . he did so at a time when Kant was exalting reason above understanding, in the name of his account of human beings as 'autonomous.' This was to place on its head the teaching of Plato in which understanding was the height of human beings: Indeed the English 'to understand' and the German *verstehen* were in their origins filled with that very sense of receptivity which Kant lessens in the name of our freedom."

6. Hall, *Thinking the Faith*, 90.

regard the claim to mastery as the height of presumption; hubris in the Greek tradition and sin (i.e. rebellion) in the Hebraic.[7]

It is, indeed, the tradition of Jerusalem that fundamentally informs Hall's theology of the cross and places it in a much broader framework of Scripture and the Hebraic-Christian tradition compared to the thought of Grant. For Hall, the tradition of Jerusalem emphasizes love as *Mitsein* (with-being)[8] and is seen in (1) "God's abiding commitment to the world," (2) God's (hidden) participation in history, and (3) the relational ontology within creation and with the creator.[9] When the cross of Christ is read through these basic precepts of Jerusalem, the radical truth of love is seen with deepest clarity. Furthermore, it is through the lens of God's *Mitsein* love (of the tradition of Jerusalem) that the *agape* (self-emptying or suffering) love of Christ on the cross comes into focus.[10] Hall is careful not to co-opt the tradition of Jerusalem into a Christian motif. Instead, he describes the ways the tradition of Jerusalem provides a lens for thinking about the cross of Christ and how both traditions reveal God as one who has not and will not abandon creation. For Hall the tradition of Jerusalem reflects the earthen, physical, and integrated anthropology of Judaism wherein there is no false division between the physical and spiritual, the mind and the heart, existence and thought. Thus, when Jesus suffered and died on the cross, he truly suffered and died in the extremity of his humanity.

Hall emphasizes the relational ontology of Jerusalem over and against the "substantialistic ontology" of Athens. In the face of Athens' false substantialism, Jerusalem emphasizes the priority of love as that

7. Hall, *Lighten Our Darkness*, 202–3.

8. Hall uses the term "*Mitsein*" to connote the relational ontology of the tradition of Jerusalem. He elaborates upon the term "Emmanuel (God-with-us)" to explore the incarnational essence of God's love as *Mitsein* (with-being). "God limits God's own self, for our sake, becoming accessible to us within the parameters of our creatureliness . . . The Emmanuel formula, however, together with the Hebraic theological-historical consciousness that lies behind it, wants to insist that what is implied here is precisely not a generalization but a radical particularization of God's gracious *Mitsein* (being with)." Hall goes on to describe how theology must necessarily be contextual, for the God about whom we think and speak is one who takes seriously the particularity of context. Hall, *Thinking the Faith*, 100. See also Hall, *Imaging God*, 116–17 and 157–58.

9. "The tradition of Jerusalem assumes that 'what is really real' is only perceivable in actual occurrences—in historical events, in lives lived . . . Jerusalem is suspicious of universals—at least they are subservient to particulars" (Hall, *Professing the Faith*, 302). Grant's emphasis on the priority of the particular over the universal is evident in the structuring and focus of his book, *Lament for a Nation*.

10. See *God and Human Suffering*, 33ff and 172ff; and *Professing the Faith*, 130–86.

which creates *ex nihilo*,[11] calls forth, and sustains being in and for relationship. "It is not a small thing whether my humanity consists in being or in loving (that is being-with)."[12] Usually when Hall uses the term "Athens," particularly in his later work, it is a short-hand way of pointing to the perceived disembodiment of thought and dismissal of matter that he sees as the downfall of ancient Greek philosophy. For Hall "Athens" represents the manifold ways that thought is falsely separated from existence, as if the former is not completely embedded in the latter. His criticism of the tradition of Athens is also related to Luther's dismissal of "speculative thought" wherein context, human experience, and historical being are not considered to be central to theological reflection and spiritual practice. For Hall, because the tradition of Athens completely misses and obscures the relational ontology at the root of existence, it thereby relays a false image of the human and of God. Further, because it misses and obscures the relationships that exist between thought and existence, there cannot but be falsity in thought about all things that grow out of this illusory ontology. Indeed, Hall's greatest concern is that the tradition of Athens obscures the truth regarding the cross of Christ. An assumed dualism between body and spirit (not to mention matter and God, existence and thought, and so on) leads to the argument that Christ did not suffer and die a human and agonizing death.

Although in his use of the term "Athens" Hall rarely distinguishes between the thought of Plato, Aristotle, and the Stoics,[13] it is clear that, when pushed, he is more favorably disposed to the thought of Plato than that of Aristotle.[14] In terms of the relationship between theology and philosophy, he understands philosophy to be the "partner of theology,"[15] offering to theology the rigorous exercise of thought. Occasionally, Hall uses the terms "Athens" and "Jerusalem" to reflect the distinction and

---

11. Hall stands in the long line of Christian thought that recognizes that only God can create *out of nothing*. Love is that which is only of God, created by God *ex nihilo*. Thus, the experience of love in life, when it is true, is the experience of God's creative power in our very hearts and minds.

12. Hall, *Lighten our Darkness*, 203.

13. See ibid.

14. See Hall, *Thinking the Faith*, 252: "All of us who confess the name of Jesus as Christ do so in language that is full of indebtedness to persons who did not or do not believe in Jesus Christ. One name alone is enough to secure the point: Plato." See also Hall, *Cross in Our Context*, 19.

15. See Hall, *Thinking the Faith*, 314–16.

interplay between philosophy and theology, thought and faith.[16] However, for the most part, he does not consider that the differences between the two traditions at their best primarily reflect a stark separation of faith and thought. Rather, they represent two aspects of thought that need each other in order for each discipline to be at its best.

Hall's Epistemology of the Cross: The Big Picture

Hall's discussions of revelation and reason, like Grant's, reflect his understanding of the doctrines of God and Creation and the relationships between them. Hall is explicit about the priority of content in method. Because there is a fundamental tension in the content of the Christian faith and story, there is also a fundamental tension in theological method.[17] Before addressing Hall's epistemology of the cross specifically through the categories of revelation and reason, it is instructive to contemplate his understanding of *continuity* and *discontinuity* in Christian life and faith.[18] Indeed, Hall's emphasis on continuity and discontinuity enables him to integrate contextual analysis into his theological method. His understanding of revelation and reason functions within his broader discussion of the continuity and discontinuity between the gospel and the world. Furthermore, a close study of Hall's epistemology of the cross makes apparent a number of other categories that have a parallel movement to those of revelation and reason: expectation and experience, hope and history, eternity and time. The relationship within each of these couplets can be most clearly accessed through his discussions of continuity and discontinuity, which provide the content and basis of his methodological thought.

For Hall it is in the categories of continuity and discontinuity that the dialectical tensions of content and form are most fully fleshed out. He explains that "while the core of the Christian message (*kerygma*) is

16. See Hall, *Lighten Our Darkness*, 202.

17. Hall, *Thinking the Faith*, 326. See also his discussion of "Knowledge of God" in *Professing the Faith*, 44–51.

18. Hall's discussions of continuity, discontinuity, and context are located within the broader theological discussions in Protestant theology, particularly throughout the last century. In numerous places throughout his corpus he engages the kerygmatic theology of Barth (and others) and the apologetic theology of Schleiermacher and Tillich. He draws out contextual factors within which these discussions are embedded and analyzes the dangers and truths of each approach that informs his theological method. See Hall, *Thinking the Faith*, 342–67, and *The Cross in our Context*, 65–72.

discontinuous with human experience, the message is nevertheless obviously intended for human beings and must therefore in some way be, or become, *continuous* with their experience."[19] In reflecting on the content of the Christian message in Scripture and in the experience of faith, Hall identifies the ways in which continuity and discontinuity function:

> The birth, and likewise the entire story at the centre of the Christian faith, serves to express the fundamental tension in Christian theology which manifests itself in theological method: continuity and discontinuity, the old and the new, accord and discord, meeting and distance, immanence and transcendence, folly and wisdom. These two poles inform the Christian story from beginning to end; and as the story is, so must the means of our telling it be. Content determines method. No method can be adequate which does not do justice to this tension . . . It is a lived tension, grounded in the faith experience itself. For on the one hand the human being who hears . . . this gospel does find it to correspond with that within . . . which has been . . . waiting for just such a kerygma: forgiveness answering guilt, mercy answering . . . condemnation, reconciliation answering alienation, love answering estrangement . . . But this continuity factor is from the outset in dialogue with its antithesis. Existential discontinuity consists not only in the realization that there is nothing automatic in the process (grace is not a foregone conclusion!) but also in the more subtle fact that, strangely, there is that within the human person which positively resists this news. For it contains a . . . searing truthfulness, a krisis (judgment) that is unnerving to the human psyche . . . The "good" news is also—under conditions of historical existence—bad news.[20]

The essential question at the root of Hall's discussions of discontinuity and continuity concerns the possibility for a point of contact between the gospel and the world. Discontinuity falls more on the side of denying the possibility for a point of contact on the human side; of assuming that "there can be no real meeting between faith and unfaith."[21] Thus, there can be no meaningful (and mutual) dialogue between Christianity and the world. Continuity falls more on the side of assuming that there is a point of contact on the human side; that there can be a meeting between faith and unfaith. Hall explores both these options dialogically as

19. Hall, *Thinking the Faith*, 327.

20. Ibid., 331.

21. Hall, *Cross in Our Context*, 61.

he elaborates upon and clarifies the content, form, and contextuality of his theology.

When Hall speaks of discontinuity, he is referring to the discontinuity that exists between the gospel and the world on two primary levels.[22] First, the discontinuity reflects the distance and otherness between God (gospel) and the world, experienced in the disruptive shock of grace that cannot but disturb us by its sheer newness and distinctiveness. This experience of discontinuity in the life of faith reflects the discontinuity in the scandal of the cross, where within the particularity of time and place God's love is revealed in the very life, suffering, and death of Jesus on the cross. "What has come to be in and through Jesus as the Christ is as '*un*natural,' as discontinuous with nature, human potentiality or . . . historical providence as a child emerging from the womb of a pure virgin."[23] The "upside-down" rule of love wholly contradicts the inclinations of the world for power and glory. There is nothing self-evident in the world or in human beings[24] that would cause one to receive the suffering of a man on a cross as the very picture of divine love in a world such as ours. "It has come to be as God's possibility not humanity's."[25] In this case, discontinuity reflects the absolute otherness of the gospel to the world. When the light of God is shone in the darkness of our lives it is astonishing in its unfamiliarity.

Second (and related to the first point), the "discontinuity factor" recognizes that the gospel—the good news of the crucified Christ—is unwelcome and unwanted by humans, particularly the powerful. This is an important point in Hall's contextual method. Though there is a resistance and refusal to love and to the truth of who we are that runs deep within the human psyche, this is especially true of the powerful, the self-assured, and the "self-made." The scandal of the cross is not that it is simply an offense to intelligence but rather that it touches on the essentials of being and "confirms what we have always suspected . . . the utter contingency of our being."[26] Our spirits are tackled at their most vulnerable psychic depths. How this is experienced—in terror or with relief—depends in large degree upon contextual factors. Demands are made by the Gospel

---

22. Both of which challenge the temptations towards natural theology.

23. Hall, *Thinking the Faith*, 328; emphasis original.

24. Ibid., 336.

25. Ibid., 328.

26. Ibid., 343.

that may seem impossible, discontinuous with life as we have known it.[27] When the light of God is shone in the darkness of our lives its revealing truth terrifies the powerful and inspires the weak.

In considering the continuity between the gospel and the world, Hall emphasizes two levels at which such continuity functions. First, he makes a case for continuity in a way that corresponds with Augustine's dictum regarding the deepest truth of the human condition: "Thou hast made us for thyself, and our hearts are restless until they repose in thee."[28] The gospel engages "that within the self that "hungers and thirsts" for just such good news."[29] This is experienced in the life of faith as that "aha!" that opens one to a deeper truth, which is known, at once, to have always been true. Hall acknowledges that questions of human purpose and meaning grow out of this place within the human that is seeking and desirous for the gospel, the good news, hope. Such questions reflect the possibility for a point of contact from the human side between the gospel and the world, between faith and unfaith. Second, Hall points out that the content of the gospel is not only experienced as that for which the soul has always yearned, but it is also that for which the whole of humanity yearns and is waiting. In receiving the fullness of the gospel into our lives we seek to communicate it to others. Or in other words, the evangelical impulse to communicate the gospel message is implicit within the experience of communion itself, received in the gospel of Christ. The good news of Christ responds to and engages the truth of the human condition.

Throughout his discussions on discontinuity and continuity, Hall is well aware of the pitfalls that can occur when one is locked into one way of thinking about the relationship between the gospel and the world. Further, he elaborates upon contextual factors in the world that can nuance the reception of grace. These factors affect the ways in which the tensions and dialogical character of discontinuity and continuity are encountered in life. The gospel is heard and experienced differently in different contexts. In contexts of power, it comes disruptively, breaking through the false presumptions upon which our empires are built. As such, for the North American Protestant church, our inability to engage the negative—that which attests to our human limit and failure, to doubt and despair and the meaningless in life—and to enter the darkness of

---

27. Ibid., 341.

28. Quoted from Augustine's *Confessions* in Hall, *Cross in our Context*, 61.

29. Hall, *Thinking the Faith*, 332.

our existential vulnerability means that the gospel comes in the most disruptive way possible. On the other hand, in contexts of vulnerability, where humility is true, and in the face of suffering, the gospel of the cross comes disruptively (and thus discontinuously) in its otherness, but not necessarily in its reception. For in the experience of authentic human vulnerability there is the possibility for greater humility and openness to receive that for which the soul longs. The false illusions that shelter the soul from accepting its limits and vulnerability do not require destruction in the same way as with the powerful and self-assured. Thus, in contexts of vulnerability and authentic humility and in the face of suffering, the discontinuity of the gospel can be experienced in a way that is life-affirming. It can therefore be received in continuity with the deepest, truest parts of ourselves.

Hall's understanding of the dynamic tension in the continuities and discontinuities between the world and the gospel is based on the fact that the gospel of Christ "has not been produced by history [the world]; nevertheless it has been well and truly introduced into the historical process and it is in the most explicit sense an historical [worldly] event."[30] Christ is not continuous with the world but *engages* it; faith is not continuous with unfaith, but *engages* it; hope is not continuous with history, but *engages* it. Such engagement does not occur in a vacuum but is lived in the world, in the very stuff of life. Therefore, regarding the question of method in theology, we cannot consider *a priori* and prescriptively that there is one way in every context to contemplate the discontinuities and continuities between the world and the gospel. Though there is definite content in the gospel and clear priorities that can be known and experienced in the world, the gospel engages us within the very particularity of life. In other words, the manner in which we are engaged with and receptive to gospel is shaped most fully by our context. It is in the dialectical movement between continuity and discontinuity that the relational dynamism between the world and the gospel, between the believer and Jesus, most fully manifests itself in theological method.

Hall's Epistemology: Dialectical and Dialogical

In his specific discussions of Christian epistemology in *Thinking the Faith*, Hall identifies the key question regarding the relationship of reason and revelation: "How, according to the Christian tradition, does the knowledge

30. Hall, *Thinking the Faith*, 328–29.

of God in God's self-revelation relate to ordinary human rationality, and vice versa?"[31] The dialectically dynamic and contextually informed relationship between reason and revelation in Hall's thought can best be explored from four distinct perspectives, represented in the discussion that follows under the headings Reason and Revelation: Distinct and Discontinuous; Revelation Seeks Reason; Reason Seeks Revelation; Revelation and Reason Seek Mutuality. Throughout this discussion it is instructive to keep in mind Hall's Anselmian definition of theology as "Faith seeking understanding." In thinking through the four angles of his epistemology, different variations on this definition come into play.[32] These four different ways of understanding the relationship between reason and revelation reflect a dialogical dynamism of thought that cannot rest but rather participates in the relationship about which it speaks, resisting attempts to master and open to receive and to wait upon God's hidden revealing.

Reason and Revelation: Distinct and Discontinuous

Hall is clear that reason and revelation are of entirely different orders. Reason cannot progressively think its way to the content of revelation. Revelation is of God and as such is *creatio ex nihilo*. Though it is experienced within history and can be thought about by human reason, revelation is not *of* history or *of* the human mind. The two are discontinuous with each other and any attempt to suggest otherwise results in falsification of reality. In his discussion of faith and theology, Hall etymologically retrieves and rethinks the term "understanding" in the definition of theology ("faith seeking understanding") to clarify that there are distinctions between content and form in ordering the relationship between reason (understanding) and revelation (faith). He contends that theology is thought about reality that "stands under" faith/revelation.[33] There is a noetic priority given to revelation that is inaccessible to reason but which reason is called to engage.[34] Reason "stands under" the content of revelation and addresses it from within its own limits and distinctiveness. In order to understand these distinctions more precisely, we need to consider Hall's interpretation of reason and revelation.

31. Ibid., 388.

32. This discussion is dependent upon a close reading of Hall's primary methodological book, *Thinking the Faith*.

33. Hall, *Thinking the Faith*, 253.

34. Ibid., 420–22.

Hall's discussions of "reason" distinguish between two types of reason, technical reason and contemplative reason[35]—a distinction that has emerged contextually with the dawning of the modern world.[36] As we shall see, even though the one type of reason is open to revelation, it remains for Hall distinct and discontinuous from revelation. Hall draws on the thought of many who make similar distinctions regarding the nature of reason in the modern world.[37] However, it is the thought of George Grant that most radically and contextually expresses the import of the distinction for Hall. In the North American context, Hall quotes Grant:

> Reason is thought of simply as an instrument. It is used for the control of nature and the adjustment of the masses to what is required of them by the commercial society. This instrumentalist view of reason is itself one of the chief influences in making our society what it is; but, equally, our society increasingly forces on its members this view of reason. It is impossible to say which comes first, this idea of reason or the mass society. They are interdependent. Thought which does not serve the interests of the economic apparatus or some established group in society is sneered at as "academic." The old idea that "the truth shall make you free," that is, the view of reason as the way in which we discover the meaning of our lives and make meaning our own, has almost entirely disappeared. In place of it we have substituted the idea of reason as a subjective tool, helping us in production, in the guidance of the masses, and in the maintenance of our power against rival empires. People educate themselves to get dominance over reason and other men. Thus scientific reason is what we mean by reason. That is why in the human field, reason

35. The term "technical reason" is drawn from Paul Tillich; see Hall, *Thinking the Faith*, 392. The term "contemplative reason" is my own; it seems to summarize or capture the definitions Hall cites. Other terms used to make these distinctions include the following: "rational thought" and "intellectual thought" (Jaspers); "intellect workers" and genuine "intellectuals" (Paul A. Baran); "calculative thinking and meditative thinking" (Heidegger); "instrumentalist reason" and "thought" (Grant); "incipient empiricism" and "intuitive reason" (Hall regarding Aquinas and Luther). Ibid., 390–99.

36. Though Hall makes much of the shifts of thought that take place with the dawning of the modern world, he also (like Grant) sees that the ancient world struggled between similar poles regarding the place and character of reason. He explores how Aquinas' Aristotelian priority of reason over belief (unlike the Augustinian-Platonic "concordat between faith and reason") triggered a whole new division between the two that has deepened in the modern era. See ibid., 275–78.

37. For instance, Karl Jaspers, Paul A. Baran, Jacques Ellul, Martin Heidegger; ibid., 392–99.

comes ever more to be thought of as social science, particularly
psychology in the practical sense. We study practical psychology in order to learn how other people's minds work so that we
can control them, and this study of psychology comes less and
less to serve its proper end, which is individual therapy.[38]

Hall tracks the historical development of the divorcing of reason from religious belief, citing the shift from reason as a kind of internal knowing of
the soul to an external knowing of the senses.[39] It is clear that for Hall, as
for others, the eclipsing of "contemplative reason" by "technical reason"
has enabled the falsification of reality and resulted in much suffering.
With other voices of the modern era, Hall seeks to retrieve contemplative
reason as the truest form of rationality for the human species.[40]

Contemplative reason is that which is concerned with questions of
meaning and purpose in life (and in death and suffering). The divine gift
of rationality to the human species is intended for thought about life's
meaning and purpose in all its particularity. That such questions are rarely welcome in the hallways of the North American academy is a fact with
dire consequences. This "flight from thinking"[41] inhibits the possibility
for theology to exist as a discipline in the academy, or for any thought
about Truth to be contemplated at any depth. For this reason, in North
America in particular, it is essential for theologians to consciously and
deliberately contend with this critique of modernity's account of reason
and to engage pre-modern alternatives.[42] In illustrating the importance
of the distinction between the two types of reason for Christian theology
Hall writes,

> Too much theology in the English-speaking world especially,
> where the philosophic tradition of empiricism-cum-pragmatism
> and the economic-industrial tradition of technologism have
> both been enormously successful, has been content to dialogue
> with a form of rationality which . . . is reductionism of the worst
> kind, and its victim is the human "thinking animal." Theology in
> our sector has been far too much at pains to make itself agree-
> able to a view of reason which insists that whatever one claims
> to "know" must be capable of empirical verification. Thus, much

38. Ibid., 398; the quotation is from Grant, *Philosophy in a Mass Age* (1960).

39. Hall, *Thinking the Faith*, 390–93.

40. Hall cites Grant on this; ibid., 397.

41. Hall is here quoting Heidegger; ibid., 395.

42. Ibid., 397.

of the theological discussion at the level of epistemology in Britain and North America has been a kind of prolonged version of that "natural theology" developed in the Middle Ages which tried to demonstrate certain religious verities . . . by reference to the evidence of the senses and the application of logic.[43]

In his reflections on contemplative reason, Hall argues that it is only this sort of reason that can engage in theology and be open to the reception of revelation. Contemplative reason asks the existential questions and engages the realities of being in history. It raises questions regarding the reality of the good and of suffering in all its grotesque and disquieting manifestations. It is in its willingness to tackle the human questions of meaning and purpose honestly that contemplative reason opens to the possibility of revelation, though it can never anticipate its coming or its content.

Hall's account of revelation is summarized in four theses that bear on his understanding of the distinctiveness of the form and content of revelation. (1) "Revelation is the basic epistemological presupposition of Christian belief and theology."[44] This thesis reflects the noetic priority of revelation and the fact that both existentially and historically Christian faith begins with revelation. Whether one speaks of the experience of faith existentially revealed through the Holy Spirit to the believer/believing community or of the historical self-revelation of God in the person of Jesus, Christian faith is the fruit of revelation. Revelation is a "disclosure" or "unveiling" of something that cannot be accessed by reason, something that was heretofore unknown. Implicit in the term "revelation" is the notion of reception. Revelation is not something that is self-generated or mastered by human thought; it is something that is given to and unveiled to human thought.[45] Christian epistemology presupposes that revelation is a divine work, not a human work.

---

43. Ibid., 399–400.

44. Ibid., 403.

45. See also ibid., 248–57. In discussing St. Augustine's famous dictum *Credo ut intelligam* ("I believe in order that I may understand"), Hall writes, "Belief here means trust in God. When Augustine goes on immediately to say, 'Indeed, unless I believed I should not understand,' he is not intending to assert (as fideism is wont to do) that nonbelievers can understand nothing of God or the things of God. That would be wholly inconsistent with Augustine's essentially Platonic epistemology. He is saying, rather, that apart from belief . . . fullness of comprehension is impossible; for this relationship, and the trust that characterizes it, is the existential basis of all theology" (ibid., 252).

(2) "The Christian understanding of revelation is at base the disclosure of a presence."[46] In his discussions of this aspect of revelation, Hall is critical of Christian theologies of glory that too easily assume that the Bible or doctrine contains and circumscribes revelation. He cites the reformers and others who are at pains to emphasize that it is only by the work and presence of the Holy Spirit (Calvin) that the Bible is transformed into the Word of God, which necessarily points beyond itself to the transcendent presence of God.

> What is revealed in Christian revelation is not, in the first place, a what but a who. A presence! The hidden mystery unveiled in external and internal event is God's own person . . . He is one who knows and wills, who acts and speaks, who as an "I" calls me "Thou," and whom I call "Thou" in return.[47]

Revelation is not the communication of a set of ideas about reality, despite the fact that such ideas are included in the experience of revelation. It is the divine-human encounter wherein the mystery of God's presence is revealed to the believer, while at the same time God's deeper mysteries are concealed—never to be possessed or manipulated by the human imagination. God's self-revelation is the revelation of an Other to whom we are other. Revelation marks the emergence of relationship between the human and God.

(3) "Revelation in the Christian understanding of it is mediated through historical events, the decisive event being the one of which Jesus as the Christ is centre."[48] There is the "scandal of particularity" at the centre of the Christian concept of revelation. Jesus the person, the Christ, is the one upon whom all our faith rests, not some trans-historical and vague deity. The very presence that is revealed to faith is identified specifically with the person of Jesus. Hall draws on Tillich's term "dependent revelation" to categorize the distinction between the particularity of the self-revelation of God in Jesus and the particularity of God's revelation to faith. The latter is known and recognized only through the former, through the Holy Spirit. Within this description Hall elaborates upon a full-bodied understanding of love in Trinitarian terms. As the love between the Father and the Son, the Holy Spirit reveals and makes present Christ's Spirit among the believing community. "Love is the essence of the

46. Ibid., 404.
47. Ibid., 406.
48. Ibid., 409.

character God manifests in the events that reveal God's presence . . . The love of God is a suffering love, agape. And there is judgment in it . . . Love needs no other ends besides itself. Love seeks the fulfillment of the beloved (not just the knowledge of its being loved)."[49] The content of revelation is love.

(4) "Revelation is that disclosure of the divine presence which grasps the whole person, not only the spirit and not only the mind, and functions in the disciple community as its 'ultimate concern.'"[50] In this section, Hall points to the fact that revelation is experienced as a gift and that it is holistic in scope. In his emphasis on the whole person, Hall is drawing on his understanding of the tradition of Jerusalem and is critical of the movements within the church and academy which have not understood the full scope of revelation and the full-orbed character of created being. The love that is known in revelation is love that embraces the whole of human being. It is not something that should be relegated to the mind to be prescriptively itemized without engaging the breadth and height of its encountering embrace. Nor is it something that ought to be relegated to the songs of the heart, without thinking about the scope of its content and the consequences of its truth. He closes his discussion of revelation by citing Grant's Weilian understanding of faith and the priority of love: "The intelligence's enlightenment by love is a terrible teaching (in the literal sense of the word). Contemplate what happens to those who have been deeply illuminated by love."[51] Hall's understanding of revelation in this instance implies a receptivity of spirit to wait upon illumination.

Revelation Seeks Reason

Despite the fact that revelation and reason are of completely different orders, the one (revelation/faith) seeks the other (reason/understanding); "faith seeks understanding." Hall contends that the content and form of revelation (the love of God in the crucified Christ) seek contemplation and communication in the world. Deep within the dynamics of revelation there is the missionary or evangelical drive to be understood and to communicate. Hall reminds us of the beginning of the church at

49. Ibid., 412–13.

50. Ibid., 415. Hall is very clearly drawing upon the thought of Paul Tillich, one of his most important teachers.

51. Ibid., 417; quoted from George Grant, *Technology and Justice*.

Pentecost and how that moment of speaking the gospel in many tongues was the very inspiration of revelation at work. The gospel is intended for human beings.[52] Further, given that love shapes the form and content of revelation, there is no option to leave it to the side and not to be inspired to spread it. This movement to communication and relationship with others reflects the very character of love. The fullness of revelation seeks to be known, understood, and communicated by the believer in all facets of life. Our minds are intended to think through and give expression and language to the content of revelation in the very concrete realities of our time and place. Love enters history and seeks to be known and manifested in history, in relationship. When revelation is received as such by reason—engaged and grappled within the very stuff of life—there is a certain "incarnational mirroring" (my term) that takes place. The kerygmatic disruption of Jesus into history is mirrored in the kerygmatic disruption of revelation into reason.

To think through the content of revelation as "being in time" is to bind oneself with the suffering of Christ. There are no easy answers. In fact one might say that there are never any full and final answers, for the experience of revelation points to the breadth of the mystery of God's love, which can never be fully understood or communicated, only waited upon and received. There is a suffering of thought here, where the gap between revelation and the limits of reason are experienced. However, the desire for revelation to be engaged, understood, and communicated in history reflects the extent to which revelation addresses the whole being of the human. Furthermore, it reflects God's activity in history and God's desire for relationship in the midst of the very limits of reason and created being. Perhaps most elemental for Hall is the extent to which revelation seeks to engage and be engaged by reason's doubts and sense of meaninglessness, which lie deep within the human. It is only by such engagement that the truth and fullness of who we are as humans—in our limits and brokenness—emerges, and we can truly trust enough to risk relationship with the divine. Moreover, the essence of revelatory truth is clarified through engagement with reason's doubts and demands in such a way that its possibilities can be thought and communicated. Trust, courage, and honesty are essential components of this movement of revelation to reason. In this way of understanding the relationship between reason and revelation, we recognize too the extent to which doubt,

52. Hall, *Thinking the Faith*, 420.

despair, and struggle with meaninglessness are reframed as possible postures of waiting upon God's illumination.

Reason Seeks Revelation

If, in keeping with the idea that "faith seeks understanding," revelation in Hall's view seeks reason, it is also true that understanding (reason) seeks faith (revelation). In elaborating on the second understanding of reason—contemplative reason—Hall argues that questions of meaning and purpose point to the longing or yearning deep within the human that seeks restlessly for wholeness/God. One of the greatest problems in North America, Hall says, is that in the face of doubt and despair this essential human restlessness and yearning have been repressed, supplanted by the fear-driven compulsion to be happy and optimistic, and have been further eclipsed by the primacy of technical reason and the philosophy of pragmatism. However, there are many sensitive souls, often those who are on the periphery of the church or who question the faith, for whom the struggle and yearning for God continues to bear witness to humanity's deepest longing and waiting. This seeking for revelation is not one that jumps back from the darkness, afraid that greater seeking will uncover only a greater abyss. Rather, human reason's yearning for revelation, in this instance, reflects openness to God's possibility and awareness both of human limit and of ultimate dependence on that which is other to the human. Further, it is a manifestation of right relation of the creature with the Creator—in a posture of receptivity, openness, waiting. It represents the mind's yearning for the illumination of love and for salvation. "For authentic Christian belief," Hall says,

> salvation is by grace alone, not by knowledge; and it entails love, not merely comprehension. We are not redeemed by what we know but by the One by whom we are known. And our being known by that One is tested, not by our "correct" answers to doctrinal questions but only by our readiness to know as we are known—to love as we are loved.[53]

The fact that reason seeks revelation in human questions of meaning and purpose in life exhibits the possibility for a point of contact between God and the creature (revelation and reason) and between faith and unfaith in theology ("apologetics"). Finally, and perhaps most importantly for Hall,

53. Hall, *Professing the Faith*, 3.

reason seeks revelation by the *via negativa*. Reason is the means by which the darkness of context and created being is engaged and taken seriously. Only by entering the darkness as it is can the true light of revelation's possibility be glimpsed. Humility, trust, honesty, receptivity, and courage mark what is essential in human reason's seeking after and waiting upon divine revelation.[54]

Revelation and Reason Seek Mutuality

As we have seen, the discontinuities and distinctions between revelation and reason highlight the "otherness" of each. It is because of their otherness—their discontinuity in content and form—that the possibility for dynamic dialectical relationship between them is enabled. Each is of a distinct order; therefore each seeks and moves towards the other by distinctive means that manifest both the discontinuities and the possibility for moments of continuity between the gospel and the world. Humans are endlessly tempted to opt for mastery and to opt out of the constant and uncomfortable dialectical tension between revelation and reason. The consequences for creaturely being of succumbing to such temptations, unfortunately, are dire.

Hall, like Grant, points to pre-modern understandings of revelation and of reason, wherein the possibilities for mutuality between them was part of what it meant to seek knowledge, to seek truth, as an important source for Christian theology.[55] Both reason and revelation are integral to the knowing that belongs to Christian faith and theology. Furthermore, knowing that is shaped by the dynamic dialectic of reason and revelation reflects the constancy of the mutual seeking between God and the human in right relation. The inner dynamics of both revelation and of reason ultimately seek and wait upon the same thing: the truth of being, which is the communion of love. As "faith seeking understanding," theology manifests the deepest desire of the human soul as it waits in its search for wholeness and for the communion of all things in heaven and upon the earth.

---

54. "'Thinking,' wrote Hannah Arendt, 'calls not only for intelligence and profundity but above all for courage.' . . . Courage in the Christian vocabulary is a gift. It is not self-achieved, it is a matter of grace" (Hall, *Thinking the Faith*, 242).

55. See ibid., 276.

Hall's Dialogical Method in Conclusion

The dialectical and dynamic relationship between revelation and reason upon which Hall insists—most clearly evident in the interplay between the four distinct understandings of their relationship with one another—ultimately reflects the liveliness of the relationship between God and the human in God's intention for creation. God seeks relationship with creation. The deepest part of the human soul yearns for relationship with God. The character of this relationship involves suffering and is recognized most powerfully from the foot of the cross. Revelation strips reason of its pretenses to self-importance and seeks its otherness as the only means by which true human knowledge of God is possible. This is not a one-time event, for the "natural" impulses of reason constantly seek human, not divine, ends. The dialectical tensions that characterize the relationship between Divine and created beings reflect not only the discontinuities between God and the world—the concrete realities of human sin, limit, and disillusionment—but also the continuities made possible by the power of love that can create relationship out of nothing and that pursues its "prey" like "the hound of heaven."[56] All on the human side that blocks, breaks, and inhibits the possibility for relationship with the Divine must be challenged. There is nothing static about the relationship between revelation and reason, between God and the human. Hall's understanding of this relationship, shaped as it is by the content of the cross, necessarily reflects multiple and dialectical tensions—tensions that cannot rest easily but rather wait with dynamic energy, resisting mastery in all its forms.

Part 1 in Conclusion: Methods of the Cross in Dialogue—Waiting

As Grant's and Hall's epistemologies have been examined by means of the categories of reason and revelation over these last two chapters, the many similarities that they share have become evident. Clearly, for both of them the relationships between revelation and reason reflect the dynamic character of the relationships between God and humanity—between the gospel and the world as mediated through the crucified Christ. Though Grant and Hall differ in emphasis and vocabulary, both consider

---

56. Ibid., 339. Hall draws this image from Francis Thompson's (1892–1935) poem, *The Hound of Heaven*.

the content and form of reason to be distinct and paradoxical,[57] while affirming nevertheless that there are ways in which reason is related to revelation and revelation to reason.[58] Finally, both stress that the ends sought by revelation and by reason are the same: unity, Oneness, communion. In the thought of both, the paradoxical and dialectical content of these four points, when they are held together, reflects a dynamic epistemology that mirrors the dynamic movement and multidimensionality of the divine-human encounter as conceived from the human side. Both understand that thought about the truth of things necessarily involves suffering as the thinker is experientially grasped by the limit of human reason, by the human yearning for the wholeness of revelation, and by the impossibility of their reconciliation from the human side. The fact that no single way of framing the relationship between reason and revelation can contain truth reflects the real limit and suffering of human reason, revealed most poignantly in the crucified Christ. For Grant and Hall alike, the cross reveals both the reality of the paradox ("contradiction" [Grant] or "discontinuity" [Hall]) and the possibility for mediation ("the whole"[Grant] or "continuity" [Hall]) between God and the world. Furthermore, the cross manifests the power of love, which is not of this world yet is intended for this world. The dynamic epistemology of the cross, apparent in the work of both of them, reflects a struggle to be open, to wait for, and receive the illumination of love's revealing when it comes. Indeed, content shapes form and form elucidates content.

Both Grant's and Hall's epistemologies of the cross are contextually engaged, challenging their readers to contemplate the falsities implicit in the modern vision of reality in terms of its understanding of the interplay between reason and revelation. The false epistemologies of modernity are considered by each to be manifestations of the theology of glory—attempts, that is, to master that which cannot be mastered by human science and technical reason. Truth cannot be known by such means because thought has itself lost its essential purpose. Further, both look to the pre-modern traditions of faith—Athens and Jerusalem—to articulate truer orderings of the relation of reason to revelation in the theology of the cross. In so doing, they each seek to draw their readers into critical and constructive postures of being so as to contemplate more deeply the questions of human purpose and meaning in the modern

57. In this chapter, see the sections entitled "Thinking about Athens and Jerusalem" and "Reason and Revelation: Distinct and Discontinuous."

58. In this chapter, see the section entitled "Hall's Epistemology of the Cross."

North American context. Implicit in their discussions on reason and revelation are considerations of the relationship between the particular and the universal and of the way in which the two can and cannot intersect and be thought. For both, the particular (that is, the time-and-place context) is the arena for glimpsing the universal (eternity). However, what this glimpsing reveals is the hidden presence of God in places unexpected. These glimpses are given by revelation to reason (and recognized in faith) in the very concreteness of human lives and relationships in time and space. The theology of the cross takes the world and the limits of creaturely being seriously as the place for God's revealing presence to be received and apprehended.

On first glance it is evident that the differences between Grant's and Hall's epistemologies of the cross derive from differences in their disciplines, vocabularies, and audiences. Succinctly summarized, their differences may be seen to illustrate the differences between the respective traditions of Athens and Jerusalem—philosophy and theology. Indeed, much could be said about these differences and about the impact Athens' (Plato's) more spatially oriented vision of reality and Jerusalem's more temporally (or historically) oriented vision have had upon Grant's and Hall's distinctive articulations of the relationships between things, especially (in this discussion) between reason and revelation.[59] Furthermore, much could be said about the differences in language of the two and the extent to which different vocabularies not only reflect but also enable differences in meaning. However, it is instructive, I believe, to take a step back and to consider their differences in terms of the complementarity of their purposes and contexts. Grant's philosophy and Hall's theology manifest two different but complementary entry points into the questions of human hope, purpose, and meaning in contemporary North America. Plainly stated, whereas Grant's philosophy represents the side of "unfaith seeking faith," Hall's theology represents the side of "faith seeking unfaith." Both Grant and Hall are engaged in articulating the apologetic intersection between God and the human, between the gospel and the world, and between the church/ faith and culture. But this apologetic stance is one that functions negatively (through the *via negativa*), clearing the way so as to serve the

---

59. While I do not pursue the course of thought here, it is one that deserves further attention. Grant describes time in Platonic terms as "the moving image of eternity"; see, for example, Cayley, *George Grant in Conversation*, 46. Hall refers to the "moving edge of time," " the mystery of the future"; see *Thinking the Faith*, 49.

kerygmatic possibility.[60] For both Grant and Hall, apologetic engagement of the negative is a means by which to "create a climate in which the real scandal of the *kerygma* can be encountered,"[61] a climate within which thought waits upon disruptive engagement.

Grant's philosophy provides him with a way to speak to the "unfaith" of modern liberal North America, to name the loss of faith, along with the dire effects and trajectory of faithlessness, and to intimate the possibilities of faith for thought and life in the North American context. He seeks to strip away the illusions of North American-style modern liberalism so as to lead people to taste their inner longing for faith. For Grant, the ancient synthesis of reason and revelation (philosophy and theology) and their common yearning for truth offers a framework by which to engage the modern world from outside its own points of reference. It is this perspective, grounded as it is in the theology of the cross, that enables him to name the manifestations of the theology of glory in North American life and thought in the seeking after mastery. For the most part, Grant is concerned with negating moves (*via negativa*) by which the "glorious" pretenses of modern liberalism (in all its manifold expressions in North American society), including the false pretensions of its "unfaith," are stripped away. His work is intended to draw us into a place of humility—and even into an abyss of sorts—where we wait upon the possibility of dreaming new dreams and seeing new visions outside the parameters of modern liberalism. Grant leads us to name the darkness as darkness, to call the thing what it is, such that the deeper truths of our meaning and purpose might open us anew to each other and our life together in creation.

Hall's theology represents the perspective of "faith seeking unfaith." In speaking primarily to those in the once-mainline churches (and on the periphery of the church) in North America, Hall sees the extent to which people in the church live in a state of denial in which they repress the knowledge of the darkness at many levels. Not only is "the negative" repressed and glossed over in our analysis of the world, but it is also repressed

---

60. I am indebted to Hall's discussions of apologetic and kerygmatic theology and the place of the *via negativa* as the apologetic engagement of the world—the means by which the way is cleared so as to await the coming of *kerygma*. See ibid., 336–67. As well, Hall's discussion of the meeting of "faith and unfaith" no doubt inspired me to consider the relationship between his work and Grant's work in this manner. See, for example, Hall, *Cross in our Context*, 61.

61. Hall, *Thinking the Faith*, 342.

in our own spiritual lives and our individual and collective quest for meaning. Our inability to engage the negative dimensions of life reflects the extent to which a theology of glory functions to blind us to the truth of things and to block us from living a truer, deeper, and more meaningful faith. We presume to master things of faith that cannot be mastered by human thought and we are unable to be honest about the depth of our confusion and despair. Like Grant from the other side, Hall recognizes the import of both existential and historical dialogue between faith and unfaith in our context such that the church might serve the world and serve God in greater truth, faith, and distinctiveness. His understanding of the theology of the cross through the lens of the ancient tradition of Jerusalem enables him to engage the darkness—the doubt, the failure, the sense of purposelessness and meaninglessness—that lies deep within the human in such a way that it may be seen for what it is. Like Grant, Hall recognizes that this internal darkness (read "unfaith") on a personal and collective level has real life (external) consequences that wreak havoc in the world. Hall is explicit in naming the extent to which the true light of Christ can only be seen from within the very darkness of this world. At one point he describes the task of theology today as the attempt to comprehend the madness—the human need to destroy.[62] As such, by the *via negativa*, he draws us into the darkness of the North American liberal church and psyche, so as to wait upon the true light of Christ hidden within this very darkness.

> It is better for us to go into the night. Not "gently" (Dylan Thomas), not heroically either, like the dying Goethe, and certainly not as if we enjoyed it! But as it is darker, let us see what meaning the darkness might contain for us. Instead of attempting vainly to prolong the modern illusion of Light, we might profitably explore the significance of our present disillusionment. It is possible—given the strange logic of biblical faith—that there could be more honest hope in our despair, more good in our experienced evil, more strength in our hard-to-admit weakness, more life in our dying than in all the pathetic attempts of a disintegrating Babylon to appear young and vigorous.[63]

"Faith seeks unfaith"—the reality of doubt, meaninglessness, darkness—so as to keep its feet firmly on the ground and its soul waiting and open to receive, in humility, the true light of Christ crucified. It is by such waiting at the foot of the cross in the face of the doubt, meaninglessness,

62. Ibid., 226.

63. Ibid., 241–42.

and despair of life that the possibilities for human hope, purpose, and meaning become visible.

Finally, in considering together Grant's and Hall's methods of the cross, the extent to which waiting at the foot of the cross is an appropriate metaphor for their method or form of theology is clear. This method embodies an understanding of hope within its very structure that actively waits upon and anticipates the illumination of thought by that which is outside its own possibility, while seriously engaging the real possibilities for human thought, will, and reason. The method of the cross can never settle, can never presume to "possess" what it constantly seeks, for that which it seeks is always and only given as a gift in a moment to those open to receive. In this method, the extent to which "waiting at the foot of the cross" means looking at the data of the world and discerning what "hope is not" is also clear. This waiting includes clear-sightedness regarding the terrible reality of pain, suffering, injustice, and oppression present in the world, lived and represented on the cross. In the method of the cross we recognize the extent to which human will and reason cannot lead us to hope but must be re-ordered in the face of God's presence and possibility. Indeed, hope as intimated in the method of the cross emerges as God's hidden revelation in creaturely life, as that which breaks in, as that which is unexpected, and as that deepest longing towards which the soul leans as it waits upon fullness that only God can offer. The posture of such hope is waiting—seeking, yearning, longing—the kind of waiting that rigorously engages all aspects of the will and reason so as to make way for the coming of God's possibility.

PART 2

Deconstructing Modern Mastery

Waiting on Hope

5

Theology of the Cross and Contextuality

As WE HAVE SEEN in the previous chapters, the theology of the cross is immediately suspicious of all claims of glory and mastery in the world, for they reflect a false vision of reality. The theology of the cross is the point of departure for thought about reality that seeks to "call the thing what it is." It recognizes that manifestations of the theology of glory reflect a fundamental lie about reality and the essence of relationships that posits mastery and glory, success and autonomy as the primary truth of being—that towards which the human must strive. In contrast to the theology of glory's emphasis on the triumphant potential of the human, the cross reveals both the suffering, brokenness, dependence, and vulnerability of the human condition and the power and possibility of God's love made visible in and through the very real limits of creaturely being. Furthermore, in contrast to the theology of glory's presumptions regarding God's obvious presence in (or above) the world, the cross reveals the unexpected otherness of God and the hidden presence of (God's) love in the details of life. This revelation inverts the human expectation and desire for glory and power in God and in the world that is recognized in the various manifestations of the theology of glory. Instead, it is through weakness that God's love is made perfect (2 Cor 12), through the "humbling" of the human that the beauty of God can become visible.

Luther's theology of the cross is explicit in its expectation that when one lives in the illusion of the theology of glory, one is forced to lie about life and especially about the character of good and evil in the world. The intense focus and vast outlay of energy required to maintain an illusion in such discord with the truth of things can lead only to denial or despair on a massive scale. In the theology of glory, one's hope is placed in that which is hopeless—that which, beneath all the stunning accoutrements, is limited, finite, and incapable of sustaining the burden of human yearning. When in discord with the truth of things, the fearful among us cannot but repress or deny the darkness of life by means of an optimism based on falsity, the powerful among us cannot but be tempted by illusions of grandeur, and the honest among us cannot but despair in the face of the very real cycles of suffering and violence in the world. In response to the cultural milieu of our context, then, Grant and Hall see denial, nihilism, and despair as pervasive postures of being in North America today.

The Particular and Universal

The theology of the cross is always an intentionally contextual theology, for it prioritizes the particular as the primary location for reflection upon the truth of things. It is within the particularity of historical experience that manifestations of the theology of glory function and wreak havoc on the world, calling "good evil and evil good." It is here too that the possibility for "calling the thing what it is" can become a reality. And finally, it is only here within the concrete realities of time and place that glimpsing the hidden intimations of the eternal beauty of God is a possibility. This is true of the cross of Christ and it is true of all of life. Indeed, the cross of Christ reveals that it is only in the particularity of human life that the love of God matters and has teeth (so to speak). The present historical experience is held up precisely because it is here that the revealing of God's hidden presence is a possibility. In Luther's experiential mysticism of the cross[1] the possibility of encounter with the hidden God fills each moment with the impossible possibility of graceful encounter. Furthermore, the particularity of present human experience is the location for the manifestations of sin and struggles with temptation that have concrete historical ramifications in life. As we have seen, Luther's theses regarding the theology of glory and the theology of the cross emphasize historical reality as that upon which the truth of the cross is laid, intimating the hidden presence of God in the very essence of the particular.

---

1. See Hoffmann, *Luther and the Mystics.* In Luther's preface to an edition of the *Theologia Germanica* by Johann Tauler, Luther claims for late medieval Germanic mysticism, by which he was deeply influenced, a "wisdom of experience" much greater than all the theological reasoning of his day. See *Luther's Works,* 31:75–76, and the introduction by Harold Grimm, in Luther, *Luther's Works,* 31:73–74.

Nevertheless, the theology of the cross does posit some universal content about the particularity of things as revealed on the cross of Christ. No matter what the details of "particularity" may be in a given historical context, with the theology of the cross there is a "universality" regarding the struggle inherent in the human condition and the character of the mediating movement of God's love in the world. As humans we are constantly caught by the contradiction between two realities that function at different levels of being in the daily realities of each of our lives. At the deepest level lies the reality that we are but dust—powerless, limited, dependent in creation and before God, living by grace alone. At another level lies the reality that we are powerful, rational creatures, with freedom to choose, to affect, and to shape the world and ourselves by the effort of our wills through the work of our hands and minds. The theology of glory inverts the proper ordering of these levels of being and emphasizes the latter over the former, placing priority on the power and knowledge of the human and presupposing the possibility for humans to fix whatever is amiss and to find absolute fulfillment in themselves. In lying about the right ordering of reality, the theology of glory explicitly denies the deepest truth about who we are as humans and implicitly denies the possibility of God's true presence and otherness being meaningfully mediated in the world. The theology of the cross, on the other hand, prioritizes the former, deepest level of being as the means through which truth is made visible in the world—reflecting, from the human side, the distinctions between God and creation, eternity and time, and so on. It is only in accepting and facing the limits of being human that the beauty of God's grace (and our partaking of it) can possibly come into view and that human will and agency can be rightly ordered. This is the universal framework within which the particularity of being finds itself. It represents a very real struggle, in which the illusions of the theology of glory constantly seek to blind us to the reality recognized in the theology of the cross.

Theologians of the cross engage their historical contexts with this foundational understanding of the human condition and the character of God's hidden presence in the world, based upon the revelation of God in and through the crucified Christ. Accordingly, they take their historical location seriously as they seek out the manifestations of the theology of glory in all its many guises and begin to discern reality through the lens of the cross. It is the particularity of historical being in its manifold dimensions that is the arena in which the sinful expressions of the theology of glory are exposed, the reality of suffering becomes visible, and the possibility of God's hidden presence in the world is revealed. The "universal" truth of the human condition, recognized most poignantly in the cross of Christ, is the framework in which the particularity of life is raised up as the very means and medium in which the hiddenness of God (in some sense the truest universal) is present. Grounded in the theology of the cross, we see the extent to which the particular and the universal dynamically intersect one another. It is important to reiterate, however, that the theology of the cross places more weight on the particular than on the universal.[2] Indeed, it is only in the fragmented particularity of this world and of creaturely being that the universal "at-oneness" of reality may be glimpsed by faith, for it is first and foremost in the particularity of the tragic and heinous murder of the specific person of Jesus that God's hidden and mysterious love is made known.[3] The theology of the cross is always a contextual theology concerned with calling "the thing what it is" in a given context and situation.

The Hermeneutic of the Cross: A Contextual Lens

It may be instructive to consider that theologians of the cross look at the world through a hermeneutic of the cross that draws into stark relief the manifestations of the theology of glory in all its forms. This is a contextual hermeneutic that brings the reality of suffering, limit, and fragility to bear upon all apprehensions of reality. Consequently, where recognition of suffering, human limit, and fragility are invisible in human life and

---

2. Both Hall and Grant consider that the particular is the means to the contemplation of the universal. Grant, for example, emphasizes that it is primarily through loving one's own that one becomes open to the possibility of loving the whole. See *Lament for a Nation*; see also Emberley, ed., *By Loving our Own*. In keeping, Grant understands art as a particular means to the universal. See Grant, "Celine's Trilogy," as well as his "Canadian Fate and Imperialism," in *Technology and Empire*. Hall discusses the priority of the particular over the universal in the theology of the cross more specifically, arguing that its emphasis on the "scandal of particularity" makes the theology of the cross truly contextual. See Hall, *Thinking the Faith*, 148–57.

3. As Hall puts it, "The cross remains the fundamental statement both of the human condition and of divine redemption. The function of the resurrection is that it establishes Christ's cross as a saving event. Thus what the triumphalist mentality identifies as the negative, dark and therefore penultimate point of the Christian story . . . is itself already astonishingly positive. *Omnia bona in cruce abscondita sunt* (Luther): everything good is already there—but hidden beneath its opposite and therefore accessible only to faith" ("Cross and Contemporary Culture," 191).

relationships, the theologian of the cross presumes the reigning presence of the theology of glory in all its power and persuasiveness. Wherever life looks glorious and humans look masterful, theologians of the cross are suspicious; there they seek to uncover the truth of things, hidden behind the platitudes of this world. The pervasive reality of suffering in the world undercuts all prideful pretensions that desire to ignore, repress, or gloss over the wretchedness of life in this realm. It is only through an engagement with the darkness of life in its suffering, brokenness, and tragedy that the truth of things in this realm can be apprehended and spoken, including intimations of beauty and goodness. The theologian who employs a hermeneutic of the cross cannot honestly apprehend beauty without the tragic dimensions of life interpenetrating and deepening her apprehension. Further, it is in a spirit of humility, with human prideful ways broken to pieces, that reality may be glimpsed as it is.

I'll share a brief example of this hermeneutic at work. On my screen saver I have a picture of a large snow-covered cross nestled in a wintery evergreen forest. On first glance it appears to be a lovely Canadian Christian image. One could feel a kind of sentimental gush in seeing the cross softly contoured by the gentle snow amidst the vast rugged northern forest. In earlier years one might even have imagined with awe the glorious missionizing work of "the faithful" bringing the Gospel to this land. However, when we begin to hear the story of that cross and its context, a whole different picture emerges. The photograph was taken in an Aboriginal village in the northern Cariboo of British Columbia. It stands within a community whose members have all been brutalized by the Indian residential school system where churches worked with the Canadian government to destroy aboriginal identity and culture over many generations. In this particular community, sexual abuse in the church-run school was rampant. The wounds of the brutality inflicted by the church on the people continue to run deep, with devastating effect. Yet, in this place, within this community, the people have chosen for a cross to stand tall in the very centre of the village—tragic and terrifying; ordinary and ambiguous; breath-taking and quietly beautiful. The layers of meaning surge forth. Is it a devastating reminder—a remembrance of "never again"? Is it an ambivalent kind of shoulder-shrugging indifference? Is it a sign of solidarity, of hope in love's possibility when all seems lost? Yes—all this and more.

A hermeneutic of the cross enables the theologian to discern the prideful expressions of the theology of glory in all the spheres of human life and relationships in the world—political, spiritual, social, interpersonal, economic, geographical, religious, and so on. There is no corner of human life that need be left unexplored by this searching hermeneutic. Indeed, the truth of things revealed on the cross of Christ includes the whole of human being, life, and intra- and extra-human relationships. All human efforts to control, compartmentalize, manage, and relativize aspects of being are subverted by the breadth of revelation in the cross of Christ. Where the epistemology of the cross discussed in Part 1 emphasizes the interiority of the theologian, the stripping away of illusions of human reason, and a patient and trusting humbling of her knowing as a means to open to the possibility for hope-filled encounter, the hermeneutic of the cross emphasizes the exteriority of life, the stripping away of illusions of the human will, and a patient humbling of the will as a means to consent to the true ordering of reality.

The hermeneutic of the cross also enables the theologian who recognizes the absence or invisibility of the cross and of suffering in a given time and place to anticipate that the falsifying work of the theology of glory is at play. The hermeneutic of the cross demonstrates that the theologian's first and foremost task is to deconstruct the edifices of the theology of glory in all its guises in the world. This is the critical and negating task wherein the theologian engages the realities of his time and place in a negative apologetic. In uncovering the theology of glory, the theologian of the cross moves negatively (or critically), naming and unpacking what is wrong in the world. The priority of the *via negativa* cannot be over-emphasized in the theology of the cross. However, the critical, negating task of this theology should not be considered as an end unto itself. Indeed, for theologians of the cross, the *via negativa* represents a confessional or repentant turning toward God. It is the means by which relationships can be properly re-ordered to consent to true reality and God's promised intrusion can be awaited. Indeed, by negating the falsity in the world, this *via negativa* clears the way for an encounter with truth—truth that is not *of* this world, but that is found hidden beneath its opposite *in* this world. The negative apologetic of theologians of the cross enables them to strip away all that inhibits humans from living in right relationship (the theology of glory) so as to wait upon the possibility for kerygmatic encounter in the cruciform reality of God (the theology of the cross).

Grant and Hall on the North American Context

As the foregoing discussion has shown, Grant and Hall clearly share an emphasis on contextual analysis that is directed toward the uncovering of the manifold expressions of the theology of glory in contemporary North America. Moreover, both Grant and Hall have similar basic assumptions regarding the relationships between the particular and universal,[4] and both understand the truth of the human condition and reality in terms of the revelation of the cross of Christ. Indeed, they are both concerned with the extent to which the truth of things revealed in suffering and in the cross is obscured in our context by the domination and proliferation of the theology of glory; the work of both engages their context with a hermeneutic of the cross so as to make evident the darkness *as* darkness in contemporary North America. Both Grant and Hall, furthermore, name the extent to which a theology of glory has been and is being manifested throughout the church as well as the public sphere and indicate the dire consequences of such glory. As theologians of the cross, they recognize the priority of the *via negativa*. By engaging the theology of glory critically, they seek to release us of its illusory power, to "call the thing what it is," and thereby to prepare the path for a truer way of being in the world. Finally, both Grant and Hall see that denial, nihilism, and despair are distinctive responses to contextual theologies of glory. Each of these responses produces suffering—internal spiritual suffering in a crisis of meaning and purpose in life and external physical suffering in disordered political, social, economic, and ecological relationships.

What is perhaps most striking about the similarities between the two (despite the many differences, to be explored later) is that both Grant and Hall argue that it is the false image of the human as "master" that

---

4. There are, of course, differences in the ways each accesses the particular and the universal in his work. As a public philosopher, Grant's focus on the particular tends to be *extremely* particular and his focus on the universal *extremely* universal. For example, Grant devotes the first four chapters of *Lament for a Nation* to the dynamics of personalities and decision-making around a particular situation; he devotes the last two on the universals of Necessity and the Good (in relation to particular actions of the Canadian Parliament). As a theologian, Hall points not only to the extremes of the particular and universal but also to the mediation of the universal in the particular. Grant's essays often flow from a particular event within the Canadian public realm, while Hall's focus is more methodological and global in scope. Hall's particular way into the universal is most elementally the "scandal of particularity" in the cross and the person of Christ and in the believer's life. See *Thinking the Faith*, 148–52.

marks the deepest *problematique* of the North American context.[5] "Mastery" is the term that both Grant and Hall use that most fully captures the organizing principle of the expressions of the theology of glory in our context.[6] It reflects the primacy of the will in the modern image of the human and the purpose of the human being in our context (our thought and action). In the North American context, "mastery over human and non-human nature" (Grant) provides the content and direction of our (false) hope. Both Grant and Hall consider that the confidence in human mastery to overcome chance to bring about a new and better world for all has been the focus of our hope as a continent and has shaped our expectations for the future,[7] not to mention our understanding of human thought as technical reason.[8]

"Mastery" in our context means "the domination of the human will over necessity and over chance."[9] At various points throughout Western history and especially in the modern era, it has been assumed that human reason can discern the good and that our wills can naturally serve the good ends that our intellect discerns. As the previous discussions have shown, Grant and Hall are critical of the use of reason to master that which is beyond human knowing. Where our reason sees the failure of such good ends, education is intended to enable us to learn from our mistakes in an ongoing movement toward goodness that our wills will enact. To use the term "mastery" as a motif of meaning in our context reflects an entire way of understanding ourselves in relation to the world— ourselves, creation, and God. We master human and non-human nature toward an assumed good end discerned by our reason and enacted by

---

5. The term "master" is meant not to convey an exclusivist/sexist image but merely to evoke the idea of "mastery" (with its intentional allusion to Nietzsche's "Thus Spake Zarathustra").

6. Grant and Hall also use a range of other terms to convey this idea, including conquest, power, tyranny, and control.

7. "Mastery over the world would enable men [*sic*] to build a society in which all members would be freed from the tyranny of labour and for benefits of leisure. . . . This great hope has sustained the continent morally until recently and still the rhetoric is used to obscure the emptiness . . . to all but the claims of mastery" (Grant, "The University Curriculum," in *Technology and Empire*, 130).

8. Hall relies a great deal on Grant's cultural analysis in his work. Grant describes "mastery" as "society's faith," the quest of which for many still serves the hope of human perfecting. Ibid., 113.

9. That is, mastery over human and non-human nature (necessity) and over the circumstances of life that we cannot control or predict in advance (chance).

our wills.[10] It is the glory of the human will/mastery that is worshipped in the most elemental expressions of the theology of glory in the North American context. It is this that shapes our understanding of hope, of ourselves, and what we are intended for as human beings.

The recognition by both Grant and Hall of the domination by the human will in the modern understanding of the human is fundamentally shaped by a hermeneutic of the cross. This hermeneutic as we have seen is suspicious of all that prioritizes human reason and the will and the glorious possibilities of the human in ways that eclipse finitude, the reality of suffering, and the possibility of grace. In the modern West, we have found ourselves living in a context that glorifies and seeks to glorify the human will to power and the human desire to control human and non-human nature so as to build a better future that is worthy of our hope. "The central dream still publicly holds," says Grant; "North America stands for the future of hope, a people of good will bringing the liberation of progress to the world."[11] In their contextual analysis, Grant and Hall explore the implications of this dream. By means of the *via negativa,* they uncover myriad ways in which the image of the human as master undergirds our efforts to make meaning and interpret human purpose in life in the modern West. And finally, in their contextual analysis Grant and Hall share the perspective that North American society and church are in crisis, a crisis caused by the falsity, fragmentation, and failure of the theology of glory in our context—our hope in mastery. In discerning the true nature of our context, Grant and Hall see that the systems of meaning and purpose within which we as a society and as a church have placed our hope are no longer viable. The uncovering of the falsity and fragmentation of the theology of glory confronts us with a crisis of hope and meaning—an abyss; and we do not know where to turn for vision that provides an alternative to the vision of mastery. Denial, nihilism, and despair tempt us, and we can find no reason to hope, nor any reality within which to hope.

The following two chapters explore Grant's and Hall's contextual analysis respectively, along with the ways they see the theology of glory in the form of human mastery dominating the North American landscape.[12] For both Grant and Hall, it is in naming the falsity of the image

10. For a helpful discussion of this idea, see Hall, "From Mastery to Passivity," in *Professing the Faith,* 280.

11. Grant, "In Defence of North America," in *Technology and Empire,* 27.

12. Grant's cultural analysis is central to Hall's critical approach to the context. I do not repeat Grant's analysis in my chapter on Hall. However, throughout the discussion

of mastery in all its guises, in recognizing its devastating effects on inner and outer being, and in analyzing the crisis of hope its dismantling has left behind that we may be opened to "saying what the thing is" and to waiting upon illumination at the foot of the cross

---

on Grant there are footnotes highlighting Hall's perspective on the topic at hand and where it can be found in his corpus. Hall's indebtedness to Grant is noted, among other places, in *Bound and Free: A Theologian's Journey*, 47 (see also 143n27.)

6

Grant on Mastery
and the Possibility of Hope

What I don't think I emphasized sufficiently [yesterday] is what a dark era this appears to me, what a *dark* era! That the age of progress has ended up in *this*, do you see what I mean? And that it's deeply tied to what I call the science that issues from the conquest of human and non-human nature. This is to most people in the world, the hope of the world, as much the hope in Asia as well as in North America; but it seems to me that it is particularly serious for the Western world . . . It's tied up with this fact, the idea that everything proceeds from the Idea of the Good and that Being is therefore good. That has gone.[1]

THROUGHOUT HIS CORPUS, GRANT is concerned with bringing to light the darkness *as* darkness in our context. He seeks to deconstruct the illusions of glory within which we live in North America, to name the moral-spiritual bankruptcy and tyranny of which we are a part, and to offer us glimpses of what has been lost in the modern experiment. In Grant's deconstruction, the mastery or conquest of chance by the human will is the fundamental lie upon which the modern experiment has been constructed and within which its hope has been construed. In retrieving riches from the traditions of both Athens and Jerusalem, he critiques the modern idolatry of the human will. For Grant, the torturous image of Jesus at Gethsemane surrendering his will to God—"Not my will but

1. Grant, "George Grant on Religion," 53.

thine be done"[2]—is the picture of true freedom of the will and constitutes a foundation upon which he builds his critical contextual analysis.

Grant outlines throughout his corpus how trust in mastery over human and non-human nature has become that within which we place our
hope as a people and understand our sense of purpose and meaning. His
writings track the ways that western modernity is particularly taken with
the metaphor of mastery as an organizing principle of meaning. Grant
sees that the relationship between human mastery (will) and hope (purpose and meaning) has been exceedingly powerful in North America
because of some of the "primals" out of which our distinctiveness has
been born. The priority of the human will and its expression in mastery
stands as the most elemental core of the modern experiment; this has
been manifested in North America as nowhere else.[3] In summarizing
some of the key impulses of our context, Grant focuses on the hidden
problem, the idea that human beings are constituted by will.

> In writing of the positive influence of Protestantism on our liber-
> alism, one is forced to touch, however hesitantly, upon the most
> difficult matter which faces anybody who wishes to understand
> technology. This is the attempt to articulate that primal western
> affirmation which stands shaping our whole civilization, before
> modern science and technology, before liberalism and capital-
> ism, before our philosophies and theologies. It is present in all
> of us, and yet hidden to all of us; it originates somewhere and
> sometime which nobody seems quite to know. Nobody has been
> able to bring it into the full light of understanding. In all its un-
> fathomedness, the closest I can come to it is the affirmation of
> human beings as "will."[4]

In keeping with the primacy of the will and the emphasis on the
efficacy of human "doing," Grant argues, there is less a tradition of contemplation and more a tradition of action in the North American context. As a result, the possibility for self-critique, rigorous thought, and

---

2. Grant, *George Grant in Process*, 108.

3. Hall draws on Grant's analysis in his recognition that the *imago hominis* of the
modern world is that of the master. In a number of places he tracks how it came to be
that the image of the human as master is the one that corresponds with the officially
optimistic society of North America. See Hall, *Lighten Our Darkness*, 6–14; *Imaging
God*, 161ff; *Waiting for Gospel*, 45, 120.

4. Grant, *English-Speaking Justice*, 63–64.

recognition of what it is we are a part of in our context has been cur-
tailed.[5] Our sense of meaning and purpose, driven by the priority of the
human will, is focused on action and doing and not on thinking and being. Grant's attempts at critical contemplative contextual analysis emerge
in a context not given to such depth and breadth of thought.

Furthermore, the prioritizing of the human will in the modern
West has effectively eclipsed the idea of God, Eternity, in thought and
in action. Consequently our thought and action (or, at least, that which
is permitted and even celebrated in the public realm) are increasingly
tyrannical and morally bankrupt. "Mastery means masterlessness."[6] It
assumes the potential for limitlessness in the human.[7] Where there is
no sense of the transcendent God—the One who circumscribes creaturely limit, who constitutes that by which we are measured, in whom
(and out of whom) absolute truth, beauty, and goodness are found—we
can only move toward a moral-spiritual abyss wherein tyranny rules. In
his deconstruction, Grant not only analyzes and explains how this has
happened through the modern West,[8] but he also focuses his thought
on specific ways that this moral-spiritual bankruptcy and blind tyranny
are being manifested and causing suffering in our context.[9] As a means
both to give us distance from our modern presumptions and to whet our
appetites for the possibility of something other, Grant describes what it
is that has been lost in the modern experiment. His descriptions of loss
focus on intimations of deprivation that can be intuited in the cracking
foundations of modernity. As a theologian of the cross, Grant recognizes
that our loss of hope at this stage of the modern experiment reflects both
the loss of our souls in the dominating paradigm of mastery and the collapse of mastery as a functional metaphor of meaning and the source
of hope. Yet Grant sees that it is only by recognizing our loss that the

5. Hall draws on Grant's analysis of the North American impulse of action over
thought. He is critical of the lack of rigorous thought in the North American context
(see Hall, *Lighten our Darkness*, 18–22) and takes up Grant's challenge that the most
central task of thought in North America is to think through what it is that we have
become with the dawning of the technological society.

6. "Obedience," 25.

7. Hall discusses this in *Professing the Faith*, 190.

8. See Grant's *English-Speaking Justice* and *Time as History*, in which he follows
the history of ideas through the modern West and contrasts these with the ancients.

9. See, for example, Grant's essays on abortion, euthanasia, the universalizing and
homogenizing impulses of empire, technology, education, the language of values, and
rights in *Technology and Empire* and *Technology and Justice*.

internal longing of our souls may be ignited to hope by the truth of who we are—creatures fitted for love and not mastery.

This chapter explores the manifestations of the theology of glory, its failure, and the possibility of hope in Grant's critique of the North American context under the following headings: Mastery, Hope, and the Conquest of the "New World"; Mastery, Hope, and Empire in Canada; Mastery, Hope, and Religion; Mastery, Hope, and Freedom; Mastery, Hope, and History; Mastery, Hope, and Justice; and Mastery, Hope, and Technology. While these categories are interrelated—they cannot really be spoken of in isolation—they do call attention to some of the key categories of Grant's own contextual critique. Each section considers its topic in relation to understandings of hope in modernity and to false hope, despair, and loss in the face of the breakdown of the modern vision of the world. This deconstructive move in each instance manifests a posture of hope that waits upon other possibilities than those given in the modern experiment. The concluding section summarizes Grant's thinking on the crisis of meaning and hope that must be faced at the end of the modern era in the West and draw out the ways he begins to point to waiting as a posture of hope for today.

Mastery, Hope, and the Conquest of the "New World"[10]

In considering the influence of the theology of glory as mastery in the North American context it is helpful to understand how Grant sees the connection between mastery and hope in the primal story of our origin as a continent. In North America there is a consciousness among those having come from elsewhere of having "made the land our own."[11] Non-aboriginal Americans and Canadians, though diverse in the expression of freedom, share the experience of having crossed the ocean and "conquered

10. The use of the terminology "New World" in Grant's work reflects the perspective of the historically dominant peoples of the West. Obviously, such language does not grow out of the experience of First Peoples of this continent. Throughout his work, however, while not being particularly cognizant of the biased language he uses, he critiques the "new world" mentality of the Europeans which quickly emphasized mastery over the land (and its people) and the "conquest" of the new world to create a "new world" *parousia* shaped by human will, imagination, and determination. In using his "New World" terminology here, I seek to remember this primal impulse of newcomers to this land—to master history (land and people) so as to create a "new world" on earth. Hall, though he would affirm the content of Grant's perspective on some North American primals, is far more sensitive to the Euro-centricity of such language.

11. Grant, "In Defence of North America," in *Technology and Empire*, 17.

new land."[12] Through the action of our hands and the power of our wills, non-aboriginal peoples have "tamed" this broad land for habitation. This conquering relation to the land (and the people of the land) has left its mark within us.[13] "If the will to mastery is essential to the modern," Grant says, then "our wills were burnished in the battle with the land."[14]

The meeting of the alien yet conquerable land with English-speaking (especially Calvinist) Protestants brought with it "a particular non-Mediterranean Europeanness of the 17th century which was itself the beginning of something new."[15] The "worldly asceticism" and priority of the will in English-speaking Calvinism merged, Grant explains, with political capitalism, and with the empiricism and the practical utilitarianism of the new science.[16] Furthermore, Grant argues that in North America the Calvinist doctrine of providence and emphasis on the will (divine and human) combined with a sense of evolutionary progress that was oriented to a future *telos* to be realized on earth. A driving practical optimism[17] and trust in technology as the means to create the "Kingdom of

12. "We are still enfolded with the Americans in the deep sharing of having crossed the ocean and conquered the new land . . . All of us made some break in coming . . . not only in giving up the old but in entering into the majestic continent which could not be ours in the way that the old had been" (ibid.).

13. Ibid.

14. Ibid., 17–18. Indeed, it is not only in relation to the land that this conquering primal exists, but in relation to the people of the land, the first nations' people, who also were conquered in the conquering of the land.

15. Ibid., 19.

16. See Hall, "The Amalgamation of Protestantism and Americanism," in *Thinking the Faith*, 165–96. "It could be supposed . . . that Christianity in the New World context might have told a story very different from the triumphant tale of historical progressivism. This did not in fact occur . . . The most influential expressions of the Christian faith in North America were those which could provide a spiritual buttress to the secular mythology of progress and mastery . . . that means, above all, Calvinism. For a particular brand of covenant theology in the Calvinist tradition could lend itself to the sense of divine election and destiny which captures the heart of the New World's citizenry" (ibid., 165). See also Athanasiadis, *George Grant and the Theology of the Cross*, 59–61, 116–17, 172, 173.

17. Grant writes a great deal on the official optimism of the North American context and the extent to which optimism has been confused with and has eclipsed the meaning and substance of true hope in our context. This feature of Grant's cultural analysis is picked up by Hall and highlighted dramatically as a central and blinding feature of the North American context. See particularly *Philosophy in the Mass Age*; *Time as History*, 43; and "The University Curriculum," in *Technology and Empire*. Hall's adaptation of Grant's understanding of optimism will be examined in the next chapter.

man [sic]," he explains, "fitted us to welcome an unlimited modernity."[18] The vast land of Canada held within it limitless possibilities, and these possibilities, Grant argues, were increasingly realized in North America through the proliferation of technology.[19]

The fact that we are a society that has no known history before the age of progress, Grant argues, combined with our hope in the "New World," has contributed to our optimism as a people. From the age of progress we inherited an optimistic view of the human will, a sense of inevitability regarding the progress and the culmination of history in a good end. This has shaped North American notions of hope.

> It is not difficult to describe the spirit of Europe in the last century [nineteenth century], for it has found its apotheosis in the externalized society we now have in North America. In outward action that spirit transformed life by creating the new technological society. In thought, this spirit built a world which put its faith in the external and raised up myths such as evolution and progress which glorify the external and state that man can be entirely understood as object. Man [sic] was not a problem to himself, for his difficulties, like those of other problems, would be solved automatically as he manipulated nature. Another scientific discovery, another hospital, another committee and gradually all would be well.[20]

The conquest of North America took place at the height of this optimism of the enlightenment and was considered to be the tangible realization of the modern hope in which equality, freedom, and goodness would abound. All the failed hopes for Western civilization could at last be realized in the so-called New World of North America. For the last one hundred years, our optimism and sense of limitless possibilities has been re-affirmed by generations of new immigrants, for whom the quest for the good life of affluence and freedom have merged in this "New World."[21]

18. Grant, "In Defence of North America" in *Technology and Empire*, 25.

19. "As we can see from our present situation, the Calvinist pioneers were building in English-speaking North America a society which would be more completely and quickly dominated by technology than any other. Yet at the same time, the absence of philosophy in North America meant an absence of the extreme forms of nihilism. North American society was until recently both more innocent and more barren than Europe" (Grant, "The University Curriculum," in *Technology and Empire*, 122).

20. Grant, "Jean-Paul Sartre," in *Architects of Modern Thought*, 67. Instead of inserting "[sic]" multiple times throughout this quotation I have opted to include it only once.

21. Grant, "In Defence of North America," *Technology and Empire*, 38.

Grant reminds us that despite the present-day cynicism and struggle with despair that abounds in the public realm, we must not forget the substance of our primal events in coming to the New World and making it our own. North America was "an incarnation of hope and equality that settlers had not found in Europe . . . there was an expectation of a new independence in which all would be free."[22]

Grant sees the extent to which this mastery over the land and its "resources" has become tyrannical in the realization that New World optimism, now that it has been tested by real life challenges, has turned away from awe and towards despair.

> Now when from that primal has come forth what is present before us; when the victory over the land leaves most of us in metropoloi where widely spread consumption vies with confusion and squalor . . . when the disciplined among us drive to an unlimited technological future in which technical reason has become so universal that it has closed down openness and awe, questioning and listening . . . one must remember now the hope . . . of that primal encounter.[23]

Externally, the consequences of our hope in mastery over the land have been manifested in ecological devastation, in the continuous expansion of cities, and in the real suffering of human and non-human beings. Our hope in the "New World" is undermined by the reality within which we live. In relating to the land and its people as resources or commodities to be exploited for utilitarian purposing, the vision of Canada has been thwarted and obscured. Internally, our conquering relation to the land (as well as to the people of the land) has blinded us to its beauty and to its possibility as an arena in which God's hidden presence might be revealed. It undermines the possibility for relationships of reverence and awe in creation. Furthermore, as the tyrannical assumption of mastery over the land more deeply takes hold of our collective soul, we are becoming more deeply imprisoned by its assumptions and unable to see beyond its all-pervasive purview.

In attempting to expose to us what we have lost, Grant works on several levels. First, he reminds us of the great dreams out of which North America emerged. On one level he is critical of these dreams. However, on another level he argues that the *great dreams* of the dawning of liberal

22. "In Defence of North America," in *Technology and Empire*, 24.

23. Ibid.

modernity are better than the *absence of dreams* of the present age of technological liberalism. The former, at least, are based upon intimations of the Good in the "New World" hope for equality and freedom for all. The latter, on the contrary, are based on despair and indifference resulting from the idea of the absence of the idea of the Good. On yet another and more pervasive level, he calls on the traditions of Athens and Jerusalem to contemplate what it is that has been lost in this modern equation of hope and mastery over the land. When we master the land, he argues, we know the land only as an "object" to be held up before us to give us its reasons for being so as to be used for human purposes.[24] Similarly, I must add, when we master a people, we know the people only as objects to be used for our purposes. We cannot, therefore, love their "otherness" and God-givenness. We cannot love the beauty in the other and catch glimpses of the Whole that is hidden within and within which all is held. The land itself, as that which is of God's gifting, hides within it the impossible possibility of God's revealing. When our relation to the land (and its people) is one of mastery and conquest, we cannot be attentive or consent to the otherness of the land as that which is *not* intended for human willful purposing, but is the very gift of God in our midst.

Mastery, Hope, and Empire in Canada

In considering the relationship of mastery and hope in terms of the Empire and the Canadian ethos, it is helpful to consider especially Grant's works *Lament for a Nation*, "In Defence of North America," and "Canadian Fate and Imperialism." Though Canada shares many primals with the United States, Grant summarizes some central distinctions that must be recollected so as to inspire Canadian resistance to the tyranny of the Empire. Such resistance itself witnesses to the possibility of another way than that of the Empire.

> Our (Canadian) hope lay in the belief that on the northern half of this continent we could build a community which had a stronger sense of the common good and of public order than was possible under the individualism of the capitalist dream. The original sources of that hope . . . lay in certain British traditions which had been denied in the American revolution. But the American liberalism which we had to oppose, itself came out of the British tradition . . . The sense of the common good

24. See, for example, Grant, "Faith and the Multiversity," in *Technology and Justice*.

standing against capitalist individualism depended . . . on a tradition of British conservatism which was itself largely beaten in
Great Britain by the time it was inherited by Canadians. Our
pioneering conditions also made individualist capitalist greed
the overwhelming force among our elite.[25]

As Canadians, we know ourselves as distinct from, yet sharing much
with, the former English-speaking empire (Britain) and the present
English-speaking empire (the United States).[26] Grant recognizes the "impossibility of Canada," while at the same time reminding us of the primal
Canadian hope of building a nation that drew from the best traditions of
each of these empires yet was not consumed by them.

In his *Lament for a Nation*, Grant laments the loss of the sovereignty of Canada to the expansionist power of the American Empire
and the loss of our hope in Canada. As a nation on the periphery of the
Empire of mastery, we are invested, for better and for worse, in the destiny of that Empire. The universalizing and homogenizing[27] influence
of the empire is powerful; it certainly has real effects in the world. Our
loss of sovereignty in Canada is directly related to the power of mastery
in the Empire. It is something that we are called to resist but that is also
far larger than we can understand. "Indeed," Grant writes, "our involvement with the American Empire goes deeper than a simple economic
and political basis; it depends on the very faith that gives meaning and
purpose to the lives of Western [people]."[28] That faith is the belief in
human mastery that must be made manifest in our progress through
"technique." The realization of the American Empire manifests mastery
in its most insidious form.[29]

In lamenting the loss of Canada as a project within which to focus
our hope, Grant seeks to remind us of what it is we are giving up. He does

25. Introduction to *Lament for a Nation*, x. It is unfortunate that Grant does not
lament the loss of First Nations traditions. His general critique of the globalizing and
homogenizing influence of Empire would have very much reflected the First Nations'
experience of empire. He comes at it from a distinctly British Canadian perspective,
one that ultimately reaps social, economic, etc. benefits from being a member of the
dominating people.

26. Grant, "Canadian Fate and Imperialism," in *Technology and Empire*, 63.

27. When Grant uses "universalizing and homogenizing," he is following Leo
Strauss in recognizing that the modern liberal state has as a goal a classless state that
is universal and homogenous.

28. Ibid., 64.

29. Grant, "Introduction," *Lament for a Nation*, ix.

this not to drive us to a nihilistic despair, but as a way of honoring our distinctiveness, reminding us both of the consequences of our decision to serve the Empire and of the import of developing a healthy sense of resistance to the "givenness" of the Empire and its ways. The relationship between the love of one's own and the love of the Whole comes into play throughout this discussion. For Grant, it is through the love of the particular, "one's own" (a particular place, person, or nation, for example), that one may be opened to love of the Whole (universal). Accordingly, in recollecting what it is we are losing in allowing the Empire to have its way on Canadian soil[30] and in lamenting this loss, Grant seeks to kindle "love for our own" distinctive origins and possibilities so as to open us to see beyond the tyranny manifested in Empire.

Mastery, Hope, and Religion[31]

In considering Grant's understanding of the relationship between mastery, hope, and religion in his critique of the theology of glory in our context, we must consider Grant's analysis of the "religion of progress" that has dominated the spirit of English-speaking North America. Grant argues that the ideology of progress, pursued and practiced as a religion, enables the technological society. In his essay "Religion and the State," Grant draws on an ancient definition of religion as that which "binds together"—in other words, "as that system of belief (whether true or false) which binds together the life of individuals and gives to those lives whatever consistency of purpose they may have."[32] In a technological society, the religion of progress (i.e., the faith in human mastery over chance) is that which binds together the meaning and purpose of North American public institutions.

> The believers in the religion of progress, mastery and power [assume] their religion to be self-evidently true to all [people] of good will, they are forceful in advocating that it should be the public religion. They work for the coming of the universal

30. The impetus for writing *Lament for a Nation* was the Canadian parliament agreeing to allow the U.S. to test missiles on Canadian soil.

31. Like Grant, Hall tracks the links between the Calvinist emphasis on the providence of God and the development of the "religion of progress" in North America. See Hall, "*Providentia Dei* and the Religion of Progress," in *Professing the Faith*, 83–88, and "Mythology and Providential Beginnings," in *Professing the Faith*, 112–19.

32. Grant, "Religion and the State," in *Technology and Empire*, 46.

and homogenous state with enthusiasm; they await its coming with expectation. Such a belief, of course, appears nonsense to those of us (Christian or non-Christian) who hold the conservative principle that belief in a "higher" divine power is a minimum public necessity if there is to be constitutional government . . . The religion of progress may have been able to kill Christianity in the consciousness of many, but it has not succeeded in substituting any other lasting system of meaning.[33]

Grant goes on to describe the religion of progress as "the ever-increasing externalizing of ourselves."[34] Ultimately the religion of progress is a belief in positive outcomes and the belief that "the conquest of human and non-human nature will give existence meaning,"[35] a meaning that will be inevitably and progressively good.

Most strikingly, Grant is incisive in his criticism of North American liberal Christianity, which he considers to be driven more by the religion of progress than by the fundamentals of the Christian faith. The religion of progress is "the only Christianity that technological liberalism would allow to survive publically . . . [It] played the flatterer of modernity."[36] Such religion in English-speaking North America is a kind of opiate to the people (Marx), if you will, blinding us to the idolatry of our mastery on the one hand and to the deeper truth of Christianity, on the other.[37]

The religion of progress is one of the most overt expressions of the theology of glory in the North American context.[38] In it we see the fusion of religion with the presumption of human mastery. Grant outlines the extent to which Calvinist Protestantism enabled the primacy of human mastery to be combined with the religion of progress in the North American context. In Calvinist Protestantism (as with the Western tradition in general, according to Grant),[39] God is considered to be "will" above

33. Ibid., 58.

34. Ibid., 59.

35. Grant, "Canadian Fate and Imperialism," in *Technology and Empire*, 77.

36. Grant, "Religion and the State," in *Technology and Empire*, 44.

37. Hall's critique of liberal Protestantism in modernity is deeply indebted to Grant's analysis of the religion of progress. See, for instance, "Official Religion of the Officially Optimistic Society" in *Lighten Our Darkness*, 45–105.

38. Hall draws heavily on Grant's analysis of the religion of progress in his work, which forms a central component of his cultural critique. See, for example, *Lighten Our Darkness*, 16–18.

39. Grant's reading of Philip Sherrard led him to see that the Latin West from the beginning was inclined to understand God as a god of will, placing priority on the will

all else. The exaltation of will in the divinity reflects the exaltation of the will in the human (despite its intention to the contrary in the latter case). This is most obvious in the Protestant work ethic. Calvinist Protestantism was, above all, a practical faith which emphasized the will—"action" and "doing"—as the outward expression of the inward assurance of salvation. Calvin's doctrine of predestination highlighted the hidden God by whose inscrutable will people are elected to salvation or damnation. Such a doctrine should have led to the conclusion that human action was of no consequence to election. However, in North America predestination and an emphasis on the Fall did not lead to quietism but rather to an emphasis on doing. As such, in the dominant ethos of North America, people "sought in practicality the assurance that they were indeed recipients of grace."[40] The Calvinist emphasis on the priesthood of all believers further encouraged a worldly asceticism in which saints (i.e., all believers) were to live practical lives pleasing to God.[41] The inherent egalitarianism of Calvinism, which also held that all believers were capable of grasping the essential truth of revelation, served the vision of equality in the New World.[42] Increasingly, the emphasis on practicality and the outward expression of salvation in works led to a focus in education on technical knowledge, which emphasized the importance of technique for effectiveness in the world.[43] Furthermore, a predestinarian progressive view of election combined with a belief that outward signs of election were discernable in works, leading in turn to a triumphant optimism that refused to question itself.

However, progressivist ideology gradually became cut off from its more Christian Calvinist roots. The idea of a transcendent God providentially ordering the world came to be understood as God moving within history, progressively moving history to a certain good end. In the Calvinist doctrine of providence, God's will was understood to be inscrutable in the world, a matter of faith invisible in the realm of human life. Under the influence of North American progressive liberalism, however, God's will began to be considered "scrutable"—that is, evident within human actions, especially the pursuit of freedom in history. Grant believes

---

and power of God over the essence and love of God. Athanasiadis, *George Grant and the Theology of the Cross*, 137, 198.

40. Grant, "American Morality," in *Philosophy in the Mass Age*, 77.

41. Ibid.

42. See Hall, *Confessing the Faith*, 165.

43 Grant, "American Morality," in *Philosophy in the Mass Age*, 79.

that in North America the doctrine of providence as it intersected with liberalism developed into the doctrine of progress, which entails a purely historicized notion of the Good, driven by the human goal of freedom. Furthermore, the exaltation of willed action fed a pragmatic optimism in which truth began to be understood according to the efficacy of action: "Our ideas are true when and insofar as they are effective in action."[44] How the human uses his or her practical freedom in history increasingly became the focus of the understanding of truth, expressing the truly modern history-making spirit of North America. The fact that truth was no longer understood to be one, eternal, and unchanging, but rather resided in the practical outcomes of willed action, means that there is no final certainty and no final purpose by which humans are measured. The results of the human will enacted in the world have become the measure of truth within the dominant ethos of North America.

The optimism that in the religion of progress masquerades as hope crumbles when the human will fails to bring the good into being. Grant sees that we are living in a time when the evidence of such failure surrounds us, attesting to its inevitability. The disintegration of this expression of the theology of glory as it has been interwoven with the motif of mastery in religion is the cause of much suffering, both externally and internally. Externally, we have become morally bankrupt and tyrannical in our relativism, preserving little sense of right and wrong in the public sphere. Our recourse to the "values" language of Nietzsche[45] enables us to hide the fact that the Good is irrelevant to our thought and lives. Yet our moral bankruptcy and tyrannical treatment of life is everywhere evident: in the tyranny of the empire in the name of "freedom" in Vietnam and Canada;[46] in public debate on abortion and euthanasia in which the appropriate killing of the vulnerable is posited;[47] and in our approach to education in which the public language of modern liberalism, which ceases to allow the existence of any other system of meaning, cripples the thought of the young and old alike.[48]

44. Ibid., 83.

45. Grant attributes "values" language to Nietzsche in "Nietzsche and the Ancients," in *Technology and Justice*, 90.

46. See Grant, *Lament for a Nation* and his essays in *Technology and Empire*.

47. See Grant, "Language of Euthanasia" and "Abortion and Rights," in *Technology and Empire*.

48. Grant, "Religion and the State" and "University Curriculum," in *Technology and Empire*, and "Faith and the Multiversity," in *Technology and Justice*.

Grant sees that this breakdown in the religion of progress is being internally manifested within the soul of North America in the experience of despair. Despair sets in when the falsity of the religion of progress is found out. There appears to be nothing enduring within which to place our hope, nothing outside the superficiality of the market by which to measure our sense of meaning and purpose. The desire to place our trust in something bigger than ourselves moves deeply within us, but this yearning and searching cannot find an object of trust. The eclipsing of the language of the good (which is the recognition of eternity in thought) is a consequence of the prioritizing of the human will "to do for the sake of doing." Where the religious manifestation of mastery initially assumed that good human action reflected God's providential salvation, in the religion of progress human action toward desirable outcomes itself has come to be understood as the means through which God acts in the world and moves history toward greater goodness. As God (the Good/truth) becomes increasingly equated with human action toward desirable human outcomes in history, the idea of God/the Good as a transcendent reality, other to the human, is eclipsed. Without a sense of the Good and eternal beyond our own will to do, our source of hope is utterly lost to us. The failure of this vision of life plunges us into an abyss of despair, unable to see beyond the crumbling walls of our self-made dream.

> How can we escape the fact that the necessary end product of the religion of progress is not hope, but a society of existentialists who know themselves in their own self-consciousness but know the world entirely as despair? In other words, when the religion of progress becomes the public religion we cannot look forward to a vital religious pluralism, but to a monism of meaninglessness. And what becomes of the constitutional state in a society where more and more persons face their own existence as meaningless? Surely, the basic problem of our society is the problem of individuals finding meaning in their existence.[49]

In seeking to re-collect what it is we have lost in the religion of progress (and conversely showing us what it is that we might taste again with the pending destruction of the religion of progress), Grant invites us to remember the traditions of Athens and Jerusalem. What we have lost in the demise of the religion of progress is only that small part of Christianity that modern liberalism allowed to survive as the "flatterer

---

49. Grant, "Religion and the State," in *Technology and Empire*, 58.

of modernity."[50] Through the traditions of Athens and Jerusalem, Grant raises before us the horizon of eternity within which human being, thought, and action are truly known. He challenges us to contemplate its loss in the religion of progress and invites us to seek out its meaning and truth. The horizon of eternity marks our limit and otherness, relativizes all within a much larger Whole, and is indeed the truth by which all is measured, and good and evil are known.

Mastery, Hope, and Freedom[51]

In considering the relationship between mastery, freedom, and hope in Grant's criticism of the theology of glory in the North American context, we must pay particular attention to his political critiques of modern liberalism.[52] At the root of modern liberalism, Grant argues, lies the affirmation that freedom is the essence of the human. Liberalism is "a set of beliefs which proceed from the central assumption that [human] essence is freedom and therefore that what chiefly concerns [the human] in this life is to shape the world as we want it."[53] As Grant unpacks the meaning of "freedom" in our context, it is clear that it has two distinctive sides: (1) freedom is liberation from tyranny, and (2) freedom is the capacity of the human will to act towards its own autonomous fulfillment. Ironically, what we see now is the paradoxical realization of the freedom of the will as the tyranny of the will. That against which freedom had been understood is increasingly becoming that by which freedom is defined.

In early formulations of liberalism, the assumption that the human will is a "good will" drove a positive vision of the possibility for active human agency to bring about the good in society. Our hope as a society was built upon visions of the future realization of freedom for all. According to Grant, this development in liberalism took place in two stages. The first stage is ascribed to thinkers such as Locke and Hobbes

50. Ibid., 44.

51. Hall critiques the understanding of freedom in the dominant ethos of North America. He emphasizes that true human freedom is found in bondage to God, not in things externally determined. See Hall, *Professing the Faith*, 25–28. "To propose that we are creatures of destiny is to run headlong into the most sacred concept of the English-speaking world, especially of the United States of America: freedom" (Hall, *Bound and Free*, 65).

52. See most notably *Technology and Empire*, *English-Speaking Justice*, and *Technology and Justice*.

53. Preface to *Technology and Empire*, 114.

who redefine human nature so that the pre-modern understanding of Divine "createdness" and creaturely dependence is eliminated. The human becomes viewed as one who is constituted both by a fear of death and by a selfish need for self-preservation. This fear and need compel humans to come together so as to "contract," co-operate, and combine their efforts and thereby maximize their individual preservation, instead of competing and killing each other. The second stage in liberalism, represented by Kant and Rousseau, Grant argues, sees the human will and nature as more positively motivated. Kant in particular posits that the human will is motivated by the highest of moral concerns; when it is autonomous, unencumbered by social constraints and convention, it will naturally seek the greater good of all beyond itself. Kant's approach, then, is to develop the critical thinking that will promote the freedom of the will for the greater freedom of all to be achieved. This was the vision of hope toward which we would move. Kant's ideas about the freedom and goodness of the will provided social contract theory with the means by which the right and freedom of a human being to do as she or he wanted came to terms with the right and freedom of others to do as they wanted. Thus, in the contractarian view, the state is intended primarily to keep individual rights in balance.[54] The idea of an inherent limit to human action, being, and thought is denied in this conception of the human. Rather, human limit is understood contractually; fundamentally, it exists only to ensure that the rights of other human beings are not jeopardized by the exercise of one's own rights. Otherwise, anything is permissible. In analyzing liberalism in this way, Grant highlights the falseness and danger of the idea that the autonomous, free human will can lead to the good of all,[55] and he critiques the lack of morality embedded in liberalism, wherein there is nothing that can be considered absolutely wrong under any circumstance.

Grant sees the falseness of the hope of liberalism and struggles to understand "why it is that liberalism remains the dominating political morality of the English-speaking world, and yet is so little sustained by any foundational affirmations."[56] Grant argues that freedom (or liberty) in North America is understood to be the highest good, the language by which meaning is derived. However, the content of that good is in-

---

54. Grant, "Faith and the Multiversity," in *Technology and Justice*, 59.

55. Grant, *English-Speaking Justice*, 27.

56. Ibid., 48.

creasingly negligible. Where once liberalism (particularly in the church) held within it remnants of the Good that focused thought and action upon charity towards others, the secularization of North America and the drive of technology have resulted in a freedom that has increasingly become "freedom for freedom's sake," without any sense outside its own dynamism by which it can be discerned and bound to a larger Good. Increasingly in liberalism, freedom is the expression of the dynamic limitlessness of the human, without substantial content.[57] Its dynamism is self-referential such that it lacks any means of self-critique. "As freedom is the highest term in modern language it can no longer be so enfolded [in questions outside its own dynamism]. There is, therefore, no possibility of answering the question: freedom for what purposes?" The answer to that self-referential question inevitably is: "an unlimited freedom to make the world as we want it in a universe indifferent to what purposes we choose."[58] Needless to say, freedom, mastery, and hope (as the power to do as we will) have become so interwoven in our context that their distinctions are virtually invisible.

In Grant's engagement of the work of political philosopher Leo Strauss, he recognizes the extent to which "freedom as mastery" in our context has driven the tyrannical "universalizing and homogenizing" impulses of the Empire in the world. What liberalism seeks is a universal and homogenous state without classes.[59] In the context of North America, "the purpose of action becomes the building of the universal and homogenous state—a society in which all are free and equal and increasingly able to realize their concrete individuality."[60] Under the auspices of bringing freedom and equality to all, the homogenizing and universalizing impulses of the liberal dream tyrannize the world. In his critique of the war in Vietnam and in *Lament for a Nation*, for instance, Grant decries the consequences of the universalizing and homogenizing tyranny of the Empire that is being unleashed across the globe. "What is

---

57. Grant, "Law, Freedom and Progress," in *Philosophy in the Mass Age*, 90.

58. Grant, "A Platitude," in *Technology and Empire*, 138. "[T]he situation of liberalism in which it is increasingly difficult for our freedom to have any content by which to judge technique except in their own terms is present in all advanced industrial countries. But it is particularly pressing for us because our tradition of liberalism was molded from practicality" ("In Defence of North America," in *Technology and Empire*, 34).

59. Grant, *Technology and Empire*, 87.

60. Grant, "In Defence of North America," in *Technology and Empire*, 33.

being done in Vietnam," he reminds us, "is being done by the English-speaking empire and in the name of liberal democracy."[61] Implicit in the liberal vision of freedom and equality for all is the tyranny of the universal and homogenous state. Vietnam experienced it in the devastating suffering of a people, and Canada is experiencing it in suffering the loss of identity as a distinctive nation. The paradox—that it is in the proud name of freedom and equality that the Empire is inhumanly and unjustly destroying lives—reflects the extent to which the tyranny of mastery has blinded us to truth and imprisoned us in its falsity. We have been mastered by notions of mastery. Grant sees that despite the public language to the contrary,

> technological progress is now being pursued not first and foremost to free all [people] from work and disease, but for the investigation and conquest of infinite spaces around us. The vastness of such a task suggests that society is committed to unlimited technological progress for its own sake.[62]

Tyranny has no ends but its own continuous self-propulsion. At least in Marxism (which according to Grant grew from the same liberal modern root as capitalism) there is a good end towards which action moves and by which it is given meaning.[63] To a certain degree, the extent to which the tyrannical trajectory of unmoored liberalism is visible is reflected in an experience of cynicism, despair, and in some cases resistance in the public realm. The challenge is this: how do we begin to think outside the dynamism and language of the liberalism that so shape our consciousness and sense of hope and purpose, yet is unable to provide meaningful content as to what it is we seek in the pursuit of freedom?

In the context of North America, the total eclipse of God/Good (the One who marks the limit and offers the content of our freedom) means that the highest end for the human becomes merely the avoidance of that which we do not like—discomfort, suffering, death.[64] The idea of limit (i.e., a limit to human freedom) is the idea of God. God is that which we cannot manipulate. God is the limit of our "right" to change the world.

---

61. "Canadian Fate and Imperialism," in *Technology and Empire*, 65.

62. Grant, "Tyranny and Wisdom," in *Technology and Empire*, 101.

63. Grant, "Temporality and Technological Man," in *Time As History*, 26. Grant argues in many places that Marxist-communism, American liberalism, and national socialism all stem from the same image of the human as master, the same flawed theological basis (ibid., 16–27).

64. Grant, *English-Speaking Justice*, 60–61.

Without God any action is permissible.[65] Because God is absent from the idea of purpose for the human, North American public consciousness (in both church and society) has no sense of "what humans are fitted for."[66]

For Grant it is clear that there is confusion regarding the essence of the human (and, thus, the God-human relationship) at the root of the modern experiment.[67] Freedom understood in terms of the human will in modern liberalism does not constitute the essence of the human in truth. To gain perspective on liberalism from beyond its own dynamism, Grant draws upon the traditions of Athens and Jerusalem to contemplate what has been lost in this manifestation of the theology of glory of modern liberalism.[68] Grant recognizes that "reverence rather than freedom is the matrix of human nobility."[69] The experience of reverence describes a posture of being in relationship with all that exists—God and the world. Freedom, in the tradition of Athens, is only "our potential indifference to God . . . For Plato freedom is not our essence. Freedom is the liberty of indifference to the Good, the ability to turn away from what we have sighted."[70] Freedom, in the tradition of Jerusalem, is that which comes to the inner soul through the revelation of truth: "The truth shall make you free." (John 8:32) Though it has external and political manifestations, in the traditions of the Ancients freedom is not in the first place understood to be an external state of political liberty and equality. Nor is it thought of in terms of the will and that which can be experienced through the working of the human action to change the world. Rather, freedom is considered in terms of the truth of God, its bearing on the human soul, and how this is lived out and mediated in relationships. It is in accepting the limits of our creaturehood before God, in receiving the gift of being

---

65. Grant, "The Limits of Progress," in *Philosophy in the Mass Age*, 73.

66. Grant, *English-Speaking Justice*, 24–36.

67. "The reason why modern liberalism is the only language that can seem respectable in the public realm is because the dominant people in our society still take for granted that they find in it the best expression of moral truth. This must be stated unequivocally because some of us often find ourselves on the opposite side of particular issues from that espoused by the liberal majority, and do not accept the deepest premises, which undergird liberalism, concerning what human beings are" (ibid., 7–8).

68. Grant, "Religion and the State," in *Technology and Empire*, 43: "Faced at an early age by the barrenness of the all-pervading liberalism, I had spent much of my life looking for a more adequate stance. In so doing I touched the wonderful truths of Athens and Jerusalem."

69. Ibid., 43ff.

70. Grant, "Faith and the Multiversity," in *Technology and Justice*, 55.

and the limits of our wills, that we taste the truth that seeks to make us free. The possibility of our indifference to God derives from the relational freedom given us with God. However, such a turning away from truth means that instead of living in the truth of God, we are living in a lie about who we are and what it is that we are intended for. The impartiality of God's love[71] for each and for all is the *only* ground by which true freedom and equality can be contemplated and enacted in the world. For Grant, therefore, reverence for (God's gift of) life is that which marks the highest purpose of the human, not the freedom of the will.

Mastery, Hope, and History[72]

In considering Grant's understanding of the relationships between modern conceptions of history, mastery, and hope, we must turn to his book *Time as History*. In this book Grant deconstructs the meaning of "time as history" in order to "illuminate our waking and sleeping hours in technical society."[73] He is clear that "time as history" represents a fundamental shift in the thought of the modern West, particularly as it is manifested in North America. It is in this conception of time and history that the image of the human as "master" comes to its fullest recognition. "To enucleate the conception of time as history," Grant says, "must . . . be to think our orientation to the future together with the will to mastery."[74] He recognizes that the notion of "time as history" came to fruition in the West as a distortion of its origins in ancient Greek and Biblical traditions.[75]

71. Grant draws the focus on the "impartiality of God's love" from Simone Weil. See Weil, *Waiting for God*, 87; *Notebooks of Simone Weil*, 254; *Intimations of Christianity among the Ancient Greeks*, 185ff.; *Need for Roots*, 288. Grant reviewed a copy of Weil's *Waiting for God* in the 1950s and from that point on, he says, she became a central authority for him on matters theological and philosophical. Cayley, *George Grant in Conversation*, 172–87.

72. Hall stands in agreement with Grant's analysis of the central place of history in modern thought and the extent to which this shift in thought shapes human life in the modern West. "The dominant note in modern culture . . . is not so much confidence in reason as faith in history. The conception of redemptive history informs the most diverse forms of modern culture . . . The glorification of history combined with the exhortation to work urges us to take responsibility upon ourselves for the mastery thrust upon us by history" (*Lighten Our Darkness*, 22, and *Professing the Faith*, 563ff.).

73. Grant, *Time as History*, 15.

74. Ibid., 17.

75. Ibid., 29–41. In his earlier work, *Philosophy in a Mass Age*, Grant describes how the notion of "time as history" originated in the combined traditions of Athens

Grant turns to the work of Nietzsche to help deconstruct what it is we are living when we conceptualize time as history. Though Grant admits that Nietzsche's work is "dangerous," it is Nietzsche more than any other who has thought through the darkness of the modern project to its end. In order to recognize what's wrong in the modern West, argues Grant, we must engage Nietzsche's thought.

> In Nietzsche's work themes that must be thought in thinking
> time as history are raised to beautiful explicitness: the mastery
> of human and non-human nature in experimental science and
> technique, the primacy of the will, [the human] as the creator of
> his [or her] own values, the finality of becoming, the assertion
> that potentiality is higher than actuality, that motion is nobler
> than rest, that dynamism rather than peace is the height.[76]

Grant argues that the word "will" in English both means "power" and indicates the future tense. The word "will" brings into focus the extent to which, in the modern project, these two notions of will have come together in our understanding of hope. Hope is placed in an imaginable future, which *will* happen. Furthermore, it is the human *will* that has the power to determine and create that imagined future.[77] With "time as history," conceptions of hope are historicized in the future. The source of hope, that within which we place our trust to bring about the imagined future, is the human will. Creating novelty or "making history" is the highest task of the human. However, unlike progressive notions of history wherein the creation of novelty is understood to be part of history's movement toward an inevitable good end,[78] Nietzsche dismisses notions of unfolding purpose for history as he dismisses the idea of eternity. In-

---

and Jerusalem. Though with the increasing manifestation of nihilism and despair in the public realm, Grant's thinking on the concept of "time as history" deepened, developing significantly between the writing of the two books, his early conception of the relationships is helpful for our discussion. "This view of time as history was brought out from the narrow confines of the Jewish people into the mainstream of Western civilization by Christianity. This is what the doctrine of the Trinity is: it incorporates into the timeless God of the Greeks, the God of project and of suffering; that is, the God of love. The sense of the unique importance of historical events was made absolute by the Incarnation. Our redemption has been achieved once and for all in his passion and death. This was not going to be repeated an infinite number of times. It was a unique and irreversible event" ("History as Progress," in *Philosophy in the Mass Age*, 41–42).

76. Grant, *Time as History*, 57.

77. Ibid., 20–24.

78. Ibid., 25.

deed, the idea of purpose for history merely reflects the "historicization" of eternity (or the collapsing of the vertical into the horizontal dimension of being). "God is dead" and thus the only horizons of meaning are those which are human-made.[79] Purpose is created by the will and is not engrained in the nature of things. The idea of mastery is the recognition that all horizons are only horizons. It is only the power of the human will that makes history.[80]

As Nietzsche understands, the only things that are final are the absence of permanence, the constancy of change, and the sheer relativism of history. To think (and live) time as history means that we must accept the "finality of becoming." Thus, hope as it has been construed in modern North America is meaningless, for without eternity there is no end point toward which human purpose can be directed and within which it can be recognized. There is no actuality, only a constancy of becoming. Indeed the conception of time as history (and later, "historicism") is the dominant conception undergirding our technological society and shaping the way we understand our lives, individually and collectively.

> I mean by historicism the modern doctrine that all thought about the whole belongs only to a particular dynamic situation. Its opposite may loosely be called Platonism—the teaching that thought in its perfection is impersonal and stands above every context. Historicism appears to me as the highest methodological principle of that destiny I have called "technology."[81]

Grant focuses on "values" language[82] as a means of deconstructing the emptiness of the relativism within which we think and live. The use of values language, he argues, is a way to project an image of the

79. Hall argues that the "death of God" is really a way of talking about the death of the true idea of the human at the dawning of the age of human mastery. *Lighten Our Darkness*, xxxix.

80. Hall quotes Grant to emphasize the same point: "Mastery comes at the same time as the recognition that horizons are only horizons. Most [humans], when they face the fact that their purposes are not cosmically sustained, find that darkness falls upon their wills" (Grant in Hall, *Lighten Our Darkness*, 26).

81. Grant, "Philosophy and Culture," 181. This essay is a different version of "Thinking about Technology," in *Technology and Justice*.

82. Grant's critique of values language is found in many places in his work. The most focused accounts may be found in "Part II," in *English-Speaking Justice*, 13–47; and "Value and Technology," in *Conference Proceedings: Welfare Services in a Changing Technology*. See also Athanasiadis, *George Grant and the Theology of the Cross*, 127, and Athanasiadis, "Political Philosophy and Theology," 27.

good without it actually being present.[83] Consequently, values language is changeable and relative; it lacks a connection to anything beyond the historical individual and her or his experience. Values language, Grant argues, is a way to mitigate the chaos of history's constant dynamism and to impose anthropomorphic explanations to order life. Nietzsche recognizes that in the trajectory of modernity that the complete oblivion of eternity is inevitable; therefore, everything that modern liberalism has espoused is meaningless, for it is entirely based upon the remnants of a more ancient tradition that has now been made defunct by modern technological liberalism itself. "What is wisdom," Grant asks, "when we have overcome the idea of eternity?"[84] Nietzsche questions what reasons or evidence sustain the belief that all people are equal or should be free. Science cannot give us this content. It is always ambiguous. Ultimately, with the oblivion of eternity, Nietzsche argues, humans are "beyond good and evil": it is only our will to power that creates meaning, gives purpose, and is the source of our hope. Hope is attached only to the human will to do and to enact its own purposes in life. However, this pathway is open to only a few whose mastery and will to power are the greatest. The greatest among us, Nietzsche argues, will take our revenge on "time as history" by loving it. Our mastery of history will be complete in our loving of history as that within which we create ourselves. Nietzsche posits that it is only those who love fate (*amor fati*)—and who love time as the eternal recurrence of the same—who will rise; only they deserve to be masters of the world. Most, however, will fail, falling into a spirit of "happy" indifference ("last people"), revenge, or resentment ("nihilists").

Grant considers that the notion of time as history fundamentally constitutes "what's wrong" in North American society and reflects a manifestation of the theology of glory. Time as history, in the Nietzschean understanding, has become the dominant paradigm in our technological society. In his critique Grant draws upon the traditions of Athens and Jerusalem,

---

83. Hall's analysis of "values" language in relation to the good is similar to Grant's: "Even the language of 'values,' which has replaced the classical language of 'the good,' can seem oppressive to those whose values (whose 'rights'!) are incommensurate with the expressed values of the majority. That anyone should feel obliged to work out his or her attitude to abortion, for example, in relation to a system of belief that imposes millennia of tradition upon the free-floating individual seems to most 'moderns' absurd. But if the profession of Christian faith means what we have claimed it means, then precisely such an obligation is built into faith itself" (Hall, *Confessing the Faith*, 266. See also Hall, *Professing the Faith*, 119).

84. *Time as History*, 43.

which he sees have been distorted in the modern account of history.[85] In so doing, he offers distance and perspective for seeing "what the thing is" and draws out the intimations of deprival and loss in this modern vision. First, Grant questions how anyone could love fate—the timeless recurrence of the same—and how loving fate would free us from revenge. Love is not something that originates in our wills, he argues. Thus, having the idea or will to love something does not result in actually loving it. As humans we cannot will to love, for love is that which is given us from beyond. Love is drawn out of us by beauty, itself an intimation of eternity.

> I do not understand how anybody could love fate, unless within the details of our fates there could appear, however rarely, intimations that they are illumined, intimations, that is, of perfection (call it if you will God) in which our desires for good find their rest and fulfillment. I do not say anything about the relation of that perfection to the necessities of existing, except that there must be some relation; nor do I state how or when the light of that perfection could break into the ambiguities and afflictions of any particular person. I simply state the argument for perfection (sometimes called the ontological argument): namely, that human beings are not beyond good and evil, and that the desire for good is a broken hope without perfection, because only the desire to become perfect does in fact make us less imperfect. This means that the absurdities of time—its joys as well as its diremptions—are to be taken not simply as history, but as enfolded in an unchanging meaning, which is untouched by potentiality or change.[86]

Grant remembers the ancient traditions of Plato and Christianity and draws out the different accounts of reason at play. Where the ancient accounts considered reason to be ultimately passive and "receptivity" to be the height of thought, modern accounts of reason concentrate on action and the purpose of reason to serve the will in controlling and making history.[87] In the ancient account, historical time is enfolded in eternity,

---

85. It should be noted that it is Nietzsche, more than any other, who dismisses Plato and whose critique shapes the dominant stereotypes of Plato common in the modern North American academy. Grant challenges this reading of Plato directly in his essay "Nietzsche and the Ancients," in *Technology and Justice*.

86. Grant, *Time as History*, 60.

87. Grant's analysis of the convergence of knowing and making in the language of technology highlights negatively the novelty of such distorted notions of thought. See "Knowing and Making"; see also "Faith and the Multiversity," in *Technology and*

which is unchanging—the context within which history finds its purpose, the truth behind which historicism cannot go. In recollecting the horizon of eternity—transcendent and other to historical time, though mysteriously mediated in it—Grant reorients our posture of being in the world and seeks to recover the essence of that within which true hope can abide. To live in time enfolded in eternity means to wait in a spirit of receptivity and love within the Whole. It means to be open to reverence and to the surrendering of our wills to remembering, thinking, and loving the good. Grant closes his essay with a question to Nietzsche and to the modern world: "Perhaps the essential question regarding the modern project is not Nietzsche's—who deserve to be masters of the earth?—but the very question of mastery itself."[88]

Mastery, Hope, and Justice

In many of his writings Grant contemplates the meaning of justice and the way in which a society's understanding of justice—of right and wrong and the consequences thereof—gives content to the conception of hope and meaning, particularly as they exist politically and socially in human life together. It is the understanding of right and wrong, good and evil that reveals the highest purpose as well as the greatest temptations of a society, both individually and collectively. It is the concept of justice that shapes how we live in the world together with each other and with non-human beings. In the modern liberal state, as we have seen, the ideas of freedom and equality shape the purpose of life together. Social contract theory is based on the political balancing of externally realized individual rights derived from "calculated self-interest" that precludes harm to others and considers death to be the enemy. External political arrangements are determined, therefore, by the balancing and presumed goodness of individual self-interests.[89] However, Grant raises questions regarding the extent to which the individualism of the contract theory satisfies the human soul.

> Is not the present retreat into the private realm not only a recognition of the impotence of the individual, but also a desire to leave the aridity of a realm where all relations are contractual,

Justice, 35–77.

88. Grant, *Time as History*, 69.

89. Grant, *English-Speaking Justice*, 43–45.

and to seek the comfort of the private where the supracontrac-
tual is possible?[90]

Regarding North American political life, Grant challenges the "Rous-
seauian" assumption that individual self-interest is naturally related to the
interest of all. He is critical of the liberal ideologies of justice grounded
in Locke's social contract theory and in Rousseau's positive account of the
human within the social contract. His critique of John Rawls's *A Theory
of Justice*[91] most powerfully encapsulates his thinking, which challenges
the North American notions of justice at their core. Grant argues against
both Rawls' reading of Kant and his basic premise about justice, namely
that there is a natural connection between self-interest and the interest
of the whole. Grant questions whether such a notion of justice can truly
be derived from the modern priority on calculated self-interest without
the order of the transcendent to ground this concept. In modern liberal
ideology, justice means *fairness*. However, Grant argues that the only true
ground for justice as fairness in society is the impartiality of God's love
for each and for all. When this dimension of eternity is not the ground of
justice, fairness is not possible. Grant sees that with the eclipse of eternity
in liberal ideology, rights have increasingly become relativized according
to power, while understandings of good and evil have become replaced by
"values" language defined by the powerful. The modern liberal ideology of
Rawls assumes that to serve the rights and self-interest of one will naturally
serve the rights and self-interest of all. However, Grant questions whether
people who are unable to speak for themselves can really be treated equally
when a person's worth is grounded in nothing greater than the order of
this world. In the case of the voiceless and those who are unable to fight for
themselves (fetuses *in utero*, the mentally challenged, and the young, for
example), the relativized "morality" of the powerful cannot help but reign
supreme. Who will ensure the rights of the voiceless and powerless? Surely
not the powerful.

Grant's essays "The Language of Euthanasia" and "Abortion and
Rights"[92] both critique the extent to which the so-called justice of calculated self-interest, based on the morality of "the will to power" enabled by
technology and the technological imagination, is winning out in North

90. Ibid., 11.

91. Ibid., 13–47. Grant considers Rawls to be a key spokesperson for the ruling
intelligentsia of North American public life.

92. Grant, *Technology and Justice*, 103–30.

America. As the idea of justice based in the transcendent ordering of reality collapses, immorality reigns in the guise of morality—"calling evil good and good evil." When justice is understood naively as the self-interest of the one serving the self-interest of the all and as that which enables people to be fairly and equally treated in society, we are blinded to the truth of things. Such "justice" is actually based upon the calculated self-interest of the powerful in society over and against the more vulnerable and weaker other; thus injustice parades as justice. When calculated self-interest is placed at the heart of the liberal understanding of justice, the tyranny of the self goes unchecked. The liberal ideology of justice domesticates the tyranny of the self such that it is held in balance with the "tyranny of other selves" of equal power, and over and against those who are not powerful. One way or the other, on the basis of calculated self-interest, the self is at the centre of the universe and otherness ceases to exist in any meaningful way. Grant raises questions that go to the heart of the failure of the liberal conception of justice and its relation to hopelessness in society: "How can foundations of justice be laid when rational humans are not given the conception of the highest good?"[93]

In an essay later in life Grant challenges the prevalent Nietzschean notion of justice functioning in North American society.[94] He argues that concerns about quality of life are replacing concerns about justice. For Plato, justice is based on the equality of each person before the Good (the essential source). Even the word "person," Grant argues, recognizes a value not made but given from beyond. According to Grant, the true origin of the term "person" is rooted in the doctrine of the Trinity and the mutual relations of "persons" bound and distinguished according to the dynamics of love. Nietzsche's concept of the quality of life, on the other hand, is based upon the judgment of certain human beings over other human beings; consequently, it forecloses the possibility for true equality between people. Questions about quality of life hide the fact that tyranny (not equality) rules and enables one group to decide the criteria for the quality of life of others—to the point even of judging that the latter are not worthy to be. When the question of quality of life emerges, what is ultimate about being is not the Good but the abyss that exists beyond the relativism of power. Indeed, for Grant the true equality of all people before the Good makes decisions regarding the quality of life irrelevant.

---

93. Grant, *English-Speaking Justice*, 76ff.

94. Grant, "Nietzsche and the Ancients," in *Technology and Justice*, 79–95.

In questions of justice (as for all questions, really), what is final for Grant is not the abyss surrounding relative power but rather the Good revealed in Christ and taught by Plato.

With his deconstruction of the meaning of justice in North America, Grant strips away the lies and illusions within which we live as a society, calling into question every aspect of the modern vision. However, it is in retrieving what has been lost in the traditions of justice of Athens and Jerusalem that he offers us distance from our imprisoning notions of justice and invites us to glimpse new possibilities. In recalling Socrates' thought on justice, he reminds us that it is a "calculation of self-interest" that undergirds Socrates'[95] great dictum on justice: "It is better to suffer injustice than to inflict it." It is always in our interests to be just, argues Grant. Indeed, "justice is what we are fitted for."[96] His description of justice, however, completely inverts the "equal rights" language associated with justice in the North American context. He points to the image of Christ hanging on the cross as the foundational image of what it means to be just. Christ, like Plato's Just Man, chooses to suffer injustice rather than to inflict it.[97] Plato bases his understanding of justice on the nature of things as glimpsed through contemplation of the Whole. Justice has to do with the very inward harmony within the Whole that makes a self truly a self.[98] Against the modern idea that humans create justice, Grant argues that justice is not something we can create, master, or make happen. Justice transcends the human. Our challenge, therefore, is to bring our lives into correspondence with the greater harmony of the Whole, which justice represents. Ultimately, Grant argues, justice has to do with consenting to the order of love that binds each to the other and thereby challenges the order of necessity at every turn. Justice is made most visible on the cross of Christ and the forgiveness of the cross. It is in the excruciating forgiveness of the cross that true justice (harmony) can be glimpsed as the costly re-ordering of necessity within the larger Whole. It is in the costly revelation of forgiving love that the order of necessity is ultimately reconciled with the Good.

Grant's essay "Justice and Technology" further clarifies this harmonious binding of love in justice. Grant pairs Socrates' dictum on justice

---

95. Grant, *English-Speaking Justice*, 44.

96. Grant, "Justice and Technology," in *Theology and Technology*, 240.

97. See Plato, *Republic* 4.

98. Grant, *English-Speaking Justice*, 45.

with Jesus' words in the Matthean Beatitudes: "Happy are those who are hungry and thirsty for justice" (Matt 5:6). Grant considers this hunger and thirst for justice to be an intimation of the Good, itself mediated in the order of necessity. Furthermore, he suggests that justice, unlike beauty, initially repulses us because of the demands it makes upon us. To love one's enemies in this world not only involves suffering, but inward transformation, which always includes pain. However, "if in this world we could see justice as it is in itself, it would engulf us in loveliness."[99] The beauty of justice is the deepest intimation of the Whole—the truth within which we exist and have meaning and the truth that challenges all our worldly desires for comfort and easy living.

> Its demands make it often unattractive both to our conveniences and in our apprehension of the situations that call for our response. Because the harmony of beauty is in some sense immediately apprehended, it is the means whereby we are led to that more complete harmony which is justice itself . . . We must understand that justice is in some sense other to us, and has a cutting edge which often seems to be turned in on our very selves . . . I cannot imagine any conditions in which some lack of harmony in some human being would not be putting claims upon us—the meeting of which would carry us wither we would not. But as soon as justice as otherness is expressed in that negation, we must hold with it the positive affirmation that we can know justice as our need in the sense that it is necessary to happiness, and we can have intimations of loving its harmony.[100]

Grant uses the ontological argument both positively and negatively to affirm the intimation of the Good to our intuitions. On the one hand, he speaks of the beauty of true justice, which draws and opens us to its otherness and to glimpsing the harmonious happiness of the Whole, hidden beneath its opposite. On the other hand, he argues that because we can think of "things that must never be done under any circumstances," we bespeak the possibility of the opposite—for glimpses of the Good to be "intimated in the ordinary occurrences of space and time." Furthermore, thinking about justice, argues Grant, is not the same as loving it and, therefore, knowing it. "Justice is an unchanging measure of all our times and places, and our love of it defines us."[101] But our need of an

99. Grant, "Justice and Technology," in *Theology and Technology*, 241.

100. Ibid.

101. Ibid., 245.

unchanging good that calls us to pay its price is theoretically incongruent with what is thought in "technology." To think of justice as that order that seeks harmony within the Whole based on the law and order of love is completely incongruent with technological notions of justice. In the latter case there is no place for the mediating love of "o/Otherness" and for justice to be anything other than that of human making and mastering. Grant closes his essay by calling us again to contemplation, to wrestling with the hiddenness of truth in this realm so as to await the "otherness" of its blessing. "I must finally say that the thought which is the task of most of us and is indeed important, always waits upon something of a different order—that thought which has been transfigured by hungering and thirsting for justice."[102]

Mastery, Hope, and Technology[103]

The corpus of Grant's published works reveals different aspects of his response to the question, "What are the modern assumptions which at one and the same time exalted freedom and encouraged that cybernetic mastery which now threatens freedom?"[104] For Grant, responding to this question, and understanding what it is that humans have become in the technological civilization, is the central task of thought in the contemporary North American context. Paradoxically, however, our very attachment to technology in itself inhibits our ability to think about our attachment to technology. "To exist in North America," writes Grant, "is an amazing and enthralling fate . . . What we have built and become in so short a time calls forth amazement in the face of its novelty." The "technical achievement" of our civilization, which has far outstripped that of any previous civilization, is not, however, merely "external to us." Rather, "it molds us in what we are, not only at the heart of our animality in the

---

102. Ibid.

103. Grant's thought on technology is greatly influenced by the work of Jacques Ellul (See Athanasiadis, *George Grant and the Theology of the Cross*, 124–26, 182–242) and later by Martin Heidegger (see Grant, "Thinking about Technology," in *Technology and Justice*). Hall integrates much of Grant's thought on technology into his own. The considerations regarding the extent to which reason has been co-opted by technology is reflected in his elaborations on "technical reason" (Tillich). See Hall, *Thinking the Faith*, 392ff.

104. Grant, *English-Speaking Justice*, 10.

propagation and continuance of our species, but in our actions, thoughts and imaginings."[105]

Technology, which for Grant is bound to the idea of mastery that he critiques, functions metaphorically as the fullest manifestation of the theology of glory; it represents both the human will to power over chance (that is, other human and non-human nature) and the yearning of humans to create ourselves and our own environment. The instrument for the builders of modernity, technology was originally thought to be the means to liberation, the means by which humans would overcome chance and master their environment for human flourishing. However, as the understanding of freedom became increasingly determined by the human will—disconnected from conceptions of the good and purpose—the human will to do and to master has become increasingly attached to and (again paradoxically) determined by technology. No longer an instrument or a means to an end, technology has become its own end, a manifestation of the human will to make and master the world that is attached to nothing beyond its own dynamism.[106] Nowhere is this more evident than in the motto of the technological world: "because we can, we must."[107] The North American imagination, Grant argues, is under the power of technology and the drive to technology; our minds have become entrapped in technological reason wherein knowledge is meaningful only insofar as it serves the making of things, preferably the making of novel things. The presumption is that these novel things serve humanity's flourishing. "What makes the drive to technology so strong is that it is carried on by people who still identify what they are doing with the liberation of humankind."[108] This is a presumption, however, that Grant questions.

105. Grant, "In Defence of North America," in *Technology and Empire*, 15. Another excellent essay on this topic is "Thinking about Technology," in *Technology and Justice*, 11–34.

106. A billboard along the Gardiner Expressway in Toronto (July 2005) read, "A long history of *creating* the future. Bell Mobility."

107. See Grant, "In Defence of North America," in *Technology and Empire*, 15.

108. Grant, "In Defence of North America," in *Technology and Empire*, 27. "The dynamism of technology has gradually become the dominant purpose in western society," Grant writes, "because the most influential men [*sic*] in that civilization have believed for the last centuries that the mastery of chance was the chief means for improving the race . . . [It is] difficult to estimate how much the quest for mastery is still believed to serve the hope of human perfecting" (see Grant, "The University Curriculum," 113).

What is most powerful and shocking in Grant's critique of technology in the North American context is the extent to which as a society we do not even know that we are under its grip, a delusion that blinds us to the truth of things. For example, think of the excitement and fervor generated by the releasing of a new iPhone or iPad or any number of other technological gadgets. For what purpose? To what end? Technology has become an end unto itself, serving no greater good. For Grant, the most frightful fact is that in our pursuit of mastery over technology, technology has mastered us. He recognizes that we are so bound within our technical reasoning that we cannot see the extent to which we have been mastered by it. "The mastery once thought of as a means becomes increasingly the public end."[109] The modern assumption that the science of technological reason is something external to us and does not shape the very way we think and engage the world is the biggest lie of the modern era and one within which we continue to function. In the grip of technology, we have lost true freedom—even those remnants found in early liberalism. In deconstructing this reality for the public, Grant unpacks the language we commonly use, analyzes the assumptions therein, and shows how deeply technological reason, in contrast with the thought of the ancients, has alienated us from truth and imprisoned us in its lie. For instance, in "Thinking about Technology," which is perhaps the most illuminating of Grant's language analyses, he considers a paradigmatic sentence: "The computer does not impose upon us the ways it should be used." Grant's analysis of this sentence shows how fully it lies about reality and reflects the imprisoning of our thought in modern technological liberalism.

Grant makes the link between the insidious power of technological reason and "the modern understanding of things in terms of necessity and chance," which, he argues, "has led not only to our conquest of nature, but to an understanding of things outside the idea of purpose."[110] Yet "the elimination of final purpose from the scientific study of the human and non-human things" had "consequences," changing "the public understanding of what it was to live." In general, "we took our science pragmatically," Grant observes, "as if its effect on us could be limited to the external."[111] Elsewhere, Grant expands on the confusion of purpose that lies at the heart of the technological society:

109. Ibid., 133.

110. Grant, "Faith and the Multiversity," in *Technology and Justice*, 44.

111. Grant, "In Defence of North America," in *Technology and Justice*, 37.

> It is now generally assumed that the [human] race has meaning (call it if you will purpose) only on the condition that we view ourselves as purposive and that none of these views are truths concerning the nature of things, but only ideologies which we create to justify our man-made [*sic*] purposes. There is no objective purpose to human or non-human nature which men [*sic*] can come to know and in terms of which the various occasions of life can be ordered. Purpose and value are creations of the human will in an essentially purposeless world.[112]

The trajectory of such purposeless technological reasoning in our context, argues Grant, can only lead to greater suffering and to our demise as a species, a demise that is already well underway. "As our liberal horizons fade in the winter of nihilism," Grant writes, "and as the dominating amongst us see themselves with no horizon except their own creating of the world, the pure will to technology . . . more and more gives sole content to creating." The result is "the closing down of willing to all content except the desire to make the future by mastery, and the closing down of all thinking which transcends calculation."[113]

Grant foresees the contours of the crisis of despair that is coming to be in the modern equation of hope with technological mastery as our sense of human purpose is narrowed and truncated.

> Purpose for the majority will be found in the subsidiary ethos of the fun culture. It will meet the needs of those who live in affluence but are removed from any directing of society. One is tempted to state that the North American motto is: "the orgasm at home and napalm abroad," but in the nervous mobile society, people have only so much capacity for orgasm, and the flickering messages of the performing arts will fill the interstices. They provide the entertainment and release which technological society requires. The public purpose of art will not be to lead [people] into the meaning of things, but to titillate, cajole and shock them into fitting into a world in which the question of meaning is not relevant.[114]

The possibility for true hope in a context such as ours has been extinguished by the darkness of the human will to power. What can be done when we can no longer hope in the possibilities of the human will? This is

---

112. Grant, "University Curriculum," in *Technology and Justice*, 128.

113. Grant, "In Defence of North America," in *Technology and Justice*, 40.

114. "University Curriculum," in *Technology and Justice*, 127.

the question that faces us at this point of crisis in North America. But for Grant this question can only be addressed fully when considered in relation to "the eternal fire that flames forth in the Gospels."[115] Thus Grant seeks to show us what it is we have become in technological civilization in contrast to what it is we have been fitted for within the greater order of the Whole, so as to inspire us to wait upon renewed possibilities for being human in this broken and beloved world.

Grant in Conclusion: Mastery Has Mastered Us

From the earliest of his writings to the end, what is most clear for Grant is the fact that we have reached a point of crisis in North America that reflects the consequences of living according to the false vision of the human as master.[116] The theology of glory has been insidiously manifested in all facets of life through the motif of mastery. In the destruction of modern liberalism, we see the destruction of the theology of glory based on human mastery over chance. However, in the aftermath of its destruction what is coming to be is more terrifying than that which went before it. What is coming to be and is even now wreaking havoc internally and externally on life is the primacy of mastery for its own sake. More than anything else, for Grant it is the extremity of *this* crisis that is novel in our context.

While in the origins of the modern project the domination of human and non-human nature was intended to serve a higher good, mastery has become its own end. Our understanding of ourselves in relationship with each other, with other nations and people, with the environment, and with other non-human being has been warped by the modern manifestation of the human as master. Our politics, our relationship with technology, our thought, and our friendships are all dominated and shaped by understanding ourselves and our purpose—individually and collectively—as created to be masters of the earth. Though the species has wrestled with the image of the human as master since the beginning of time, it is in modern North America that this image has come to dominate the imagination to such a degree that we have ceased to be able to see it for what it is or to recognize its hold on us. Thus we are driving ourselves to

---

115. Grant, *English-Speaking Justice*, 2.

116. For an example from the beginning of Grant's career (1956), see "Uses of Freedom," 525. For an example from the end of his career (1986), see "Philosophy and Culture," 173.

our own demise—and causing as well the demise of non-human creation. Grant sees the extent to which the demon of mastery has *internally* taken possession of our souls and is having its way *externally* in the concrete realities of our life together.

The crisis is leading to the demise and great suffering of the species—spiritually and socio-politically, in our thought and in our action, in our relationship with God and with each other. For Grant these internal and external dimensions of being cannot be torn asunder.[117] In the global crises of suffering, violence, injustice, and ecological devastation Grant recognizes the "external" consequences of the unbridled dominance of the human will in the world, born in the modern vision of the human. "Internally," we are suffering a crisis of meaning individually and as a society. We no longer have a sense of purpose and meaning for life. Dominated by the promise of human mastery, our imaginations face an abyss beyond which we are unable to see. The "external" suffering feeds "internal" suffering and the "internal" suffering feeds "external" suffering.[118] In the mastery of technological liberalism, death is at play in our souls and in our bodies, in our spirits, and in our relationships with human and non-human being. This is the result of the dominating rule of the theology of glory in North America and the abyss that remains.

What is most frightful about the crisis we are living within is that we have been mastered by mastery and are blind to the severity of the crisis, despite the fact that the signs are everywhere around us. "In this crisis of our present lives in North America," Grant writes, "an effort is required to think what we have become."[119] The dynamism of mastery in all its forms has closed down possibilities for true thought about ourselves and our context—who we are and what we are becoming in the technological world. This theology of glory has such a stranglehold on our thought that we are incapable of recognizing it for what it is—a lie that calls "evil good and good evil."

---

117. "Whatever the distinction between outward and inward may mean," Grant writes, "if there be a crisis it is a crisis about what we are and what we are becoming, both inward and outward" (*Time as History*, 8).

118. Grant describes the doubting of the modern experiment as manifest in "outward problems of cities, water and air, poverty, monstrous weapons, and expanding populations" and such "inward difficulties as banality in education, alienation from meaning, and widespread nihilism" (ibid., 7).

119. Ibid., 8.

The unfolding of the sciences which issue in the conquest of human and non-human nature—what I have hypostasized as "technology"—can be predicted. What that unfolding will disclose in detail cannot be. What that novel unfolding means as part of the whole is everywhere opaque. Indeed its very novelty has put in question the idea that openness to the whole is the mark of the philosopher. The first necessity in any understanding of this great novelty is to recognize that it is not something external to us. The representation of technology as an array of external instruments lying at the free disposal of the species that created them is the chief way that North Americans close down the possibility of understanding what is happening. Rather "technology" is an account of the whole in terms of which we are led to our apprehension of everything that is. Here our language falters because we moderns have so long ridiculed the use of such words as "destiny," "fate," etc. . . . It sounds ridiculous to say that technology is our "fate." Yet if we do not understand how much we are enwrapped in all we think and desire in this novel "destiny," then our philosophy simply becomes a part of it.[120]

In his work Grant seeks to unpack the crisis from outside the dynamism of technological liberalism. He seeks to name it for what it is, shock us into recognition before it is too late, and challenge us to re-order our thought about technological society so that it might be open to serve a larger good beyond the mechanisms of the technological imagination.

In identifying North America as the apex of the technological society, the centre of the world-wide crisis, Grant urges us to take up the calling that is particular to our context:

We live then in the most realized technological society which has yet been; one which is, moreover, the chief imperial centre from which technique is spread around the world. It might seem then that because we are destined so to be, we might also be the people best able to comprehend what it is to be so. Because we are first and fully there, the need might seem to press upon us to try to know where we are in this new found land which is so obviously "terra incognita." Yet the very substance of our existing which has made us leaders in technique, stands as a barrier to any thinking which might be able to comprehend technique from beyond its own dynamism.[121]

120. Grant, "Philosophy and Culture," 175–76.

121. Grant, "In Defence of North America," in *Technology and Empire*, 40. All but last sentence is quoted in Hall, *Lighten our Darkness*, 221.

Though he recognizes the forces in society that make such thought virtually impossible, he never ceases calling us to the task of genuine thought about who we are and what we are becoming. In this act and its challenge, Grant witnesses to the hidden possibility of hope in our context—a waiting upon that which is beyond our capacity to master.

For Grant, it is Nietzsche like no other who understood the character and dynamics of modernity. If one is to understand modernity, Grant argues, one must read Nietzsche.[122] "A hundred years ago," Grant asserts, "Nietzsche first spoke what is now explicit in western modernity."[123] To a large degree it is the thought of Nietzsche (and Heidegger's interpretation of it) as it contrasts that of the ancients that frames Grant's critical thinking on the crises in our context—the *via negativa* by which Grant recognizes what is wrong with things as they are in North America. Yet Grant cautions that "one should teach Nietzsche within the understanding that he is a teacher of evil."[124] Nietzsche is one who has been "mastered by mastery" and sees "mastery of the earth" as the highest purpose of the human. Grant urges that "one should not flirt with Nietzsche . . . but teach him in the full recognition that his thought presages the conception of justice which more and more unveils itself in the technological west."[125] For our purposes it is helpful to recognize that it is most decisively in his dialogue with Nietzsche that Grant sees the extremity of the crisis of hope (that is, of meaning and purpose) in North America; and it is in his critique of and distance from Nietzsche that he sees the possibility for true hope to emerge.

Nietzsche foresaw the demise of modern liberalism in the coming to be of the "last people,"[126] "the nihilists," and the "*ubermenschen*." These three categories reflect different human responses to the motif of mastery in modernity. Grant critiques the third of these Nietzschean categories (*ubermenschen*, or "supermen," the idea within which Nietzsche placed his hope) in *Time as History* and clarifies the impossibility that such figures will actually emerge, given that the love and hope that they are to

---

122. "There is no escape from reading Nietzsche if one would understand modernity" (Grant, "Nietzsche and the Ancients," in *Technology and Justice*, 89).

123. Ibid., 90.

124. Ibid., 91.

125. Ibid., 95.

126. Where appropriate I will refer to the "last people" in my text and insert it within square brackets in Grant's text.

embody[127] are impossible within the confines of the modern vision of reality. Love, Grant argues, comes from that which transcends the human and the dynamics of mastery;[128] the sheer possibility of love, therefore, undermines Nietzsche's entire construct. Grant does, however, find Nietzsche's categories of "last people" and "nihilists" to be accurate descriptions of two of the human responses to modernity's paradigm of mastery as it is being manifested in contemporary North America.[129] While the majority of people slip into the slothful comfort of the last people, entertained in mind-numbing ease by the mammoth entertainment industry, those with power tend toward the restless, amoral dynamism of pure technique, courting the nihilist "will to will" at every turn.

The last people, Grant sees, are those who have retreated from meaningful participation in public life into their "happy" state of indifference.

> The last [people] are those who have inherited the ideas of happiness and equality from the doctrine of progress. But because this happiness is to be realized by all . . . the conception of its content has to be shrunk to fit what can be realized by all. The sights for human fulfillment have to be lowered. Happiness can be achieved only at the cost of . . . all the potentialities for nobility and greatness. The last [people] will gradually come to be the majority in any realized technical society. Nietzsche's description of these last [people] in Zarathustra has perhaps more meaning for us than it had for his contemporaries who read it in 1883 . . . "'We have discovered happiness,' say the last [people] and blink." . . . The central fact about the last [people] is that they cannot despise themselves. Because they cannot despise themselves they cannot rise above a petty view of happiness. They can thus inoculate themselves against the abyss of existing . . . They think that they have emancipated themselves from Christianity; in fact they are products of Christianity in its secularized form. They will be the growing majority in the northern hemisphere as the modern age unfolds. The little they ask of life (only entertainment and comfort) will give them endurance. This is

127. This is reflected also in their lack of resentment and in their forgiveness of necessity/chance.

128. See the discussion of *Time as History* under the heading "Mastery, Hope, and History" earlier in this chapter.

129. See, for example, Grant's prophetic description of North American society at the opening of this chapter, "Mastery Has Mastered Us."

the price the race has to pay for overcoming two millennia of Christianity.[130]

In contemporary North America, the last people's happy indifference and blindness to the crises that everywhere strangle the earth and its inhabitants enables the exacerbation of the crises and the tyranny of the nihilist's drive toward mastery and destruction of the earth. To the last people, questions of meaning and purpose are "silly" and superfluous.

The nihilists are those who would rather "will nothing than have nothing to will." The paradigm of mastery has so possessed them that they cannot see beyond its dynamism. Grant considers that the tyrannical yearnings for the universal and homogenous state reflect this nihilist tendency (particularly as this is practiced in wars of the Empire throughout the globe). The drive toward nihilism is also implied in the "motto" of the limitless destiny of the technological society mentioned earlier: "Because we can, we must." Grant describes the nihilists thus:

> These are those who understand that they can know nothing about what is good to will . . . [People] have no given content for their willing. But because [people] are wills, the strong cannot give up their willing. [People] would rather will nothing than have nothing to will . . . They will be resolute in their will to mastery, but they cannot know what that mastery is for. The violence of their mastery over human and non-human beings will be without end.[131]

Grant goes on to describe the way in which Nietzsche's thought illuminates the North American crises. Though such crises have arrived later in North America than in Europe, "now that they have come, they are here with intensity." The results are dire: "At the height of our present imperial destiny, the crisis of the end of modern rationalism falls upon us ineluctably. In Nietzsche's words: "the wasteland grows. The last [people] and the nihilists are everywhere in North America."[132]

Indeed, as we have seen throughout Grant's work, the will to power of the nihilists is fully critiqued. However, what is important to note in his understanding and analysis of the last people and the nihilists is that Grant does not read them with disdain and contempt or as lesser beings as Nietzsche tends to do. Grant's critique is focused upon the origins

130. Grant, *Time as History*, 44.
131. Ibid., 45–46.
132. Ibid., 46.

and character of the system of thought and meaning that has both the last people and the nihilists under its power. There is a sense in Grant's work that North Americans are both responsible for and victims of the possessing power of mastery; both responsible for and victims of the stranglehold that this theology of glory has upon us individually and collectively and the crises of hope it is everywhere inflicting. On the one hand, Grant argues, to the degree to which we are victims of mastery, its "possession" of us is far greater and more complex than any one cause, person, or group. On the other hand, to the degree to which we bear responsibility for the dominating power of mastery and the crises in the world, it is only by recognition of its falsity that its stranglehold can be broken. However, according to Grant, we cannot will this recognition of the falsity of mastery without first having been ignited by something deeper and truer than mastery itself. Indeed, in his work Grant seeks to ignite our recognition of the truth that lies hidden beneath its opposite in the very stuff of life—the truth that we are creatures "fitted for love" rather than mastery. Grant sees the last people and the nihilists from outside the paradigm of mastery itself and thus is enabled to meet them with compassion and a prophetic challenge. It is in living the truth of who they are—beings "fitted for love" (not mastery)—that they too are invited to reflect the possibility for authentic hope.

The categories of "last people" and "nihilists" are not the only categories of response to mastery that are implicit throughout Grant's work. Grant is also deeply interested in speaking to and about those in North American society who despair. Those who despair in the present order of the world are, ironically, the ones in whom Grant sees the possibility for authentic hope to emerge. In their courage to face the reality of the darkness for what it is and to know despair without trying to escape it or master it, Grant sees both the possibility for honesty "to call the thing what it is" and the means to truth. For Grant, those who despair in the ways of the world, especially as it is everywhere being manifested in the destruction of human and non-human nature, are those who have glimpsed something other than the way of mastery. Despair is much like an unrequited longing and yearning for something other than what is. Those who despair are able to lament the loss of something good that is no more. Those who despair of the ways of the world are ones for whom "intimations of deprivation" bleed through their veins in a longing for something other than what is, in a longing that itself bespeaks renewed possibility. Hidden deeply within despair there is a broken desire. Grant's work addresses Christians, others of faith, and those for whom the remnants of the Good still have meaning. In these times in North America, it is those who despair in the ways of the world and its theologies of glory who are most courageous and truthful, and thus most open to the Whole and to the grasp of eternity should it come.

> The debt of our worship of the world must now be paid and it must be paid in real coin, not in popular returns to secure religion. Our generation must pay by being faced with the absence of God and particularly among those who find that absence most frightful. It is after all, the truth of the Cross that the anguish of the soul must be made absolute before God can make it His own. It has been said of existentialism that it takes one to Golgotha to find there only two thieves dying on their crosses. Certainly I would not be content with such a vision of what happened there. Nevertheless to be at Golgotha, in despair and without vision, is better than not being there.[133]

Grant reframes the experience of despair as a hidden glimpse of hope. Those who despair are those who are familiar with the struggles between the temptations of both the last people and the nihilists. They are those who have seen in themselves the temptations of humanity, who know their own wretchedness and have tasted their longing for wholeness in the glimpse of love. At the end of mastery is a despair that is, ironically, the beginning of hope's possibility. To despair is to discover that something is unworthy of one's trust and hope and to let go of the falsity of what was. The letting go of falsity, however painful, is the beginning of opening to new unimaginable possibilities. In his recognition of the place for despair in the yearning for truth, Grant stands in continuity with Martin Luther, who connects the experience of human despair with the possibility of receiving grace: "It is certain that man [*sic*] must utterly despair of his own ability before he is prepared to receive the grace of Christ."[134]

In drawing out some of the ways Grant explicates the crises of modernity and thinks through the responses to modernity, we have considered his critique of Nietzsche's trajectory. It is most consistently through Nietzsche that Grant is able to see where modernity is headed, and it is over and against Nietzsche that we can begin to recognize a direction for Grant's understanding of authentic hope. In considering the hope for thought in the future (over and against Nietzsche's critique of liberal

---

133. Grant, "Jean-Paul Sartre," *Architects of Modern Thought*, 74.
134. Luther, Thesis 18, *Heidelberg Disputation*, 51.

modernity), Grant calls on both the traditions of Athens and Jerusalem to touch the eternal hidden beneath its opposite. "In the homogenized societies of the future," Grant writes, "the hope of philosophy will lie with those who understand that thought can partake in that which is not dependent on any dynamic context. It will lie with those who can rise above the historicism which has permeated Western thought since Nietzsche." For Grant, to "partake" in philosophy, "does not mean to stand above history as if the race originated yesterday. Rather it means touching eternity—if only the hem of its garments."[135]

And finally, in one of Grant's most powerful and provocative later essays he names the failure of Christianity in its pursuit of glory and identifies it as that which fed the idolatry implicit in modern science. Grant argues that "western Christianity simplified the divine love by identifying it too closely with immanent power in the world. Both Protestants and Catholics became triumphalist by failing to recognize the distance between the order of good and the order of necessity. So they became exclusivist and imperialist, arrogant and dynamic." Grant is categorical: "They now face the results of that failure." However, he argues, perhaps it is finally only by such an excruciating path as the one that we are on that Christianity may be led through the purifying fires of modernity to glimpse the love that is hidden beneath its opposite—the love that transcends and draws together all within the Whole.

> Modern scientists, by placing before us their seamless web of necessity and chance, which excludes the lovable, may help to reteach us the truth about the distance which separates the orders of good and necessity. One of Nietzsche's superb accounts of modern history was that Christianity had produced its own gravediggers. Christianity had prepared the soil of rationalism from which modern science came, and its discoveries showed that the Christian God was dead. That formula gets to the truth of western history, but is nevertheless not true. The web of necessity which the modern paradigm of knowledge lays before us does not tell us that God is dead, but reminds us of what western Christianity seemed to forget in its moment of pride: how powerful is the necessity which love must cross. Christianity did not produce its own gravedigger, but the means to its own purification.[136]

135. Grant, "Philosophy and Culture," 181–82.

136. Grant, "Faith and the Multiversity," in *Technology and Justice*, 77.

Indeed, Grant affirms, even the terrifying mastery of modernity is ultimately held within the embrace of eternity, whose mystery ever promises the newness of life and hope. Even though a theology of the cross refuses to ascribe a concrete, positive outcome to any process of negation (or purification), it trusts and waits upon the love that revealed itself in the last gasps of the dying Jew from Nazareth crucified on a Roman cross. Paradoxically, for Grant this vision is the basis of inexhaustibly renewable hope.

7

Hall on Mastery
and the Possibility of Hope

We read *Technology and Empire* on the eve of an approaching sabbatical leave. Perhaps, we thought, Grant was right to despair of the churches and to expect little from a theology which, in its essence, he had described as a thoroughly un-American activity. At the time he penned those lines, the North American Protestant community was being seduced by yet another "changing ripple of European thought," in this case a sloganized adaptation of the "theology of hope," by which (as he aptly put it) the professionals attempt "to revive a dying faith." We left for our sabbatical with George's devastating critique hanging over us like a summons.

Was it possible for Protestants to discover in their origins a pre-modern stand, a vantage point from which, here and there in this most problematic of societies, they might find the courage and the intellectual honesty to enter the darkness of our epoch without succumbing to ultimate anxiety and despair? That sabbatical leave was to become, in response to this question and summons, the beginning of our own modest effort to rethink the received tradition of Protestantism from a more ancient vantage point—that of Luther's *theologia crucis*. We felt that it might be possible from such a frame of reference to recover authentic Christian hope without equating it with the official philosophy of optimism and what Grant called the "religion of progress."[1]

1. Hall and Hall, "George Grant (1918–1988), A Tribute," 76–77.

IN MANY WAYS THIS statement of Douglas Hall and his wife, Rhoda Palfrey Hall, demonstrates the character of the dialogue between the critical-contextual work of Grant and Hall. Hall's work both builds upon and responds to Grant's work. As I have shown, on the one hand, it is clear that Hall recognizes much truth in Grant's critical-contextual analysis. Grant's work provided a ground for Hall's own reflections on the public manifestations of the theology of glory in the North American context and has inspired him to think through modernist triumphalism as it has been manifested in the churches and in Christian theology in general. On the other hand, Hall's work is in large measure a "response to Grant's summons" to theology and the church. Hall responds to Grant's challenge by delving into the Christian tradition, where he discovers a means to respond to the malaise of the age. He acknowledges Grant as one who "summoned" him to take the public role of theology seriously. Their differences may be seen as two sides of a conversation. Where Grant's work, as I have suggested, may be considered to be the "summons of unfaith to faith," Hall's work may be seen as a response to the summons—the response of "faith to unfaith." I do not wish to suggest here that Hall is the answer to Grant or that theology is the answer to philosophy. Nor do I wish to suggest that Grant's work is grounded somewhere outside of faith. Rather, there is a dynamic interplay represented in thinking Grant and Hall together. They both articulate different sides of a contextually engaged theology of the cross that works to tear down the illusions of the theology of glory so as to open renewed possibilities for hope to be enacted in our context. As a public intellectual, Grant represents the side of "unfaith," and in speaking the cruciform truth of our context he seeks to ignite the yearning for "faith" within the Canadian public sphere.[2] As a Christian theologian, Hall represents the side of "faith." In speaking the cruciform truth of our context he seeks to engage the "unfaith" of the church and society with a more disruptive vision of faith[3] and thereby carve out a public space for Christian theology in response to and in distinction from the anxieties of the age. Throughout this chapter, the extent to which Hall both builds upon and responds to Grant's work in his own theological articulations will become evident.

2. When I say "faith" here I mean to suggest that Grant seeks to ignite that within the human soul that yearns to trust in that which is "other" to the human and to purely historicized notions of being.

3. Hall, *Confessing the Faith*, 444–45.

Hall, like Grant, is convinced it is most fundamentally the idol of mastery that manifests the theology of glory and obscures the truth from view in the contemporary North American context, locating hope, purpose, and meaning within the image of "human superiority . . . [that] subdues the earth."[4] The central delusion regarding who we are as human beings has shaped our collective and individual self-understanding (identity) and driven our goals as a society (vocation). The defiance of human limit in the modern experiment has resulted in the idolatry of the human wherein the place of God has been usurped by the masterful and creative human will and intelligence.[5] Similar to Grant's analysis of the tyranny of the universal and homogenous state, Hall considers that the motif of mastery serves the imperialist striving of the Empire (socially, economically, politically, etc.) and can only end in serving the powerful and undermining the weak. Like Grant, he believes we are at a time of crisis in which the paradigm of mastery is breaking down and its failure is everywhere evident.

> The plain fact is that our expectations as a civilization have failed. We have not been able to sustain the dream called "America," which was dreamed by the European optimists of the Renaissance and the Enlightenment. We have floundered conspicuously and notoriously . . . For what is America, what is the New World but the dream of humanity that we can produce the perfect kingdom within the terms of reference of our own mastery? . . . We in North America have dreamed the dream for a long time. We have had time for it to take hold of us at the deepest levels of the psyche. It has shaped our life. It has driven us to a level of technological achievement undreamed of . . . . Time and the human will, prosperity, the absence of war, and the abundance of nature—all these have indulged the dream. We have taken it—or have been taken by it—beyond the reaches experienced so far by any people. And it has failed.[6]

We are disoriented from any other sense of meaning and uncertain about how to live authentically. Like Grant, Hall argues that the failure of the modern dream is causing widespread confusion, fragmentation, and uncertainty, signified by the loss of hope. The differences between Grant's and Hall's critical thought (*via negativa*) are evidenced primarily

---

4. Hall, *Professing the Faith*, 280ff.

5. Hall, *God and Human Suffering*, 49–122.

6. Hall, *Lighten Our Darkness*, 259–60.

in the focus and quantity of their material and not in its foundational content, despite their different disciplines and audiences. These differences, in part, enable the twofold relationship of Hall's work to Grant's— both building upon and responding to his summons. While Hall engages and includes the wide cultural analysis and general content of Grant's critique, he focuses more directly on the church and Christian theology and its co-optation by the theology of glory in the motif of mastery. In deconstructing the paradigm of human mastery and power in terms of theology and the church, Hall brings into view the many ways the once-mainline churches in North America have been living in the illusion of the theology of glory in their religious elevation of the paradigm of mastery. In his analysis Hall highlights the impact of "the religion of progress"[7] and further thinks through the truth and implications of "official optimism" as it is manifested in the North American churches. Finally, in noting the continuity between North American society and the North American church in its domination by mastery, Hall urges that the church be stripped of its pretensions of mastery and re-oriented to the cross of Christ. It is only in this way that the church may discern its true identity, purpose, and meaning.

Another distinction between Grant and Hall that has partly enabled the dynamic relationship between their work can be seen in the types, language, and quantity of materials each has published. Given that Hall has published far more than Grant ever did, Hall has needed to be far more explicit about his method and more linear in his articulation of its content. Where Grant left questions of method as a background issue and focused more on the content of his philosophy to be tested by life, Hall explicitly engages questions of method throughout his corpus. He is intentional about thinking through the coherence between content and form, while being cognizant of the human limits implicit in such a task. Furthermore, where Grant's analysis of the dynamics of despair and the possibility of hope are peppered throughout his work and implicit in all he writes, Hall's analysis of these dynamics is explicit, particularly as it pertains to the North American church. Finally, and importantly, while writing a great deal of critical theological reflection, Hall is more intentional than Grant in articulating possible constructive moves that grow out of his critical analysis.

---

7. Hall, *Thinking the Faith*, 164. Hall references Grant on the "religion of progress" throughout his work.

Both recognize the North American tendency toward "anti-intellectualism" (pro-activism)[8] and craving for novelty,[9] both of which can inhibit rigorous thought about existence. This is true as much in the church as outside the church. For both Grant and Hall, the fact that as a society we are ignorant of our own ignorance compounds the sense of crisis. The modern experiment supplies no resources for thinking through critically, engaging, and facing the dynamics of the crisis that bears down upon us. Without a tradition of rigorous thought in our context, we are caught up in the self-perpetuating cycle of *doing*, unable to think through the fearful realities of which we are a part.

Both Grant and Hall bring the theology of the cross to bear on the modern consciousness such that they are enabled to "think outside the box" of modernity. Where Grant draws on the traditions of Athens (Plato) and Jerusalem (the Gospels) to give language to the truth of the cross and to provide us with a critical distance for recognizing "what's wrong" in our context, Hall explicitly draws on the "thin tradition" of the theology of the cross (in the tradition of Jerusalem) to carve out a critical distance for discerning our context. If faced with courage and honesty, Hall argues, this thin tradition may provide the means for the Protestant church to respond to the crisis of these times and take on a priestly role of guiding the North American public into the darkness of these times. "There is no greater public task for theology in North America today than to help to provide a people indoctrinated in the modern mythology of light with a frame of reference for the honest exploration of its actual darkness."[10] In tending to the cross of Christ the church may be opened to discern its role in the larger society—to truly be in the world but not of the world, to be authentic "faith" engaging the pervasive realities of "unfaith."

As a means to establish the parameters of Hall's analyses of mastery and in an effort to build upon (and not repeat) the content already presented on Grant, I open this discussion where I left off my discussion of Grant in chapter 6, exploring (from Hall's perspective) the nature of the crisis within which we find ourselves in North America. Hall's critique of mastery and his analysis of the crisis in all instances is framed by the categories of "optimism" and "despair" which, for him, characterize dominant responses amidst the crisis of these times. It is fundamentally

---

8. Hall, *Thinking the Faith*, 13–14, 48.

9. Ibid., 22.

10. Ibid., 36.

over and against optimism and despair in our context that the contours of authentic hope come into view. Having established this framework I will go on to present Hall's critical theology of the cross, considering the relationships between mastery, hope, and the central doctrinal areas: God, Christ, the resurrection, the human (*imago hominis*), the church and mission, and eschatology. Following a discussion of his critical analysis, each section closes by pointing to the constructive moves that Hall suggests, guided by the theology of the cross.

Fear of the Darkness: Hall on the Crisis of Hope

Hall's understanding of "crisis" is articulated in his book *The Canada Crisis*.[11] For Hall, to be in crisis is not necessarily a bad thing, particularly in our context, where he believes we have been living in denial and in repressive illusion for far too long. Indeed, he sees that the possibility for authentic hope can emerge only from crisis and the uncertainty that surrounds it. "This is a book about Canada, and it is one of hope," he begins. "If that sounds strange—given *The Canada Crisis*—it is only because we underestimate the positive side of most human crises. To me, a Canada in crisis contains far more to be hopeful about than our hundred odd years of official hope and rhetorical unity!"[12] He goes on to explore the ways the language of "crisis" marks a critical moment or turning point of extremity in life. An individual, group, or nation can only be in crisis if an outcome is uncertain. Crisis marks the moment of recognition wherein circumstances will turn in one direction or another—to death and failure or to new life. In the case of the Canada crisis, Hall says "Canada may die [or disappear]; but on the other hand it may . . . find itself."[13] Throughout his work, it is clear that Hall maintains this perspective on the character of crisis, especially in our North American context. To be able to name something as a "crisis" shows honesty and courage in the face of uncertainty. It also reflects a moment when the ambiguity and darkness of life can no longer be ignored and must be entered and grappled with directly. In identifying our context as one in crisis, Hall seeks to draw us into a state of attentiveness—alert to the dynamics at play, seeking understanding so

---

11. Hall, *Canada Crisis: A Christian Perspective*. This book was written by Hall in response the Canadian struggle for identity and purpose as a nation.

12. Ibid., 15.

13. Ibid., 19.

as to enter the darkness with courage and with openness toward the possibility of true hope within the darkness.

Hall is explicit that the catastrophic suffering of creation and the possibility of global destruction reflects the novelty and extent of the crisis of our times. Like Grant, he makes a connection between ecological and inter-human suffering and devastation and the motif of mastery that dominates the primary image of the human in the West. The suffering of creation is the external sign and consequence of the unbridled human will to conquer and control nature. In seeing the world (with human mastery at the centre) as predictable and self-sustaining, we have considered our species to be the "lords and possessors of nature" who need not settle for a derivative mastery of the Other.[14] We North Americans, in our idolatry of power, have lost a sense of both our limits and of the true meaning and purpose of our lives. The crises of our times are forcing us to recognize that mastery is not the purpose of human life. Yet the response to this question of human purpose appears to be only an abyss. With the crisis of human purpose and meaning comes a crisis of hope. Our modern understanding of hope has been tied up with an optimistic faith in human mastery's capacity ultimately to solve all of life's problems. However, today the idea of human mastery over chance is increasingly suspect.

Hope, says Hall, exists within the dialogical relationship between *expectation* and *experience*.[15] Expectation refers to the anticipation of the future. Experience refers to that which is known in the present and the past. In the officially optimistic society, the relationship between expectancy and experience was to be a positive interaction wherein the expectation for future good was fed by the experience of past and present good mediated by human ingenuity and will. However, the crisis of our context exists because, instead of a positive or even dialogical relationship between expectancy and experience, there is only a relationship of contradiction—an irreconcilable gap between our experience of negation in the past and present and our vision of a glorious and triumphant future. This is true of the wider society and it is true of the church. Today the tension between expectancy and experience reflects the two opposing images of the human that wrestle within the societal ethos of North America: as the noble pinnacle of history marching toward full realization of human greatness within history, and as a vacuity, or nothingness,

---

14. Hall, *Lighten Our Darkness*, 14.

15. For a discussion of this, see ibid., 28–39.

enmeshed in historical processes that are ultimately meaningless.[16] At present, the West lives within this contradiction between expectancy and experience, the recognition of which is producing a vacuum. Far from opening up new possibilities, the emerging recognition of the contradiction is leading to the proliferation of "last people" (seeking to repress and escape the darkness) and, worse, nihilists (seeking, in their resentment, to take revenge on the darkness). The mere recognition of negation and of the contradiction between expectation and experience is not, in itself, enough to inspire a truer *imago hominis* for our times. "There is nothing in the operative traditions of our culture to enable us as a people to encounter at the level of conscious reflection the prolonged experience of negation," Hall observes. "Our expectations are overwhelmingly positive, while our experiences are, increasingly and profoundly, negative. The dialogue between expectation and experience, upon which civilization depends, has had to be stifled for want of courage to confront openly this discrepancy."[17] Indeed, recognition of the discrepancy brings forth despair. Hall characterizes the crisis as a crisis of despair compounded by a refusal to acknowledge our despair.[18]

Our expectation of life has been shaped by the triumphant promises of liberal modernity (the theology of glory, the religion of progress) within which we assume a progressive and inevitable good to be manifested in the world. Though this optimism for the world *may* have been appropriate in past times, Hall argues, today it can no longer face the *data of despair* that everywhere abound. In the larger society, generally speaking, the optimistic "hope" for the future has been replaced by fear of the future, a "future shock,"[19] in which fear, not hope, marks the orientation to the future. The past and present experience of the data of despair can no longer be absorbed into an expectation for a future good.

What does this have to do with mastery? Basically, the central dynamic of the crisis may be found in the terrifying disconnect between the expectation of mastery and the experience of mastery.[20] Like Grant, Hall recognizes that the most fundamental problem that lies at the root of the crisis of our present day is the falsity of the human image as master

---

16. Ibid., xxxi.

17. Ibid., 45.

18. Hall, *Canada Crisis*, 113.

19. Hall, *God and Human Suffering*, 45.

20. Hall, *Lighten Our Darkness*, 28–39.

at the centre of all things. However, because our expectations for life are still so deeply shaped by the optimistic promises of mastery, we are blind to the future possibility without this dominating metaphor closing in on us. Expectancy in the modern schema says that human mastery will contribute to create the ideal in the future. Yet, when as a species we attempt to master the future, the result is destruction, which we see evidenced all around us. The experience of negation (of the possibilities for human mastery) is so powerful that expectancy for the future is eclipsed. However, in the officially optimistic society the experience of negation and failure is not one we permit ourselves to face. When we have no way to enter the darkness of the contradiction between expectation and experience, this crisis of contradiction is met either with repressive optimism, nihilism, or despair[21]—all of which, in the end, are responses to the falsity of mastery itself.

Generally in his considerations of the crisis, Hall starts with the big picture of the global and North American context and gradually focuses in on the North American once-mainline church (and on its periphery) and the particular contours of the crisis for people of faith.[22] Hall is acutely aware of the extent to which the once-mainline churches in our context have precipitated and internalized the optimistic outlook of the modern vision of the human and of history as a whole. This religion of progress has insisted upon a positive outlook and outcome to everything. He uses and expands upon Grant's analysis of mainline Christianity as "the official religion of the officially optimistic society."[23] Hall argues that "the modern mythology of light" has been particularly fierce in the church, creating a people who repress the negative and avoid the experience of failure. These escapist ways of being in the world are motivated, on the one hand, by an intense fear of the darkness of existence and, on the other hand, by a lack of any meaningful way to think about the darkness of life. Hall suggests that even more than the general public, the once-mainline church has been blinded by the optimism of liberal triumphal religion

21. For increasingly disestablished churches, for whom nihilism is not really an option, the greater struggle is between optimism and despair. Hall, *Has the Church a Future?*; *Future of the Church: Where Are We Headed?*, 24–37; *End of Christendom and the Future of Christianity*, 9–18, 56; *Confessing the Faith*; and *Christian Mission: The Stewardship of Life in the Kingdom of Death*, 31–40.

22. See, for example, chapters 1–3 in Hall, *Lighten Our Darkness*; and Hall, *Cross in our Context*, 157–78.

23. See chapter 3, "Official Relgion of the Officially Optimistic Society," in Hall, *Lighten our Darkness*, 45–98; and Hall, *Confessing the Faith*, 226–40.

and therefore is unable to see the reality of the darkness. The pathos of our context, Hall challenges, "is not that we have failed but that we can't bring ourselves as a people to contemplate the failure" and, therefore, we are more dangerous.[24]

Further to this, Hall (with Grant) argues that in society generally, and especially in the church, there has been confusion between optimism and hope.[25] The fact that the modern conception of hope is tied to notions of human mastery and control has created a situation in which authentic hope is virtually impossible, for there is no way to think outside the box of the modern experiment. In his early work, *Lighten Our Darkness*, Hall discusses at length the confusion of hope and optimism: "We belong to a society that was assured it could hope. Hope would not disappoint us, for we were participants in a process, and the end of the process was good . . . [We were told to] think positively and eliminate radical negativity."[26] Throughout modernity, hope was understood to be concentrated on the future—the expectancy side—the vision of which was to give content and direction to our action in the present. We worked in the present for our good outcome in the future—the realm of God on earth, the world for Christ. Hope had to do with having a positive outlook and the possibility to bring into being a positive desired outcome. However, as "the official religion of the officially optimistic society," Christendom is unable to face the darkness and negation that constitute the dominant character of contemporary experience.[27] In our novel context, the extent of global crisis is truly staggering, and the obsession with the positive is met increasingly with negation. Appeals to positive or optimistic outcomes are increasingly trite and meaningless. In order for the church to acknowledge its own falsity and the manifold ways it has in the past and continues now to bow to the theology of glory, the church must face its nagging failure, its experience of negation and hopelessness in the face of the crisis.

Two helpful categories Hall uses to further explore these dynamics are *covert despair* and *overt despair*.[28] These categories help to uncover the faces of despair that are manifested in the world today and the ways

24 Hall, *Lighten Our Darkness*, xxii.

25. Throughout his corpus Hall uses the terms "false hope" and "(official) optimism" almost interchangeably.

26 Hall, *Lighten Our Darkness*, 27.

27. Ibid., 46.

28. Among many places he discusses this, see Hall, "Hope From Old Sources for a New Century" and "Despair as a Pervasive Ailment." See also Hall, *Christian Mission*.

these forms of despair are interconnected. *Covert despair* is the form of despair that most characterizes the inner spirit of the North American (particularly) middle class and the powerful. It moves, almost imperceptibly, within the souls of the powerful of the world. It is despair that is everywhere within the North American Empire. It is characterized by a sense of meaninglessness and lack of purpose in any larger Good. Hall challenges the once-mainline church of North America to recognize the covert despair that is hidden beneath an official optimism. This despair is that which is found hidden beneath the happy optimism of the "last people" and even beneath the wretched resentment of the nihilist. *Overt despair*, on the other hand, can be recognized throughout the world in the experience of abject poverty, oppression, injustice, and violence in situations where people have been so beaten down by the tribulations of life that their despair cannot be hidden.[29]

The intersection of mastery with the experience of covert despair and overt despair is an important one for Hall. In the latter case, human mastery over history and nature results in the real and concrete suffering of people and creation. Those who live in overt despair suffer the consequences of the tyranny of mastery manifested externally in social, economic, and political systems of injustice. Overt despair reflects the external suffering of mastery. On the other hand, covert despair reflects the internal suffering of mastery. Where on the outside there may be no obvious signs of despair,[30] Hall argues that the primary suffering of the "powerful" is internally manifested in a sense of purposelessness, meaninglessness, and hopelessness.[31] Covert despair has external consequences that precipitate the experience of overt despair. When the powerful have no way to understand their purpose and nothing outside themselves in which to hope, they are drawn into ways of being that result in perpetuating the suffering of the other (human and creation). The crises of the world manifested in overt and covert despair are self-perpetuating.

29. Hall, *Reality of the Gospel and the Unreality of the Churches*, 173–74.

30. Among the statistics that attest to the malaise of covert despair, Hall cites the high incidence of depression-based mental illness and suicide among the North American middle class, etc. See for example Hall, "Despair as Pervasive Ailment," 85–86.

31. See Hall, *Why Christian? For Those on the Edge of Faith*, 45–51; and *Christian Mission*, 29–45. See also Hall's discussion of Ernest Becker in *Thinking the Faith*, 176n77.

In speaking to the churches in North America, Hall underlines the fact that, as church, our greatest temptation is incessantly to repress our experience of covert despair beneath the guise of a happy optimism that continues to be thoughtlessly driven by images of a glorious future. It is in the churches of North America that Hall recognizes a particular attachment to the theology of glory in the guise of optimism. The crisis within which the church finds itself is multi-layered. The data of despair press in upon it on all fronts, whether we see this in the narrow purview of the churches' empty pews, crumbling buildings, and uncertain future, or in the wider and more global context of violence and ecological devastation. As we stumble into make-work projects, attempting to keep the looming darkness at bay, our official optimism shallowly hides our covert despair and constitutes the basic lie of the church in our context that calls "evil good and good evil."

Hall seeks to draw the church into contemplating its own place in the context of global crisis of which North America is at the centre. He challenges the church to move out of its repressive optimism so that it might enter the crises of the world to await the light that can only be seen in the darkness. It is only through such a process as this that it might be grasped by its true vocation. In *Lighten Our Darkness* the central questions for Hall are these: Is it still possible for us to discern within our tradition the basis for a hope that does not have to look away from death in order to find the courage to live?[32] "Can Christianity offer anything that might contribute to the provision of a meeting ground of expectation and experience? . . . Can Christianity offer a vantage point from which to acknowledge, reflect upon and reckon with the encroaching nihil?"[33] In a context where fear of the darkness and lack of rigor dominate thought, the most important task of theological thought is bringing to light "the darkness as darkness."[34] In carving out a public space for the church's witness, Hall draws out the church's courage to face its own darkness. For him, however, "the truth of the matter is that . . . Christianity, as it has displayed itself in the life of the New World, is the greatest barrier to Christianity becoming a redemptive force in such a society, a light for our darkness."[35]

32. Hall, *Lighten our Darkness*, 1–3.

33. Ibid., 45.

34. Hall, *Thinking the Faith*, 11–14, 36.

35. Hall, *Lighten our Darkness*, 46.

In the officially optimistic society, and especially in the official religion of the officially optimistic society, our expectation is positive and our hope and sense of purpose are placed in human mastery. The experience of our context globally, continentally, and as church is overwhelmingly negative—the negation of our expectancy. The outcome of human mastery increasingly breeds hopelessness and meaninglessness. Whether we stand with shallow optimism or with despair in the face of the false idol, we still stand before the same false idol. As society and church we have no way to think through and enter the darkness of the contradiction within the terms of the modern experiment. However, the theology of the cross, which sees mastery as the theology of glory, can enable us to find a way into the darkness of our contradiction and bring the light of truth into view such that the church may truly witness in the public sphere. "There is no hope for us that does not lie through the valley of the shadow of death," Hall writes. "We citizens of the United States and Canada shall learn to hope only insofar as we submit ourselves openly to the hidden despair that informs our entire civilization."[36] Indeed, throughout his writings Hall is explicit that the darkness is truly our habitat. In recognizing our habitat of darkness as a crisis, we also recognize the unsustainability of this context and condition. It is only in facing the darkness of our context—and that means seeing in it the manifestation of mastery and the theology of glory—that we will possibly glimpse the true light that can lighten our darkness.[37]

Mastery, Hope, and Doctrine

In general, Hall distinguishes between the doctrine of the theology of glory and that of the theology of the cross by means of a primary set of categories. The doctrine of the theology of glory emphasizes sight (or certitude) over faith; finality (consummation) over hope; and power over love.[38] We can see how mastery joins these "three postures of glory" in the mastery of knowledge (sight/certitude), the mastery of time (finality/consummation) and the mastery of otherness (power). These ways of being in the world have infested Christian doctrine and the church in both its form and content throughout much of its history. For Hall, the critical task of the theologian of the cross today is to bring the falsity of triumphalistic

36. Hall, *Reality of the Gospel and the Unreality of the Churches*, 177–78.

37. Hall, *Lighten Our Darkness*, 227.

38. See, for example, Hall, *Cross in Our Context*, 214.

doctrines into full view. Only through such deconstruction does it become possible to begin to articulate doctrines of the cross wherein faith (as trust), hope (as waiting), and love (as openness) truly provide the foundation for the church in both the content of its message and its medium.

Mastery, Hope, and God

> The Christian doctrine of God has tended to accentuate the aspects of transcendence and power, as befits a patriarchally conceived deity in the service of the empire; but in doing so it has severely jeopardized the essence of God testified to in Holy Scripture, and has risked confining belief in God to contexts amenable to "positive religion."[39]

In considering Hall's critique of the doctrine of God as a manifestation of the theology of glory, I will for the most part follow the sequence of his argumentation as it is presented in *Professing the Faith*, with references to related works throughout.[40] Generally speaking, Hall argues that since the inception of Christendom, the motif of mastery has shaped theology in general and the understanding of God in particular. This influence has functioned on a number of levels of human existence as "the negation of the negative and the affirmation of the positive"—that is, of power, glory, and strength, humanly conceived. Hall sees that with the triumph of the positive in the religion of Empire, starting with the Constantinian Empire and extending to its apex in the American Empire, the theology of glory has so infected Christian theology that only a massive deconstruction of Christian doctrine may enable truth-telling in the disciple community.[41] Hall specifically identifies the power of positive religion— the triumph of the positive—in the doctrines of Christendom and most spectacularly in the religion of the American Empire. It is associated with the doctrine of God's omniscience and omnipotence wherein the negative and ambiguous dimensions of being are invisible. Positive religion is associated with the motif of mastery on a number of levels. In negating all that is negative in human existence (including ignorance, death,

---

39. Hall, *Professing the Faith*, 92.

40. My discussion draws on all of *Professing the Faith* (except for chapter 2, "Questioning the Father Almighty"), as well as Hall and Ruether, *God and the Nations* and *God and Human Suffering*; and Hall, *Imaging God: Dominion as Stewardship*.

41. For an excellent analysis of Christendom and post-Christendom, see Hall's *Confessing the Faith*, 201–64, and *The End of Christendom and the Future of Christianity*.

and ambiguity), positive religion asserts only a god whose being can be mastered by the human imagination and knowledge. The god of positive religion is one who has overcome the negative dimensions of being by a victorious positive, crushing the negative such that it ceases to be in any real way. "He" is necessarily a god of power and might who masters all that inhibits his will from being done. It is interesting to consider the transference of the motif of mastery to the doctrine of God throughout Christendom and particularly in the American Empire. Only a god of glorious power and might can triumph so fully over that which manifests the negative and ambiguous dimensions of life. Only a god of power and might is powerful enough to reflect the culmination of human striving after mastery and finality. Let us now explore more specifically the connections between mastery and positive religion in terms of the doctrine of God it presupposes.

According to Hall, positive religion involves first the triumph of "faith as certitude" over "faith as trust." Faith is (mis)construed as that by which God gives certain positive knowledge of God's self. Revelation includes no hiddenness or concealment of God's essence and activity in the world. Instead, it is a means to see, without doubt or hesitation, the positive continuity between God and the world. As positive religion developed in the "New World," the doctrine of God's providence was decreasingly understood as a means to accept and contemplate the hiddenness and unknowability of God's ways in the world and was increasingly understood as a positive account of the God-ordained doctrine of progress as bringing success upon those whom "he" favours. Because God is for us, having chosen us as the elect, our glory represents God's glory. Our success, individually and collectively, is the evidence of God being for us. In considering the conventional pathways to the knowledge of God, Hall identifies the extent to which the triumph of the positive has been stressed to the exclusion of the negative. In positive religion there is no means to account for the ambiguous, the struggle, and suffering that are part of the human experience. Furthermore, the idea of God's alterity cannot be permitted into human contemplation because alterity implies the unknowable, even ambiguous, mystery and otherness of God. The certitude of positive religion undermines the possibility of "faith as trust" constituted in the alterity of an unknowable, though revealed, other. The "faith" of positive religion in fact forecloses the possibility of true relationship with this Other.[42]

42. Hall, *Professing the Faith*, 92–101.

Second, positive religion involves the theology of glory as the triumph over non-being and victory over death. The emphasis on the resurrection of Jesus in positive religion completely obliterates the "negative" dimensions of Christian revelation and experience, particularly as these are manifested in the suffering love of Jesus. Finality replaces hope. Power replaces love. Golgotha and Gethsemane are displaced by the triumph of Easter Sunday and the victory of God over all that negates. Divine power is gloriously revealed as that which cannot be challenged by weakness, vulnerability, suffering, or struggle in any real way. Thus, God's love must necessarily be understood in terms of power that ultimately crushes its antithesis, suffering. There is no place for contemplation of "agape," suffering love, for agape contradicts power-models of love. The finality of the victory disables the contemplation of God as one who fully engages the human—even those aspects of human experience that struggle with the threat of non-being (etc.) and with thought that is discordant with the positive.

> God emerges from the tussle with death and hell as one who is above it . . . God is depicted as one who, unlike us, does not exist under the threat of nonbeing in any of its manifestations. Thus, the divine power (omnipotence) is not challenged by any lack or weakness; the divine knowledge (omniscience) is not circumscribed by ignorance, uncertainty, or inherent limitation; the divine presence (omnipresence) is not subject to the constraints of time and space; and God is not vulnerable to change or prey to passions that may be aroused by an external eventuality (immutability). Indeed, so consistently have such attributes been associated with the Deity that it has been extremely difficult for Christians to reflect upon God, "the Father Almighty," according to the primary categories of biblical Theology, which . . . are not categories of pure power; . . . they are categories that in themselves entail the subordination of power . . . to its apparent opposite, weakness.[43]

Finally, Hall argues, with the triumph of positive religion has come the triumph of finality, which has obscured the meaning and character of authentic hope. Since the dawning of Christendom, Western eschatology has emphasized realized eschatology as the future-oriented triumph of finality that is articulated either in terms of heavenly or earthly consummation and manifestation of triumph. There is no wrestling with the negating dimension of being or with the ambiguity that surrounds creaturely life.

43. Ibid., 97.

Hall argues that the "already" of eschatological discourse far outweighs the "not yet" in the doctrine of positive religion. Accordingly, Hall considers that the biblical category of "promise" has been usurped by the affirmation of "fulfillment." Finality (or consummation) replaces hope.

The doctrine of God has been one in which every trace of incompleteness and tentativeness is denied in favour of a God who dominates and is in charge, whose will is being done in heaven as upon the earth in visible and efficacious ways. Indeed, the problem remains that in squelching all that contradicts the finality of God's will and its visible manifestation, there is no way given to Christians to contemplate the contradictory and negating powers that impose themselves upon existence in each moment of every day and to seek God out in hope and in faith manifested in trust. In summarizing his "Critique of Pure Power," Hall articulates what has been lost in the domination of positive religion:

> (1) In its zeal to present the knowledge of God as a triumph over ignorance and doubt, historic Christendom forfeited the language of faith; (2) in its zeal to present the being of God as a triumph over nonbeing, historic Christendom forfeited the language of suffering love; (3) in its zeal to present the work of God as a triumph over evil, death, and sin, historic Christendom forfeited the language of hope.[44]

Hall understands that this triumph of the power of God and the positive relation between God and creation has taken place in positive religion in Christendom (and in North America in particular) for both existential and historical reasons. Existentially, the human condition is needy for fulfillment and, as such, has created a picture of God who decisively triumphs at every turn.

> There is that within us which wants and even needs the positive to triumph and which, precisely because the positive does not obviously triumph in the realities of our daily experience, creates images of triumph that bolster within us the will to affirm life despite its negations and ambiguities . . . The divine reality is held over and against the realities of earthly experience, and the resolution and victory that are absent from mundane experience are affirmed by belief as nonetheless real—as ultimate reality . . . This is the god who deserted Jesus on Calvary.[45]

---

44. Ibid., 101.

45. Ibid.

This god is an idol who is the conclusion of all our insecurities and fears, who protects us from the negative dimensions of life and keeps us thinking positively in the face of all that undermines being.

Historically, there are both philosophical and political reasons why God the Father Almighty has triumphed in Christendom. Philosophically, Hall argues that the tradition of Athens (in particular) was unable to bear the idea of a suffering God—God in relationship with the beloved and suffering creation. In the tradition of Athens, God was "transcendentalized" to such a degree that the biblical relational God of Jerusalem was eclipsed by one who was dislocated *above* time and history, disinterested in mediating *kairos* through the *chronos* time[46] of history in anything but obvious and triumphant ways, if at all. Hall considers that the doctrine of the Trinity, established in the early councils, reflected the influence of Athens and the priority of reason for the establishment of faith. Though he recognizes the attempt to reflect the mystery and intimacy—the transcendent and immanent—dimensions of God through paradox, he argues that the brain-twisting and lofty philosophical thought implicit in the doctrine effectively removed it from the experience of faith of the masses and placed it above the clouds beyond the brain power (or interest) of most Christians.[47] Such "transcendentalization" of doctrine (in both form and content) further hardened a vision of God as one *above* looking down on the entirety of creation like a puppet-master manipulating creatures and events so that "his" will on earth might be done. Like the tradition of Athens, Hall finds that the liberal western philosophical tradition has also preferred a powerful and triumphant God. "While it is true that the liberal tradition rids itself of ideas about God's wrathful judgment upon the earth, the benevolent "Grandfather All-Merciful" who replaces the "Father Almighty" wields at least as much power behind "his" ubiquitous and unquestioning love as did other renditions of God's omnipotence."[48]

It is the political co-optation of the doctrine of God, however, that Hall identifies as the most decisive of all the reasons for the ideological triumph of the positive in Christendom's doctrine of God. Power replaces love as the divine priority. Hall marks the establishment of Christianity as the official religion of the state under the reign of Constantine as the turning point, when a true doctrine of God (etc.)—that is, a doctrine

---

46. Hall, *Professing the Faith*, 104; and *Bound and Free*, 51–52.

47. Hall, "Trinitarian Thinking in Our Context."

48. Hall, *Professing the Faith*, 105.

based on the revelation in life and death of Jesus Christ and on the biblical tradition of Jerusalem—was left behind. It is in Christianity's official
alliance with the powers of the world that the motif of mastery, in the
doctrine of God, most firmly takes hold. "A religion designed to serve the
purposes of empire cannot present the spectacle of a God whose kenotic
long-suffering detracts from 'his' majesty."[49] Hall reminds his readers
that the sign of faith that Constantine saw was a vision of Christ as con-
queror, not as the servant who struggles with despair, suffering humiliation and a criminal's death. Instead, Constantine and his "theological
servants" exploited the power potential of the Christian God in order to
unite the Empire under one conquering and heroic rule of God and, in
so doing, to minimize everything reminiscent of divine vulnerability and
self-emptying.

Hall is clear that the political co-optation of Christian theology did
not end with the Roman Empire. It has been present in all subsequent empires with which Christianity has mingled. Since the fourth century up to
the twentieth, Christendom, not Christianity, has been the dominant religion of the West. It is a religion whose essence is shaped by the imperialist
impulses of empire—touting a god whose divine rule and sovereignty are
absolute. This god is unambiguously supportive of the established earthly
powers that honour him, fully in accord with the aims of the imperium,
and unassailed by self-criticism. "He is always the "Father Almighty," even
when he is grandfatherly, and he triumphs over every enemy, no matter
who, in that historical moment, the enemy happens to be."[50]

Hall outlines how the positive and political triumphalism in this image of God has been particularly captivating in North America. Though
he makes a necessary distinction regarding Canadian scepticism,[51] since
the inception of the United States as a nation there has been an indelible
link between God and "America."[52] Hall tracks historical manifestations
of the ways the positive religion of Christendom became specifically
(and exclusively) associated with America. He describes how the "mythology of providential beginnings" has informed the whole history of
the United States. Particularly following the War of Independence, the
sense that America's destiny was connected to God's own purposes was

49. Ibid., 106.

50. Ibid., 107.

51. Ibid., 108.

52. Ibid., 111.

strengthened by the perception (manifested in the victory of the war) that America alone had been singled out for leadership. However, as Hall notes, the extent to which this god of the powerful was dependent upon the success of the American experiment was less clear.

As we have noted at length before, the Protestant (particularly Calvinist and Puritan) world–view played a powerful role in the religious identification of the American Dream. Protestants internalized the "this-worldliness" of the doctrine of God's providence, which further emphasized both the God-ordained import of this life and God's direct sovereignty over this world. God was recognized to be working positively and to be present everywhere. The negating and hidden elements of the reformation doctrines of God were utterly eclipsed in the New World's positive religion. As the Age of Progress was manifested in religious understandings of providence, victory over peoples and land became increasingly identified with God's will for America to conquer. As such views developed, Hall shows, America metamorphosed from a republic to an empire, a transition which itself affected the dominant theology. He sees that, although the impulses to associate God and America were there from its origins, only much later did they become entrenched in the American self-understanding, especially in the wake of the Civil War.[53] With the birth of Empire the connection between God and America was consummated,[54] and the American motto, "in God we trust," was vindicated by American success and power in the world. Even in the present day, public political voices in America call upon the god of positive religion to lead them.[55]

How does Hall engage this discussion with the struggle between official optimism and despair that prevails in North America at present? Official optimism is the only acceptable approach to accompany positive religion. Official optimism describes the spiritual and socio-political dimensions of creaturely being in the world of positive religion. However, what happens when this fails? Hall critiques the "weakness of power" in the positive religion of God the Father Almighty. He shows how this god has died. With the death of this god of positive religion comes the death of the official optimism that propped up the deity. In such a context as

53. Ibid., 117.

54. Such concepts as America's "Manifest Destiny" represent the consummation of the politics and religion of empire.

55. Over the last several years the call for a "war on terrorism" is associated with the will of God in America's positive religion.

ours, where the mastery motif has so inserted itself in all positive notions of being (human or divinely construed), its destruction enables only the survival of the multiplicity of negations that have been so long denied. In the face of the negation of the positive and of mastery as the motif of meaning (even in its negation), despair sets in. In the absence of mastery, there appears to be nothing at all to shape the context of meaning. If the negations of life cannot be conquered by the positive, there is no way to live in hope, for the negations seem relentless. We have come to the point in which we can no longer live in the official optimism of positive religion.

In contrast to the false image of God in positive religion, namely the god of power and mastery, Hall explores the concepts of *agape* and *mitsein* as the means to construct a doctrine of God based on the revelation of God in Jesus Christ. First and foremost, it is in the suffering (*agape*) love of the cross that God's power is revealed. It is in the with-being (*mitsein*) love of Emmanuel (God-with-us) that God's presence is known. Over and against the positive and officially optimistic renditions of God's power as mastery, God's love struggles and suffers in the garden of Gethsemane and the hill of Golgotha, agonizing and dying on a cross. Over and against the providential visibility of God's presence in positive religion, God is hidden—hidden in the very darkest corners of life and death. The theology of glory with its dominating motif of mastery leaves no room for the God revealed in Jesus and in the tradition of Jerusalem— the God who stands in relation with the covenant people; the God who suffers and whose pathos weeps forth; the God whose revelation is before anything else one of concealment in the world.

Mastery, Hope, and Christ

> It has been the folly of most of Christendom that it has imagined that only a conquering Christ could meet the needs of humanity for God and salvation. We are still labouring under this pathetic illusion. In some ways, North America is its last stronghold. We think that Jesus must be strong, a winner.[56]

In considering Hall's treatment of doctrines relating to Christ and his implicit critique of the motif of mastery underlying such doctrines, we will look at his discussions of the person and the work of Christ. At a number of points, Hall is critical of the extent to which, throughout the

56. Ibid., 496.

history of the church, Christology has acted to encumber and blur what we profess with the words, "Jesus is the Christ." Hall argues that most Christology since the Council of Chalcedon has been "Christolatry"[57] —a theology of glory by which certain images of Christ have dominated and undermined the possibility for the living Christ to be recognized in our midst. He outlines how this has been true historically and how it continues to be true today in certain forms of popular American fundamentalism. Historically, he cites the fact that the official doctrine of the church pertaining to the person of Christ (the two natures) was executed at the Council of Chalcedon, a Council initiated and overseen by the Empire. Not only is he critical of the content of the doctrine, he is critical of the power politics involved in creating such official doctrine. Though he does appreciate the dialectical nuancing in the understanding of Christ's human and divine natures (and seeks to engage this in his own constructive articulations of the doctrine), he is wary of the assumptions of human mastery implicit in the creation of official doctrine. To assume that the human mind and language can encapsulate the truth about the nature of Christ suggests the prideful assertion of human will and imagination that leads to idolatry. Needless to say, that a Council overseen by the Empire would produce doctrine used to crush its opponents is not a surprise. The idolatry of power infests both the form and content of the Council's doctrine.

Though Hall elaborates upon the strengths of classical Christology (i.e., the doctrine of the two natures of Christ) at length, highlighting its potential for dialectical openness and its use of the *via negativa*,[58] he is critical of the ways the doctrine is removed from the experience of faith in the life of the believer. Instead of inspiring faith/trust in Jesus the Christ, the doctrine requires a mental assent and locates faith not in the inner experience of the believer with the living Christ but in the assent of the mind to a highly philosophical articulation of who Christ is. Related to this insight is his criticism of the extent to which this doctrine has been used to emphasize the divine nature of Christ, completely undermining conceptions of the human nature. He describes how the "divinization of Jesus of Nazareth" was influenced philosophically by the tradition of Athens, which effectively supplanted the "Hebraic matrix"

---

57. Ibid., 441.
58. Ibid., 394–403.

in the evolution of the doctrine.[59] The earthy biblical understandings of revelation (the mediation between divine and the human, or eternity and time) were usurped by Hellenistic notions. Where in the Hebraic context the broken and bound human could be the bearer of transcendent purpose, in the Hellenistic context (especially as it is reflected in the school of Alexandria) the human is "distrusted as a medium of ultimacy."[60] Thus the philosophical formulations of Athens joined forces with the political needs of the Empire and the human Jesus of Nazareth became increasingly eclipsed by the divinized Christ. This "Christology from above"[61] has been challenged in the modern era by "Christologies from below." However, he cautions that both poles must be questioned, for they each tend "to reduce the mystery of the person of Christ to typologies, and sometimes caricatures, drawn from preconceptions of divinity and humanity [assumed in idealized versions of given strata of society]." Hall goes on to argue that "Jesus Christ confronts and challenges our preconceptions of both God and ourselves. For faith, his humanity defines authentic humanity and not the other way around."[62]

Hall interprets this phenomenon in North American fundamentalism and liberalism. The most frequently articulated Christological statement in American fundamentalism is "Jesus is God," and "fundamentalist Christology is significant in North American Christianity and society, not only because it can claim the allegiance of a significant portion of the population, but . . . [because] it can seem to the general public as well as to many Christians in nonfundamentalistic denominations the purer form of Christology."[63] On the other hand, Hall is critical of liberalism's emphasis on Jesus as "the perfect man." Though he affirms liberalism's move to put forward the human Jesus, Hall challenges the way this Jesus projected a Victorian ideal rather than the Jewish working class Jesus of first century Palestine. "The problem was," Hall argues, "that Jesus for liberalism became a model of humanity so perfect, so absolute in virtue, so blameless in respect to every sin recognized by his Victorian and other champions, that in the long run the very humanity of the liberal Jesus functioned in much the same way as did the divinity of the conservative

59. Ibid., 448.

60. Ibid., 450–51.

61. Ibid., 402.

62. Ibid., 402–3.

63. Ibid., 453.

Jesus—that is, to distinguish him conspicuously from the rest of us."[64] Instead of showing us the way to authentic humanity in relationship with the Living Christ, challenging and confronting all that blocks transparency to Christ in faith, such Christology has become idolatrous, a stumbling block that limits the possibility of recognizing the true Christ in our midst. For the most part, traditional and contemporary Christology has manifested triumphalist notions of Christ and denied the darker and more ambiguous dimensions of the life, death, and resurrection of Jesus of Nazareth. It has been a Christology of positive religion, avoiding all the negative dimensions of being, and affirming only those elements that assume the import of human and divine mastery.

Hall's discussion of the work of Christ—the soteriological question—is focused around the three-fold office of Christ as prophet, priest, and king. He is critical of the ways that the official church has tended to emphasize the three-fold office in terms of the work of Christ alone and not in terms of the work of the church. This hierarchical, non-participatory ordering only acts to maintain the status quo and undermine the possibility for a spirit-inspired disciple community. As prophet, over and against images of Christ's masterful sorcery of the future or of Christ as the innocent victim, Hall contends that

> Jesus not only challenges the authority of secular authorities but he defies the religious authorities as well. Indeed, he appears as one who is ready to question all authority—not because he is against authority *in se* but because he is conscious of the propensity of authority to wield power for the sake of self-aggrandizement . . . Clearly his bias (. . . in strict continuity with the whole prophetic tradition) is in favour of the powerless, the oppressed, and the poor: . . . those . . . who do not have power but are victims of power.[65]

Hall resists the caricature of Jesus as a silent victim. Rather, he insists that in his prophetic office Jesus is "the roaring 'lion of Judah'"[66] challenging the powers that be, no matter what their political-religious stripes. In fact, Hall argues, it would be impossible to speak of Christ's priestly work without first contemplating the prophetic work which took him to the cross. In its yearning for political power and easy relations

64. Ibid., 457.
65. Ibid., 409.
66. Ibid.

between church and state, Christendom has tended to undermine the prophetic work of Jesus, preferring to highlight both his priestly work of atonement and his sovereign work as "king." In his office as prophet Jesus calls on all to face their own self-righteousness and be humbled before God and each other. This "humbling of the mighty from their thrones" is the most radical element of Christ's prophetic work. He challenges the powerful and self-righteous to be humbled inwardly and to manifest outwardly their humility of spirit in the world. Above all, it is in his suffering and death that Jesus fulfills his prophetic office—the divine intimately and passionately involved in the life of the world.

It is the office of Christ's priesthood that most occupies Hall, for it enables him to consider the doctrine of the atonement, whose contemporary expression he holds to be sorely inadequate. Whereas Hall's critique of classical Christology was articulated over and against the official doctrine of the Empire-approved Church, his treatment of the priestly work of Christ engages dialogically with the different articulations of the doctrines over the ages. In essence, I believe that his different approaches to the doctrines of the person and the priestly work of Christ reflect his recognition of the different power dynamics at play in the formulations of the two sets of doctrines. Where with the "person of Christ," the church clearly established what was held to be true and untrue doctrine, with the "work of Christ" no official doctrine has ever been established. The open-endedness of the latter doctrine enables Hall to engage the content without having first to deconstruct the power presuppositions implicit in the form and content of the doctrine and its coming to be. As a result, he is able to consider the central articulations of the atonement primarily in terms of their apologetic relationship to the contexts out of which they emerged, while at the same time critiquing their existential remoteness from the present context and noting their inappropriate power presuppositions related to their respective host contexts.

The three theories he discusses are (1) the classical theory of deliverance, ransom, *Christus Victor*, or (in contemporary terms) "liberation," associated with early Christian articulations; (2) the Latin theory of sacrificial and substitutionary atonement, associated with Anselm and later re-worked by Calvin; (3) the moral influence or demonstrative theory, associated with Abelard, which focuses on the revelation of love and Jesus as moral exemplar. These theories, at their best, reflect contextual responses to the question, "What has Christ done for us?" (or "What is the salvific meaning of the suffering and death of Christ for us?") given the particular *problematique* of each context. Each of the theories, Hall argues, drawing on Tillich,[67] responds to one dimension of human anxiety given in the human condition. The classical theory responds to the fear of death and fate with the assurance of eternal vindication through Christ's victory. The Latin theory responds to the very real anxiety of guilt and condemnation (particularly in the early and middle ages of Europe) with the assurance of forgiveness and offering of grace as the outcome of Christ's sacrifice. The moral influence theory, Hall contends, not only reflects Abelard's reaction against the previous theories and their implicit portrayal of God as a god of power but also attempts to respond to the anxiety of despair and meaninglessness of the time in terms of the love of God revealed in Christ. All of the theories respond to some dimension of human anxiety implicit in the human condition and preoccupying within their contexts. None of them is sufficient in and of itself. It is important to note that, following Tillich (and Kierkegaard), Hall considers anxiety more than anything else to be the enemy to faith. Thus, theories of the atonement attend to the particular anxiety in a given historical context and reflect a movement toward deeper faith in that same historical context. For Hall salvation in Christ that speaks to the real *problematique* of our context has to do above all else with "making humanity more human." We are being saved from living in false images of ourselves and called to live in the truth of our humanity—within the limits and possibilities of our finitude—with all the tragedy and beauty that that includes. We are called to be human, no more and no less.

In his discussions of the third office of Christ—*Christus Rex*—Hall continues his criticism of the "transcendentalization" of Jesus who, according to the authoritative Nicene creed, "sitteth at the right hand of God." There is a tendency with this doctrine to emphasize christological triumphalism[68] and patriarchy. While appreciating the import of the sovereign work of Christ's love in hidden and mysterious ways in the world, Hall is critical about the extent to which doctrines pertaining to this office have tended to emphasize an imperialistic image of Christ at work in Christian history, obscuring the image of the cross. The "lordship" of Christ is a dialectical and ultimately subversive affirmation that claims,

> appearances to the contrary, the one [who is truly sovereign] is not the fantastically bedecked and exalted emperor, surrounded

---

67. Tillich, *Courage to Be,* 32–63.
68. Hall, *Professing the Faith,* 437.

> by all the symbols and weapons of power that the world can
> devise, but one whose sovereignty expresses itself in readiness to
> serve, to the point of laying down his life for his friends. Victory
> is not dismissed from this office . . . but the victory is a victory
> very different from the kind honoured by the world . . . It is the
> victory of meekness, voluntary powerlessness, truth, and love.
> And that kind of victory is accessible only to faith, for it is neces-
> sarily "hidden beneath its opposite" (Luther).[69]

In summarizing his critique of the treatment of Jesus throughout Christendom, Hall calls for a retrieval of "Jesus, the Christ, before
Christology."[70] Just as he is critical of the dominant *imago hominis* of
Christendom and Western modernity, in his discussions of Jesus Hall
is critical of the dominant *imago christi* and calls for a transformation
of our image of Jesus. Indeed, transforming how we image Jesus would
necessarily require us to transform how we image what it means to be human. Christendom wants to place Jesus on a throne of mastery and power
or to present him as the ideal human to which we must aspire; in both
images, Jesus serves the powers that be in the world. Only a complete
deconstruction of such images can possibly clear the way for authentic
recognition of the true *imago christi* revealed in the Scriptures and to the
life of faith. In the North American context, Hall is particularly critical of
the Euro-American Protestant image of Jesus as mild-mannered, sexless,
and non-political.[71] He challenges the way false images of Jesus function
to block further the possibility for authentic faith and for the true face
of Christ to be recognized in our midst. Any Christology or soteriology
that is worthy of its calling must point beyond itself to the "Thou" that
stands at the centre of the Gospels and at the heart of faith. It must invite
us into a deeper and more authentic relationship of faith. Images of Jesus
as the ideal and masterful human to which we must aspire ultimately
undermine our humanity and urge us to serve false idols and images:

> But this Jesus only does for us, individually and collectively,
> what all highly positive images of the human do: he makes us all
> the more conscious of our weakness, absurdity and lostness. He
> may, for a time, serve empires and the rich and successful. But
> empires decline, the rich are required to give up their souls, and

69. Ibid., 438–39.

70. For a compelling discussion of this point, see also Wells, *Christic Centre*, 1, 117,
and 136–37.

71. Hall, *Professing the Faith*, 485.

the successful enjoy their success only briefly, if at all. When will we learn that Jesus, the crucified one, is with us in our decline, our extremity of soul, our failure? When will we discover the one whose power has to be manifested in weakness because it is the power of love?[72]

In this quotation we can see the ways that the motif of mastery and the *imago Christi* intersect with the experiences of false optimism and despair. Christendom's image of Christ, whether in its imperialistic or ideal manifestations, is disconnected from the earthiness of creaturely life.[73] It is an image of one to whom we can never ascend and who forever eludes us because of our "all too human" humanity. Such an image of Christ functions to push us further into the repressive ways of optimism that cannot admit failure or into the defeatist ways of despair that can only experience failure in the light of such an otherworldly ideal. Indeed, for Hall it is only an image of Christ as the human Jesus that can truly "lighten our darkness." It is only the Christ who knows negation and failure, who struggles with doubt and the agony of being, who experiences the hunger and longing of creaturely being—it is only this Christ who can truly join us, who can engage us in our humanity to offer us the bread of life. For an image of Christ to correspond with the revelation of the Jesus of the Scriptures, it must draw us toward the world—to befriend the world, to steward the world, to be committed to the world, and to undertake responsibility for the world in ways that are costly.

In his constructive work on Christology, Hall draws on the metaphor of Christ as representative. In his authentic humanity, Jesus represents God to humanity and humanity to God. For Hall, the concepts of "participation" and "solidarity" are the most central for giving shape and content to his representational Christology. Christ's representation is solidarity of the most intrinsic sort wherein his very flesh and blood—his suffering, struggle, agony, and failure—participates in our common humanity. It is precisely here in the very particularity of being that God's love is mediated. In his work and being, Jesus represents God in creation and creation before God. In his being and work, Jesus participates in our humanity and in the particularities of the human condition and stands in

72. Ibid., 496.

73. In a sermon entitled "We Would See Jesus," Hall outlines three common but false images of Jesus that function in North America Christendom: the Divine Jesus, the Conquering Jesus, and the Accepting Jesus. These three images correspond to the three atonement theories discussed above.

solidarity with the suffering of creation. Over and against the theology of glory and motif of mastery, this understanding of the person and work of Christ emphasizes the fullness of the *agape/mitsein* love of the creator for the creature and the intended love of the creature for the creator. The suffering of Jesus represents the suffering of beloved creation alienated from its Creator and the suffering of the Creator in solidarity with the fallen and suffering humanity. The love between creature and Creator is mediated and represented in the participation and solidarity revealed on the cross of Christ. In the very suffering of Jesus on the cross is the love that "at-ones" the distance and alienation that divides creature and Creator. The suffering of the cross is the pathos of love in God's participation in and solidarity with the beloved in the person and work of Christ.

This understanding of Christ as representative engages the dynamics of optimism and despair in our context. Where the motif of mastery still functions in its prideful, fearful, repressive, and optimistic forms, Christ the representative calls us to face the limits of our being—our fragility and fallenness. Christ, who participated fully in finite human being, invites us not to fear the truth of our humanity but to face it honestly for what it is, for it was within the very matter of creaturely being that God's love was (and is) made manifest. Where the motif of mastery has crumbled and slothful despair has set in, Christ the representative challenges us to remember that "matter does matter"; that God's very solidarity with humanity/creation revealed in Jesus affirms that all of life is precious, and that human action and inaction in the world do make a difference, for better or for worse. Indeed, Christ's agonizing death on the cross reflects this in the starkest way—the potentiality for evil in the human will. As followers of Christ, Hall challenges us in our action to confront all that feeds the kingdom of death and to stand in solidarity with those who suffer. In both our being and in our doing we are called through Christ to participate in the fullness of our humanity that stands over and against our temptations to mastery, false optimism, and slothful despair.

Mastery, Hope, and Resurrection

One of the areas that has been criticized in Hall's work is his treatment of Christ's resurrection.[74] In the conclusion to *Professing the Faith*, Hall writes:

74. "This is one of the questions I have about the work of Douglas John Hall in its earlier stages (see, for example, *Lighten our Darkness*). One almost gets the impression

How difficult—how almost impossible—it is to speak about the resurrection, especially "in a North American context." We have encountered this difficulty throughout; for while literally everything that I have wanted to say in this volume is dependent upon the resurrection faith of the people of the cross, the word "resurrection" can hardly be uttered in this milieu without its conjuring up whole legions of misconceptions and wrong associations.[75]

While the resurrection of the crucified Christ stands as the starting point for and presupposition of his entire project, Hall is critical about the extent to which the doctrine of the resurrection has undergirded Christian triumphalism and has been implicit in the logic of Empire. The resurrection, Hall argues, is generally seen in terms of Christ's "mastery over death." In negating the negation of Christ's suffering and affliction, it serves positive religion. The doctrine of the resurrection, more than any other piece of Christian doctrine, Hall argues, has been co-opted by the theology of glory in our context in the service of the power of mastery. The triumph of the positive, especially in North American doctrines of resurrection, serves a false *imago Christi* (of mastery) and therefore serves a false *imago hominis* (of mastery). More than any other Christian symbol, the doctrine of the resurrection has blinded us to who we are as people and as nations. When the resurrection triumph is understood to deny, repress, and avoid the depth of the darkness and creaturely suffering in the world, Hall argues, it is not the resurrection to which Christian faith corresponds. In other words, any doctrine of the resurrection that takes us away from the suffering of the world is not the resurrection of the Crucified Christ who more than anything else is *pro nobis* (for us). Instead, Hall urges, Christ's resurrection must be understood as the first and last word of the Christian faith, with the cross as the *decisive* word at its centre. The resurrection of the crucified Christ vindicates and confirms the crucifixion. For Hall, the resurrection is not something separated from the crucifixion; rather, the resurrection of Christ is that which is hidden beneath its opposite—hidden beneath the very cross of Christ. In the world as it is, it is upon the cross of Christ and the suffering of the world that we must gaze if we seek to glimpse the face of God's

---

Hall is afraid to turn to resurrection for fear it will mitigate the unrelieved negativity of the cross vis-à-vis the 'official optimism' of North America" (Forde, *On Being a Theologian of the Cross*, 18n19).

75. Hall, *Professing the Faith*, 549.

resurrecting hope.[76] The resurrection of Christ is precisely about the hidden reality of God's love and its ever new possibility to inspire hope, even and especially in situations of dire suffering. Glimpses of love and hope in this life always reflect the deepest truth of being that will one day be manifested in fullness. The call to followers is to look up from the foot of the cross and wait upon God's resurrecting hope.

Mastery, Hope, and the Imago Hominis

In several important ways, Hall's conception of the dominating *imago hominis* clears the way for the articulation of his more constructive doctrinal formulations. As we have seen, one of the central doctrines that has fed the false *imago hominis* is that of the *imago dei*.[77] Though it comes in many guises, the issue that Hall is approaching here is the intricate interconnection between our image of God, our image of ourselves, and our understanding of the purpose of life. This doctrine is based upon Genesis 1:26–27, wherein the human is the one creature "made in the image of God" and given "dominion over the fish of the sea, and over the birds of the air and over the cattle, and over all the wild animals of the earth, and over every creeping thing that creeps upon the earth." In the imperialistic imagination of Christendom, to be given dominion over the earth and its creatures meant to be given dominating power. Just as God's power came to be understood as that of Caesar, not of God—that of the tyrant, not of suffering love—so the image of the human warped into such falsity. The image of the powerful imperial God of Christendom melded with the modern image of the human as technocratic master of the environment. Thus the doctrine of the *imago dei* increasingly fed an *imago hominis* as one who (1) disregarded human involvement with nature in favour of human transcendence *over* nature; (2) divorced relationship with nature from personal relationship, leading to humanity's further estrangement from nature; (3) concentrated on human rights for authority over nature in exclusion of nature's rights for responsible authority directed by its own needs; and (4) abandoned the idea of stewardship in favour of something closer to ownership.[78]

---

76. Ibid., 549–54.

77. See Hall, *Lighten Our Darkness*, 55–71; *Imaging God*; *Steward*; *Professing the Faith*, 187–359; and *Cross in our Context*, 92–99.

78. Hall, *Lighten Our Darkness*, 55–71.

However, Hall argues, when humans are called to have dominion, we are called to "image God" by being a mirror of divine compassion and stewardship.[79] It is the image of the "steward" that most encapsulates Hall's understanding of the true *imago hominis* intended by God. The image of the steward challenges false images of prideful mastery as well as their corollary, slothful indifference. As stewards we are called to tend to, care for, and delight in the beloved creation. As stewards we are enabled to mediate God's communion love in the world. To be stewards of God's care for the world has both vocational and ontological dimensions. Indeed, the "stewardship of life in the kingdom of death" is the task for which we as followers are intended.[80] It is also true, however, that as one part of a much wider creation we humans are intended for a mutuality of relationship with the rest of creation. This is not only in our doing but also in our being; it is not only ethical but ontological. For as we live in the falsity of ownership and mastery over the earth or in the slothful despair of indifference toward the earth, we end in destroying ourselves as well as other being. Humans have been made as a part of the communion of creation; whenever we fail to live in accordance with this ontological truth we move in self-destructive and other-destructive ways. The steward cherishes otherness and resists the temptations to master or ignore other human and non-human being. In this we see the link between the image of the steward and the theology of the cross—through the very compassion that empties itself in care for the other, in this way embodying the hope that waits upon the other.

Mastery, Hope, and the Church and Mission

Hall has written on the church perhaps more than on any other topic. Theological reflection on the character and mission of the church historically, critically, and constructively was the focus of Hall's early dissertation and has since resulted in numerous books, articles, sermons, and speeches on the topic.[81] One of his most powerful critiques of the church,

79. See Hall, *Imaging God*, 88–108.

80. See Hall, *Christian Mission: The Stewardship of Life in the Kingdom of Death*.

81. Hall's works on the topic include the following: *Ecclesia Crucis: The Church of the Cross; Reality of the Gospel and the Unreality of the Churches; Has the Church a Future?; Future of the Church: Where Are We Headed?; Christian Mission: The Stewardship of Life in the Kingdom of Death; Confessing the Faith; End of Christendom and the Beginning of Christianity;* "Church: Beyond the Christian Religion"; and "An Awkward Church."

as has been evident throughout the foregoing discussion, is his critique of Christendom, during which for 1500 years the church was possessed by a model of empire rooted in the exercise of triumphant power and thus blinded to the truth of Christ. The fact that most Christian doctrine and practice has emerged from this church of Christendom gives to Hall's critical work its contours and edge. Because the infection of this triumphalist theology of glory runs deep, all thought and practice that have emerged from it are suspect. In much of Hall's critical theology, this understanding is an essential point of departure. As well, Hall understands the crisis of the present time, particularly as it pertains to the Protestant churches of North America, in terms of the breakdown of the Christendom model and the confusion that this breakdown is leaving behind. Without Christendom, wherein the church constituted a central element of society whose status and power assured its identity and purpose, the church in our times finds itself floundering. Hall seizes hold of this crisis moment in the life of the church, recognizing it as an opportunity for the church to be freed from the clutches of the theology of glory and released from its idolatry of power. While critiquing what's wrong with the captivity of the church to established Christendom, he urges the church to dis-establish itself and so move toward a truer and more authentic way of being the church of the crucified and risen One.[82] His analysis of the church of Christendom is primarily a political critique (through the lens of the cross) that challenges the implicit power assumptions in the assumed identity and purpose of the church in the world. He seeks to uncover the extent to which Christendom "calls evil good and good evil." While he retrieves pre-Constantinian resources of the Christian movement to feed the life of the present-day church, he also believes that having lived through Christendom and having contemplated itself over and against its theology of glory, the church is invited to new ways of being church that engage the present historical moment while integrating the realities of its past. As the following discussion will show, Hall's historical, critical, and constructive approaches to the church in our time lead to new insights about the marks of the church, the mission of the church, and the image of church that these considerations suggest.

Hall considers the traditional marks of the church critically and constructively in terms of the aforementioned perspective. The church is

---

82. Hall discusses the call for the church to "dis-establish itself or to be disestablished" in a number of places: *End of Christendom*, 41–42; *Confessing the Faith*, 201–64; and "Awkward Church," pt. 1.

One, Holy, Catholic, and Apostolic.[83] Once again, Hall is appreciative of this historical doctrine, drawing out the nuances of context that a deeper understanding of the truth articulated in historical expressions of doctrine requires. For example, in his treatment of the central affirmation of the Nicene Creed—"I believe in one holy catholic and apostolic church"— Hall ponders the ways in which the early Christian movement sought to discern true from false expressions of the faith. Nevertheless, the fact that such an affirmation was formulated under the imperial command of the Roman Empire in an effort to entrench Christianity as the one official religion of Rome raises concerns. The affirmation of the Church as one, for example, not only serves as an act of self-definition but also reflects the Empire's desire for unity in the service of a centralized consolidation of power. Thus in the Code of Theodosius (430 CE), the unity of the church became law, the breach of which was punishable: all people in the Roman Empire were required to be Christian. At the same time, the authority of the Emperor became commensurate with the authority of God.

Hall is critical of the church's affirmation of oneness for another reason as well. He calls attention to the hypocrisy of the church throughout the ages and at the present time in confessing unity even while it is internally divided into mutually alienated and hostile factions. At the same time, however, he asserts that the Oneness of the church cannot be created by human will or desire. Indeed, even the ecumenical movement, with its impulse for unity, can lose sight of the fact that "the oneness that the church has *en Christo* is not an ideal, it is a reality; it is not a principle but a gift, continuously being given."[84]

Regarding the holiness of the Church, Hall cautions against the temptation, past and present, to consider holiness or sanctity as a merited condition earned by the efforts of the human will and therefore to boast. Hall also warns of possible political consequences of holiness: the doctrine of the church as holy can function (like the doctrine of unity) to de-humanize and falsely divinize the powerful so as to further consolidate their power and associate it with the heavenly realm. Instead, the holiness of the church must be understood as a gift given to it from outside, by God. More than anything else, Hall argues, holiness marks the vocation of the church in the world as that which is set apart as the *koinonia*. Yet being set apart is not an end to itself, Hall cautions. Rather,

83. Hall, *Confessing the Faith*, 70–96; *Future of the Church*, 87–103.

84. Hall, *Confessing the Faith*, 75.

it is a means by which the church can be sent into the world as stewards, and as representatives of God's solidarity and love, sharing in a common creaturehood with all creation.[85]

Hall's discussion of the third mark of the church, its catholicity, explores the universality of the church. The intention here is to emphasize that the true disciple community transcends all boundaries, both natural and historical, that divide and separate people one group from another. At its best, it affirms the essential universality of the body of Christ and its incarnational openness to all.[86] The temptation of the theology of glory and its idolatry of power in terms of the catholicity of the church is for certain parts of the church to claim and assume an exclusive and true catholicity over and against other parts. The historical antagonism between the Western and Eastern church, not to mention between the Protestant and the Roman Catholic church, reflects such arrogance and lack of humility, which have resulted in much suffering. "The universal," Hall claims, "that is the body of Christ, in which 'there is neither Jew nor Greek, . . . slave nor free, . . . male nor female' . . . stands as both a criterion and a judge of every claim to universality, and particularly where the claim is based on power . . . The universality of the church, rightly understood, is premised on the assumption that the unity and ubiquity we glimpse but do not yet embody emanates from the cross and not from the throne."[87]

In discussing the fourth mark of the church, apostolicity, Hall affirms the intention of this mark to establish the priority of the biblical witness and point to a common scriptural norm for the Christian faith. In its apostolicity the church affirms its historical foundations and the particularity of its origins in certain central events. There is a historical norm to which the church refers and out of which it has developed; it is called to remember this norm in its worship and witness. However, the dark side of the mark of apostolicity emerges when the temptation of power obscures the truth of this mark by claiming an exclusive apostolicity—an access to truth by parts of the church over and against others. This is evident when apostolic succession rather than apostolic tradition is affirmed as the guide for the norm of faith. The historical, truly incarnational, foundations of the church are essential. However, when naming and claiming these becomes an end unto itself, the purpose of

85. Ibid.
86. Ibid., 79.
87. Ibid., 82–83.

their norming efficacy in the life of the believing community is lost. Hall is convinced that our era is one in which the breakdown of Christendom is challenging us to remember our roots in the scriptures and the historical church in ways that defy the power assumptions of Christendom and the modern world. Perhaps in our recollection of the apostolic tradition we may be opened to glimpse anew our identity and purpose as church.

The most essential mark of the church that, sadly though not surprisingly, is left out of the traditional marks is that of *suffering*.[88] The church in the world must be a suffering church with "the mark of the holy cross" (Luther). Hall reminds us that there is no other theme pertaining to the church that is more prevalent in the New Testament than that of suffering. The image of a suffering church undermines notions of the church's triumphant glory and mastery in the world as it is conceived in its alliance with the Empires of the world. It challenges theological formulations of the theology of glory at every turn. The mark of the suffering church intersects with the four other marks of the church in ways that draw out the true elements of each. Where the suffering of the church is not present, then the other four marks must be called into question. In order to have unity, holiness, catholicity, and apostolicity in their true incarnational and Trinitarian sense, this fifth mark of the church is indispensable.[89] Suffering is not a mark of the church that is to be sought as an end in itself. If undertaken in this way, like all the other marks of the church, it will become a manifestation of the theology of glory in the form of the "martyr complex." Rather, suffering is a consequence of discipleship. "The church is the community of the resurrection: that is, it is brought into being, continually, through the experience of dying."[90] It is what happens when the church truly stewards life within the world. To be open to the world, to care and to mediate compassion, to face honestly the agony of being and the reality of sin means that the church will suffer. This suffering of the church is a sign of its love, solidarity, and commitment to God's beloved world and its creatures.

As Hall sees it, the suffering of the church reflects its discipleship, for it is the taking up of the cross to be "delivered from the tyranny of the self through the grace of participation in something much larger than the

---

88. Hall, *Cross in Our Context*, 137–80.

89. Hall, *Confessing the Faith*, 95.

90. Hall, *Has the Church a Future?*, 176.

self: namely, the "pain of God" (Kitamori) or the groaning of creation."[91] For the disciple community, there is a representational element to this suffering. By being *in* the world but not *of* the world, the church in its suffering represents the pain of God to the world and the pain of the world to God. The church is given the grace to enter into solidarity with sinful, suffering, and broken humanity insofar as it is, itself, sinful, suffering, and broken humanity, vulnerable before God. It is through its kenotic self-emptying that the church suffers and fulfills its vocation in the world. In the North American context, where the insistence on a pain-free world is held up as the goal of life, the cross stands at the centre not in a way that legitimates pain, but in a way that opens us to the reality of suffering in the world and the pain in the very heart of God.

> So long as human beings suffer, God suffers, and so long as creation groans, the Spirit sighs. As the "body of Christ," the church is that community which is being enabled by the divine spirit to participate in God's participation . . . What we call "church," if it is "true," is that sphere in which the suffering that belongs to creaturehood and the suffering that is the consequence of the human distortion of creaturehood is beginning to be borne— willingly. That is the "logic of the cross" (Reinhold Niebuhr); and that is why the only truly indispensable mark of the church is "the possession of the holy cross."[92]

In addition to the marks of the church, the mission of the church has been an essential area of focus for Hall as he examines the intersection of church and mastery. He writes a great deal on the mission of the church and on the character of the church's engagement of and encounter with the world.[93] In his discussions of Christian mission, Hall employs the categories of faith versus sight, hope versus finality, and love versus power to help him identify the specific ways Christendom's missiology was shaped by the theology of glory and its ideology of triumph and mastery. Furthermore, these distinctions enable him to articulate a missiology of the cross wherein the cruciform obedience to faith, hope, and love come into

---

91. Hall, *Confessing the Faith*, 94.

92. Ibid., 96–97.

93. See, for example, Hall, *Christian Mission: The Stewardship of Life in the Kingdom of Death*; *Confessing the Faith*; *Cross in Our Context*; and Hall's two articles ("Canadian Context" and "Despair as Pervasive Ailment") in Brueggemann, ed., *Hope For The World*. As well, all of Hall's books on the Church address these questions of Christian mission directly.

view.[94] In many ways Hall's critical theology comes to a crescendo in his discussions of the mission of the church. He outlines how the coalition of church and empire, with its expansionist impulses, brought tyranny to many people of the earth. In the West this has been the way for 1500 years. First it was the Roman Empire, then the Holy Roman Empire, then the Spanish, Portuguese, French, and English Empires, and now it is the American Empire. Because he looks at the history of the church through the hermeneutic of the cross, Hall is particularly cognizant of the extent to which "conquering for Christ" is the heritage of both conservative and liberal Protestant churches in North America.

The North American liberal "quest for the 'kingdom of God in our time' seems to have been thoroughly imbued with the spirit of Constantinian religion, aided and abetted by the general aspirations of the modern West in the full cry of the age of progress."[95] At the turn of the twentieth century, across all parts of the church there was a sense of the imminent manifestation of the kingdom "on earth as it is in heaven." The triumphalism of the theology of glory has been in full swing throughout all eras of Christendom in the West, complete with its implicit assumption that the powerful of the earth must force their belief systems on the powerless. The church's relationship with culture throughout Christendom has tended to be at one with the powerful and with their efforts to colonize the souls and the lands of the "other," less powerful cultures and nations.

However, the breakdown of Christendom has called everything into question, so that even the term "mission" raises many red flags for those who have become sensitized to the legacy of coercion and violence in the church's mission. Many in the churches carry guilt for the arrogance of the past and struggle with the possibility of mission for the church at all. Indeed, it is all too common for North American Protestants (perhaps especially Canadians) to speak only personally about their own faith for fear of offending the "other." At the same time, the impending demise the once-mainline Protestant church in North America is facing has forced it to raise the question of mission and Jesus' call to speak the gospel. "The question implicit in this is whether, at the end of the Constantinian era, it will be possible for Protestants to discover a mode of Christian mission

---

94. Hall, *Cross in Our Context*, 192ff.

95. Hall, *Confessing the Faith*, 212.

that is not implicitly imperialistic, racist, and destructive of other cultures that may in important respects be superior to our own."[96]

In Hall's analysis of Christian mission and the church's historic relationship with cultures, we can see the poles of optimism and despair coming into play. Where Christian mission through the Constantinian Era of the West (Christendom) brought with its triumphalist ways a sense of unlimited optimism and the impulse to expand endlessly, its demise brings with it a deadening sense of despair and cynicism about church and its relationship with culture. In the joint statement of the Campbell seminar, Hall along with numerous other theologians and biblical scholars identifies despair and the failure of hope as the fundamental problem to be addressed by mission today.[97] Despair and the lack of meaning reflects the spiritual crisis at the root of much suffering in the world. As with all of his constructive work, Hall urges us toward a third way wherein the despair of the world is faced, its false optimism is negated, and hope emerges as the focus of mission. He acknowledges that mission is inherent not only in the scriptural exhortation to faith but also in the actual experience of it. Both the reception and the communication of the life-giving power of faith is part of the very faith experience itself. We are invited to use our minds "to give reason for the hope that is within us" and to be freed to speak this. "The mission of the Christian movement in the 21st century is to confess hope in action."[98] First, however, the false equation between mission and ecclesiastical expansion must be broken for a truer cruciform understanding of mission to emerge. Guided by the tradition of Jerusalem (epitomized for Hall in the thin tradition of the cross), we are reminded that Christian mission to the world must follow God's mission to the world. In our particular context, Hall cautions against the activist, goal-oriented understanding of mission wherein our human work displaces the possibility of recognizing God's hidden work in the world, along with the possibilities of prevenient grace even as these are manifested in other religions. He reminds us that "God is not equatable with any "doctrine of God," and what God is really doing in the world is not equatable with any conception of divine providence or

96. Ibid., 146.

97. Brueggemann, "Missional Questions in a Fresh Context," in Brueggemann, ed., *Hope for the World*, 7–8.

98. Brueggemann, ed., *Hope for the World*, 6.

salvation."[99] The central aspect of God's mission to the world revealed in the Christ event is its world orientation. Far from being an escape from our humanity and "creaturehood," salvation is revealed on the cross as the ultimate "yes" to the creaturely condition. "This 'yes,'" Hall cautions, "will not solve all the problems of the universe," for the very limits and nature of the human condition precludes this. However, "whatever the salvific process means ultimately, for human beings in their present estate it means the peace (*shalom*) that comes from the glad acceptance of creaturehood."[100]

Christian mission, therefore, that grows out of the world orientation of God's mission to the world has the cross of Christ as its centre in all its humble and gracious mystery. Paradoxically, in the revelation of the cross stands the true face of life, the true humanity which is the deepest part of us all. Indeed, it is as the incarnation of God's passionate commitment to life in the world that Jesus comes as God's mission, God's hope for the world. It is Jesus' very commitment to the world—to particular people in particular circumstances—that puts him on the cross to suffer and die. Following the logic of the cross, then, Hall argues that in its world-orientation and passion Christian mission must be more indirect than direct, more hidden than triumphant. He shares the motto, "In the church tell the story. In the world live the story." At the same time, however, he is clear that, when asked, we are called to give reason for the hope that is within us. He discusses how our living of the story is sure to ignite such questions if it is true to its calling. It is a calling that is both personal and collective. In the world the church as a whole must live the gospel message; the task of discerning that gospel in each context is necessary for the church's ministry and mission. Ultimately, for Hall, the church has a representational role in the world in its participation in the ministry of Jesus Christ.

In the face of the church being "disestablished," Hall calls on the church to "disestablish itself" so as to follow more intentionally the path of discipleship in Jesus and not the unreachable worldly ideals of greatness, glory, and success. Instead of seeing the disestablishment of the church as a failure, Hall challenges the church to see it as an opportunity for deeper faithfulness marked by conversion and the recovery of genuine theological thought. He urges the church to take an active role

---

99. Hall, *Confessing the Faith*, 152–53.

100. Ibid., 153–54.

in its own disestablishment—to be "providentially present" in its disestablishment.[101] Given that Christianity under Christendom has been virtually synonymous in its convictions and values with the dominant society, its disestablishment will require renewed understanding as to its genuine foundations through serious and disciplined theological reflection. In disentangling itself from Christendom and the dominant culture, the church is called to a painful though faithful vocation. The church's disentanglement is not primarily about living "over and against" the host cultures within which the church functions. It is rather a growing in faithfulness to God and the recognition of God's call. To be "*in* the world though not *of* the world" is only true in Christian mission insofar as it supports Christ's command to "go into the world." "The purpose of disengaging the disciple community from its host culture is nothing more—and nothing less!—than to re-engage that same culture."[102]

Hall emphasizes that the task of thought is to serve the mission of the church as it becomes disestablished. He is clear that the road that leads neither to "ghettoization" nor "absorption" is indeed a road less traveled, marked by struggle, contemplation, and dialogue. In its disestablishment the church will become a diaspora reality wherein it may embody in action its hope for the world. Hall emphasizes that, more than anything else, the deepening of thought will enable this walk into the unknown diaspora of disestablishment and enable the possibility of survival in the impending darkness. Survival is not guaranteed. However, to hide from or repress the reality of the church's disestablishment is to court untruth and illusion. "Thought is of the essence of the cross that North American Christians today are called to pick up and carry!"[103] Thought directed by love for the world manifests hope in action and faith in God's abiding presence.

Mastery, Hope, and Eschatology

Hall's treatment of the intersection of mastery and eschatology has been intimated throughout this entire discussion of doctrine.[104] In many ways the distinctions he is making in all his critical and constructive theology reflect his response to the deeper questions of eschatology and hope.

101. Ibid., 243.

102. Ibid., 251.

103. Ibid., 264.

104. "Eschatology is not a "doctrine" among doctrines, but a dimension of every other doctrinal area" (ibid., 457).

Eschatology typically has to do with the end of time and the created order and the relationship with time as followers of Christ. It is the doctrine within the church that best addresses two sets of questions: those pertaining to the end of history and (related to this though more important in our context) those pertaining to the meaning of history.[105] Given that the future (the not-yet), as well as its relationship to the present and past, is the object for theological reflection in this doctrine, specific discussions on the meaning and content of Christian hope appear under the rubric of eschatology. Indeed, our understanding of the meaning of history ("to what end, history?") shapes our understanding of the meaning and purpose of life and gives content to our way of being in the world—collectively, as planet, species, and individually.

Just as with all his reflections on doctrine in his treatment of eschatology, Hall is concerned with deconstructing the theology of glory and the Christian triumphalism present in many of its historical articulations. As we have seen, Hall explores the disconnect between the positive *expectations* for the future of our society and church and the actual *experience* of "future shock" in which the future appears to be heading for disaster. Despite the fact that present crises throughout the world may be relieved in some way or another, the experience of those living through the twentieth and twenty-first centuries suggests that past crises are replaced by present crises which will be replaced again by future crises.[106] The trajectory of our experience of history—its violence and devastation—is not a positive one and, when faced, will elicit despair.

In the religion of progress, Christians of the nineteenth and early twentieth centuries got caught up in a tide of euphoria as they anticipated their participation in the inauguration of the realm of God on earth. Christian hope and notions of eschatology were wrapped up in the human's ability to know with finality the vision of God's realm and to bring it into being by the actions of the will and imagination. Indeed, the dynamics of the theology of glory played themselves out in full through this

105. "The Greek word *eschatos*, like the simple English word 'end,' contains two connotations. The most common use . . . in everyday discourse, is the idea of termination: something—a vacation, a war, a life—comes to an end . . . [However] nothing ends without implicitly raising the question of its end, its purpose (. . . *telos*)." Hall goes on to describe how it is that eschatological conversations took on teleological questions with particular pointedness following the First World War and increasingly in the West as a crisis in the understanding of human/creaturely purpose became more clear. Ibid., 469ff.

106. Ibid., 454.

doctrine. Christians had the certain knowledge (sight) of the final vision towards which creation was moving; in the exercising of their power, they would bring it into being. Ultimately, Hall argues, the religion of progress reflects faith in time and the possibilities that are given in history (as opposed to faith in the crucified and risen Christ).[107] Such faith is most evident in North American doctrines of realized eschatology wherein "America" represented the cutting edge of the purposeful movement of time. However, "the twentieth century has systematically eroded that assumption; so that now, although the churches still try to behave as if it were their duty to be hopeful, it is very hard to discover sincere historical hope among Christians or anyone else."[108] Where is there any evidence of the sovereignty of divine love? Indeed, it is nowhere evident to the naked eye. Such recognition causes one to despair in history and the modern paradigm of meaning. Hall reminds us, however, to return to the biblical text, which never locates the *source* of hope within history but in that which is other to history, while being mysteriously and miraculously mediated in history. Indeed, discussions of eschatology have a necessary interest in the future. However, for followers of the cross the relationship with the future is one of openness to its alterity based on trust in God and hope in the possibilities of God's hidden and abiding commitment to the world, embodied in the image of waiting at the foot of the cross.

Over and against North American assumptions regarding the reign of God, Hall articulates what the reign of God is not. It is not "a program, a plan of action, a strategy for change. God's reign is not just a condition that is going to occur willy-nilly."[109] God's reign is also not an ideal or utopian vision. Nor, finally, is it a "merely subjective state, a metanoia of the heart, a 'spiritual' disposition."[110] Hall goes on to argue that it is easy to see in the scriptures that the reign of God "is not compatible with tyranny, gross economic disparity, the degradation of the earth and of human beings . . . It is not compatible with violence, war, slavery . . . [or] indifference to those in need, etc."[111] What he is getting at here is the centrality of

---

107. Hall asks the question, "What need had the churches of North America to dabble in the complexities of biblical eschatology when modernity had made it plain, and our cultural milieu made it mandatory to believe, that time itself progressively redeems?" (Hall, *Confessing the Faith*, 457).

108. Hall, *Confessing the Faith*, 455.

109. Ibid., 460.

110. Ibid., 461.

111. Ibid., 462.

Christ, the stories of Jesus, and the tradition of Jerusalem for providing content to understandings of the reign of God and for making it possible to discern what the reign of God is not, biblically speaking. However, Hall's cruciform emphasis on faith (trust), its posture of hope, and its expression in love do not lay down a program or concrete vision of the reign of God or the future of the world. There is hiddenness in the reign of God that does not exist triumphally for its own sake, but is *kenotic* and serves the stewarding of life in the world. Not to recognize the essential transcendence of the "reign of God," Hall warns—to risk allowing it to "become the property of some power elite," however idealistic—is to risk "substituting for the reign of God, the dominion of death."[112]

A final and important contextual focus for Hall in his discussion of eschatology is his concentration on the dynamics of the officially optimistic society and how these have come into play in North American understandings and doctrines of hope and eschatology. We have covered these distinctions in depth elsewhere; however, the essential question emerges: How it is that Christians can confess hope in the officially optimistic society, which has reflected so little upon the distinctions between optimism and hope? Exploring this question is an ongoing cause for clarification in Hall's work. "As for hope, the biblical dialogue partner of despair, it is the most difficult of all theological categories to preserve from the cooptation by the desperately optimistic."[113]

Hall points to concrete movements in the church and world that reflect the "already and not-yet" presence of the Reign of God, hidden yet revealed to the eyes of faith. He highlights the Sojourners community in Washington D. C. and various movements of Christian resistance that reflect the "already and not yet" presence of God's reign.[114] Yet, given the contextual realities of North America (namely, a craving for a map into the future, a prediction of concrete outcomes, a divine plan for history being worked out), the bulk of Hall's work is on the "not yet" of realism that refuses to "call good evil and evil good" and yearns only to call the thing "what it actually is."[115]

---

112. Ibid., 463.

113. Ibid., 465.

114. Hall, *Lighten Our Darkness*, 259, 262; *The Cross in Our Context*, 209–30.

115. Hall, "Despair as Pervasive Ailment," in Brueggemann, ed., *Hope for the World*, 83–93.

Part 2 In Conclusion: Deconstruction as Waiting

Do the critical perspectives that Grant and Hall share constitute unwarranted pessimism about the future? Do they encourage quietism? Nothing of the sort. Hall, like Grant, wants to separate the motivation and energy for concrete action in the world in the name of Christ from an outcomes-driven projection into the future of concrete visible and positive results based on human mastery. The reason for this is that both Hall and Grant have witnessed all too often in our context the disillusionment and cynicism not only of the failed masters, but of the failed activists who have become demoralized by the failure of measurable, consistent improvement toward the approximation of the reign of God on earth. To follow the One who was crucified in the world, and whose rising was witnessed only by a few, means that visible results of the reign of God in the world are the exception rather than the rule. So it is also with the reign of God as it is lived out in the faithfulness of Christ's followers during this time of the "already and not yet." Within history we can only glimpse God's reign in moments of hidden revelation until the realm of God comes and God's will is finally done on earth as it is in heaven—a happening that is totally discontinuous with the course of history and necessity, though promised to be strangely inclusive of it.

Grant and Hall's critical (and constructive) work is directed by the recognition that it is only as we deconstruct the data of the officially optimistic, dominant culture that we become free to inquire anew into the possibility of hope in our time. "Ours is a time when hope is most difficult, and most necessary."[116] The theology of the cross calls for courage to enter the darkness of the prevalent despair and the lies of optimism. It is only in walking through the valley of the shadow of death, in standing at the foot of the cross, that true hope, which is only a "hope against hope" (Rom 4:18), may emerge.[117]

As we have seen, both Grant and Hall focus on the deconstructive task of the theology of the cross, breaking down the multiple ways North American society (Grant/Hall) and church (Hall) place "hope" in the possibilities for human mastery and seek fulfillment in that which cannot satisfy. Further, they both demonstrate the extent to which this idolatrous hope in human potentiality has resulted in oppressive and destructive

---

116. Hall, *Reality of the Gospel and the Unreality of the Churches*, 173.

117. Hall refers to Paul's term, "hope against hope" regularly throughout his corpus.

ways of being in relation to other humans and creation. This deconstructive method of the *via negativa* identifies what hope *is not* by demonstrating the extent to which human mastery has resulted in destruction and suffering rather than fulfillment and the coming of "heaven on earth." In practice, their deconstructive moves reflect the idea of "hope as waiting" to which their thought points. Their focus on the "negative" in life—that which shows how things ought not to be—reflects how hope as waiting actively engages its context, paying close attention to the details of suffering caused by the constant attempts by humans to control, manipulate, and master otherness rather than to love it. This practice of deconstruction, this waiting on hope, is intended to clear the way so as to enable other ways of being to emerge. By such a clearing we may be open to be met by the One who is outside all attempts at mastery, who is the source of all hope. The deconstruction of the *via negativa* reflects a posture of trust that it is in facing and identifying "how bad the bad news is" in our world that we locate ourselves at the foot of the cross, eyes wide open to the crushing devastation of suffering and tragedy in all its forms. It is here in eager anticipation that we await and make way for the coming of hope's possibility in the unexpected. This posture of waiting at the foot of the cross is preparatory, vigilant, constantly attentive to God's hidden presence in the very midst of darkest darkness of our world. It is here, as at the foot of the cross, that God's hidden presence breaks open in a quiet and ferocious love—the beginning, middle, and end of all our hope.

While Hall focuses more on the constructive possibilities outside the parameters of human mastery, both Hall and Grant explore how the deconstruction of mastery in all its forms opens up the possibility for *that which is not* mastery to come into focus. We must wait upon this. As mastery is extinguished as the purpose of life through Grant and Hall's deconstructive moves, love emerges as that for which we are made and by which we are called into relation with all that is. Over and against mastery and at its end, love becomes visible as consent, openness, receptivity, and attentiveness to otherness—the very movement of God's hidden presence in our midst, the in-breaking of eternity in the vicissitudes of necessity. How does this understanding of love relate to hope? While Grant and Hall only ever point towards it through mostly deconstructive moves, the hope towards which they point (and for which they wait) is one that is based on waiting for and trusting in God's hidden presence and possibility in time and space. The character of God's hidden presence and possibility is love. Thus hope waits for and upon love in time and space as the sign of the hidden God, the very essence of the man called Jesus of Nazareth who hung on the cross at Golgotha in 33 CE.[118]

---

118. Clearly, we are uncertain about the exact date of Jesus crucifixion. However, what I am seeking to highlight here is the fact that this event of the cross happened in our world in a particular place at a particular time to a particular person, the very essence and love of God in concrete time, space, person.

PART 3

Waiting at the Foot of the Cross

We are there, at Golgotha that terrible day.
Waiting, as the tired, torn, and tortured bodies are thrust onto crosses.
Waiting, as Jesus, there in the centre, is lifted up—nails, crown of thorns, weak,
bleeding, mocked, heavy head . . .
gasping words . . .
I am thirsty . . .
Behold your son . . .
Forgive them, they know not . . .
Today you will be with me . . .
My God, my God why . . . ?
Into your hands I commend . . .
It is finished.

Silence.

NO!
NO.

no master to serve
no heroic vision
no new realm on earth
no fix-it solution
no triumphant cry

only the cry of absence reverberating

Hope is gone.
powerless, helpless, weak, gone
body broken
life unhinged
God absent
and the pain goes on . . .

too much to bear
Disappointment. Disillusionment. Disbelief. Humiliation. Laughable.
Pain outside and in . . .

How dare you die!!

Panicked . . . What to do?!
Hide? Run? Fight? Rage? Play dumb? Pretend?
Forget about it? Business as usual? Numb out? Laugh? Mock?

. . . . . . No.

Wait. . . .

8

Toward a Theology and Practice of Hope

IN THIS FINAL CHAPTER I begin to construct a theology of hope as "waiting at the foot of the cross" that has been intimated throughout the book so far. As we have seen, the work of both Grant and Hall is suggestive of this alternative understanding of hope. Hope as waiting at the foot of the cross builds upon their analysis of hope in our context based on the *via negativa* of the theology of the cross. This way of understanding hope both counters the impulse of modernity of hope as mastery and points toward a more faithful theology and practice of hope for today. This chapter accordingly functions as both a response to and an elaboration upon their work. Over and against hope as mastery and its failure in denial, indifference, and nihilism, hope as waiting embodies a faithful way of being—of thinking and living in relationship—necessary for people today. The survival of our planet and species may well depend on such a shift. At this juncture in history, people of faith in English-speaking North America are called to wait not just anywhere, but to wait at the foot of the cross; to interpret our context through the lens of the cross. In order to explore further a theology and practice of hope for today, I have divided this chapter into three major parts: Waiting as Hope; Waiting at the Foot of the Cross in Our Context; and Practices of Hope as Waiting for Today.

Waiting as Hope

For many shaped by the modern western imagination that typifies English-speaking North America, it is difficult to conceive of a more contradictory idea than hope as waiting. Waiting completely negates the popular understanding of hope as mastery that seeks to control aspects of creaturely life to serve a future outcome of its own making. Waiting undermines the sense that we are what we do and that we can create the world we want to inhabit. Waiting suggests passivity and inactivity rather than changing the world and making a difference. Waiting seems to undermine the power and potentiality of the human. It suggests that we are dependent upon some other for whom we wait. How can waiting be a good basis for hope?

First, waiting emerges as a contextually significant motif for hope given the failure of hope as mastery in our context. Precisely because it completely counters the common notion of hope, it is one that must be considered—especially in light of the method of the cross and the *via negativa* that have been the thrust of the book. As we have been stripping away the falsity of hope as mastery in all its forms, waiting emerges as a subversive and potentially powerful way to understand and practice hope. In our contemporary context, to consider hope as waiting is countercultural, for it undermines the habit of mastery so elemental to our way of being in the world. Waiting is the converse of mastery. Where mastery seeks self-expansion, waiting restrains the compulsion toward self-expansion. To wait counters the need to master the other and rather invites contemplation of the other. It counters the impulse to "make history" through the enacting of our wills and to "create" our own heaven on earth. Hope as waiting reflects restraint and caution regarding the compulsion of the human will and imagination to master.

Second, over and against the temptations of denial and repression, indifference and nihilism in response to the failure of hope as mastery, waiting invites a completely different response. Rather than pretending that reality is something other than what it is in order to feign hope, waiting challenges us to be honest about reality—"calling the thing what it is"—and to foster a posture of trust in the face of life's negations, trusting the coming of that for which we wait. Rather than falling into "happy" indifference and psychic numbing so nurtured by the entertainment industry and shopping culture, waiting challenges us to pay attention and to stay alert to that for which we wait in the midst of daily living. Finally, rather than lashing out against life and the repeated experience of disappointment, as is the case with nihilism, waiting suggests a posture of openness and receptivity toward all that is as we seek that for which we wait.

Third—and importantly—waiting's connection with hope is deeply rooted in the Hebrew Scriptures. There are several words that can be translated either as hope or wait. For example, "Those who wait upon the

Lord" can also be translated "Those who hope in the Lord" (Isa 40:31).[1] While it is not my intention to do an in-depth word study here, the intrinsic link between waiting and hoping in the Scriptures is instructive. This waiting-hoping includes a sense of anticipation, an active seeking and yearning for that which is to come. The character of this waiting-hoping is defined and shaped by that which is hoped for / awaited, usually identified as God's action in history to guide and to save.

What Is It That We Wait For?

While hope as waiting is powerful in and of itself, and while it offers rich possibilities in re-conceptualizing hope over and against mastery, we must recognize that hope as waiting is always related to that which is sought. In modernity, hope was generally attached to a specific outcome and vision that drove our activity into the future. We moved toward the future. We didn't wait for it to happen. The failure of this outcome-based notion of hope has left a vacuum; people no longer know what to hope for. Hope itself has become suspect. However, the concept of hope as waiting offered here is premised upon a relationship with the One for whom we hope and wait. Ultimately we wait for the One whom we cannot master or control. We wait for the One who is not defined by mastery or the enactment of will upon circumstance. We wait for God, the One revealed through the cross, who is mysteriously present in the broken and the suffering. We wait for the One present in love and forgiveness, in compassion and solidarity. We wait for the One who resists mastery in all its forms and is manifested in the hidden possibility of love in the midst of finitude and fragility. Hope as waiting is explicit that God is ultimately the source, energy, and focus of our waiting, our hoping.

Many might argue that the image of waiting for God, and especially waiting for God at the foot of the cross, points to the resurrection. We wait at the foot of the cross for Jesus to be resurrected. This is both true and not true. Indeed, the resurrection of Jesus points to God's possibility in time that comes unexpectedly, not in a loud and victorious way but in a hidden and quiet way revealed to a few followers. As has been intimated

---

1. Each of the four Hebrew words that connect hoping and waiting has a slightly different emphasis: expectant waiting-hoping that yearns eagerly (see Isa 40:31); waiting-hoping that is related to looking closely, even inspecting (see Ps 119:166); hoping-waiting that emphasizes patience (see Isa 30:18); hoping-waiting that longs for fulfillment (see Ps 31:24). I am grateful to my colleague Brian Irwin for his guidance in interpreting Hebrew words for hope.

throughout this book, the theology of the cross rejects all triumphalist interpretations of God, particularly those that suggest that the resurrection is a triumph over the cross, where the resurrection overcomes, masters, and has victory over the cross. Such interpretations lie both about the way things are in the world and about the stories of Jesus in the Scriptures. They tend to turn us away from the world rather than toward the world. When the centrality of the cross is denied in our understanding of God's revelation in Jesus, we are effectively taken away from the reality of suffering in our own contexts and lives. Instead, the resurrection points to God's hiddenness in the cross: newness of life where only death is present; potential and possibility when all seems lost. To wait on this God of cross and resurrection means waiting for and seeking out glimpses of God's presence in day-to-day relationships and situations, while also trusting God with the fullness of all that is.

Hope as Waiting for O/other

As stated above, the waiting of hope is ultimately a waiting for, a hoping in, God. How we conceptualize and understand God and the intersection with creaturely life is of utmost importance. Hope as waiting based on a theology of the cross suggests an intrinsic link between waiting for God as Other and waiting for "otherness" in our lives and relationships. Indeed, waiting upon glimpses of God (the Other) in others is central to hope as waiting for the O/other. In order for such otherness to come into view, it must be seen with eyes of love: love as openness, attentiveness, and reverence, not love as mastery, power, and control, which are so often confused in understandings of love in modernity. Let us consider the dynamics of what it means to "wait for" the Other (God) and how this shapes and intersects with our waiting for the other (human and non-human being).

First, when our primary vocation is understood in terms of waiting, we are not focused on seeking mastery over the O/other, whether in our conceptions of God or of other human and non-human being. We wait in trust in such a way that the otherness of being can come into view. Love (rather than mastery) and trust (rather than fear) are essential for otherness to be recognized and received. When we recognize beauty in another, we are glimpsing the beauty or image of God in that other. True otherness is received when love is ignited and beauty is glimpsed in the other or is seen hidden beneath its opposite. Second, to wait assumes a posture of receptivity and openness to otherness. It presupposes the essential "unmasterableness" of the O/other, resists the compulsions within that seek to master, and works to wait in openness and receptivity. Third, there is an intrinsic correspondence between the posture of relationship toward both *Other* and *other*. The relational ontology of "waiting for" the Other is manifested in the character of our lived relationships with others. To wait for the O/other is wrapped up with loving the O/other, for it is by love that truth is discerned and true knowing happens. Far from the technological reasoning of science in modernity, to wait for O/other(ness) means paying attention in reverence to the other and not "holding the other up as an object to give its reasons for being."[2]

At the same time, some distinctions must be made between our relationship to Other (God) and our relationship to others (human and non-human being) in our characterization of hope as waiting. In waiting for God, there is the sense of belonging to God and being in relationship with God that has a particular direction and priority to it. Waiting for God implies a relationship of acknowledged and ultimate dependence. We wait for God upon whom our life hangs. In our relationship with the whole (the otherness of creation within which we exist), there is a corresponding relationship of dependence. That is, our lives are dependent on the whole of the created order, and thus living with attentiveness to this dynamic, in reverence, is part of what waiting as hope for the world means. At the same time, our relationship with other distinctive human beings is not one of ultimate dependence, but one of creaturely interdependence.

Hope as Waiting in Relation to Time and History

In relation to conceptions of time and history, the concept of hope as waiting completely counters the modern manifestations of the theology of glory in which history is "made" by the efforts of the human will. When we wait, there is no room for a "history-making spirit" in which the ends are seen to justify the means and the present is used to serve the future.[3] History happens and humans, of course, participate, embedded in the cause-and-effect relationships governed by chance. Each moment of life has consequences. What history tells us is that matter matters. This is

2. See Grant, "Knowing and Making," and "Thinking About Technology," in *Technology and Justice*, 11–34.

3. See Grant, *Philosophy in a Mass Age*, 90–104.

true in daily interactions, and, as the Christian confession reveals, this is true in the heart of God. However, assuming a posture of waiting within history means that we participate in it without presuming mastery and exerting control over it. To wait reflects a specific relationship with time and history such that alterity and creaturely limit can come into view.

In relation to time, we stand within it and are called to wait in attentive alertness to the present moment. We cannot control time any more easily than we can conjure up a magical realm here on earth. Part of living in time means accepting its alterity, or the limits that its otherness places upon us. To live in a posture of waiting in time means to live without resentment against the limits implicit in the relationship between being and time. Part of the problem with the modern conception of time as history is that it manifests human resentment toward time and reflects a lashing out against the limits time places upon being in finitude. In conceiving of time as history and intersecting time with the human will to power in the "making of history," humans could feign mastery over the limits of time and finitude. This lie about reality has precipitated other lies. To wait means to live in relation to time, honoring its alterity and the parameters within which we exist.

When contemplating the character of waiting as hope today, the future must be thought through in terms that serve the present and not visa versa. Just as the reality of Christ's resurrection turns us back to the cross and helps us to recognize the power of love in the weakness of the cross, so any anticipation of the future must turn us back to the present life of faith and hope in the world. Part of the failure of the modern vision of history is the extent to which the present is understood only in terms of future possibility and utilitarian purposing. Not only does this misconception tempt us at the level of the will; it also makes it impossible to see the present with attentiveness to its detail and with alertness to what lies hidden within it—both the beautiful and the tragic. The seeds of the future are hidden within the soil of the present, for both good and ill. In our waiting we are called to pay attention, to recognize the seeds of good and ill, and to attend to them accordingly in the present.

Not only does hope as waiting counter the "history-making" spirit of modernity, but it also completely negates the meaning of hope (and faith) in the modern religion of progress. There is, after all, nothing inevitable about the movement of history. There is not some promised outcome for which we wait and towards which history will inevitably turn. When we wait, therefore, we do not stand in a posture of trust to history, but to the One who is Other to history. God, as revealed in the crucified and risen One, breaks into history while also being mysteriously hidden within it. Waiting in history with a posture of trust elicits a hermeneutic of suspicion regarding conceptions of history based on assumptions of mastery through either human or divine action.

Hope as Waiting: Passive and Active

The most common criticism of hope as waiting is the concern that it presupposes inactivity and passivity in life, especially in the face of injustice. This is not the case. In fact, both the inward experience of waiting as hope and its outward manifestation involve a dynamic interplay. The waiting of hope is experienced internally by an ultimate faith and trust in God. This internal waiting is both passive and active. It is passive in that it lets God be God, Other to us and to our ideas of who God "should" be and how God "should" act. It is active in that it actively resists the compulsion to be as God by the vigilant practice of the *via negativa*, which strips away the soul's pretensions to finality and mastery. As such, it ever seeks to be open to receive God's otherness and presence as it meets us in daily life.

On the other hand, the waiting of hope is externally manifested in both passive and active ways. It is passive in that it is prepared to take a breath, to step back, to discern before responding in action. Such waiting as hope is mindful of the propensity for reactivity and fear to compel humans to run after various actions in order to feel like "something is being done," so as to feign hope. In such situations, hope as waiting has a "passive" flavor that seeks to wait upon discernment, open and attentive to other perspectives, trusting in the midst of ambiguity that a pathway will emerge. Such hope as waiting is experienced in the very midst of these processes, in openness and attentiveness in relationship with others, and not primarily as the outcome of them.

Hope as waiting is externally manifested in an active attentiveness and resistance to all that seeks mastery or suggest finality on a human level. Just as the *via negativa* internally strips away such pretensions, externally it calls us to challenge and resist all that functions with a sense of ultimacy and with the use of force over otherness. In the face of force and oppression we are called to resist, to challenge, to act on behalf of those who are vulnerable and suffering (including both human and non-human life). The goal is to do so in such a way that the use of mastery, force, and power is undermined; to act in compassion, love, and solidarity. These ways of relating manifest God's way in the world revealed in Jesus and the fullness of waiting as hope. Some examples in our world of such action can be seen in the work of international aid workers and groups like Doctors without Borders, which sends physicians into situations of violence and extremity to care for those in need—at great personal risk. The work of caring for victims in such contexts in itself critiques the use of power to oppress and victimize. It sets up a completely different way of relating based on love, compassion, and solidarity in the midst of mastery and power having their way. This kind of active hope as waiting breeds more hope, faith, and love in contexts of fear and suffering. Indeed, such waiting as hope stands at the foot of the cross, for it is shaped by the critique of force and mastery emerging from the cross, where God is revealed through broken and forgiving human flesh.

Hope as Waiting: Trust, Receptivity, Openness, Attentiveness, Reverence

As has been suggested throughout this chapter, as well as the book as a whole, trust, receptivity, openness, attentiveness, and reverence are central features of hope as waiting. In contrast to the temptations of mastery to fix, to control, to lash out, or even to run away that grow out of an existential fear of finitude and dependence, hope as waiting grows from an elemental trust—trust in God, trust in love's possibility in life, trust in the face of the darkness. These postures of being reflect how to live in relationship in the world based on hope as waiting and the revelation of the cross. As we have seen, such ways of being in the world completely undermine and critique, and can even unhinge and transform, the power of mastery and force in the world. The message of the cross tells us that power, mastery, and force feed sin, evil, and suffering. Wherever they are exercised, there are negative consequences and relationships that are not being lived as they are made to be lived. This is true in personal as well as local, national, and global relationships, and this is also true in our relationship with the land, sea, and sky, and with ourselves in time.

The call to live in trust, receptivity, openness, attentiveness, and reverence is not straightforward in our world. It calls for discernment and courage. It also calls for a willingness to take responsibility and to recognize the consequences when we fail—as we will often do, given our humanity and the web of necessities in which we participate. To live out of these postures of hope as waiting requires a willingness to confess, to repent, and to receive forgiveness when fear, power, force, and mastery become part of our way of relating to others. This too is not easy, for we must be prepared to be brought to our knees in humility again and again, to be taken to the foot of the cross. It is here that our hope as waiting will be renewed in the voice from the cross of compassion, love, and forgiveness.

Waiting at the Foot of the Cross in Our Context

The preceding section has considered some aspects of what it means to wait at the foot of the cross in our context; this section will explore specific ways the cross shapes our interpretation of God's presence in the world and what this means for practices of living in hope. While the theology of the cross is suspicious of positive or constructive theological claims and always seeks to interpret human activity and thought through the *via negativa*, it is important to give content to the revelation of God in the cross of Jesus in order to discern what it means to wait at the foot of the cross in our context.

The vision of God revealed on the cross is of one who has been defeated by the power of the world. This is not a God who works by such force. Rather, God revealed here is barely visible for those who seek a God of power and glory. The power of force in the world is judged and condemned at Golgotha. So too are all our expectations of such a God and our prioritizing of such power in the world. This is what the *via negativa* attends to and what we have discussed at length. We cannot look to the cross and easily see any sign of hope worth waiting for. However, it is when we are at the end of such "easy hope" that we are called to wait in trust, openness, and attentiveness more intentionally.

Hidden beneath the suffering of the cross is the presence of God. We wait upon such revealing. God, through the lens of the cross, is one who is particularly present in solidarity with those who suffer and are abandoned, humiliated, and betrayed by the power and coercion of the world. This God revealed in Jesus is in deep relationship with the beloved creation. Hidden beneath the terribleness of this image is the beauty of one who continues to speak in love and compassion, forgiveness, utter transparency, and deep trust in the face injustice and suffering. In Jesus' resurrection, God vindicates what is revealed on the cross. This is God's way in the world. This is what we are called to wait upon in the world.

Waiting at the foot of the cross in our context means paying particular attention to suffering and being in solidarity with those who are suffering in our world, for God is present there. It means paying attention to the vulnerable, those in whom the fragility and finitude of life is most present. It means seeking to follow the difficult path of love and compassion, forgiveness and transparency in relation to others. It means resisting power, coercion, and mastery in all its forms, within and without, and as we live out such understandings in our theology, churches, and worship practices, as well as in the public sphere. It means never easily presuming that we can recognize God's presence as anything more than a glimpse in an unexpected way. It means being open and attentive to otherness and to the hidden beauty of God in all, as well as to the distortions that hide God's beauty in others and ourselves. It means trusting enough to wait and to be present in the midst of the deepest darkness and sorrow in our world and resisting the temptations to ignore, repress, or run from how bad the bad news is. We need to be prepared to "call the thing what it is" and to continue to be honest and to trust in spite of how dark the darkness is or may become.

Waiting at the foot of the cross in our context means being prepared to confess and repent when we have acted in ways of mastery and fear rather than love and trust—to make amends and receive forgiveness. When we reach our limit or end, it means being prepared to entrust our endings to God. It means trusting in the transforming energy of love in all its forms and enacting it. It means maintaining a harsh critique of all projects, analyses, and plans that propose to offer final solutions. It means deconstructing and resisting all that seeks to "pretty things up" in the world and ignores the reality of suffering and the darkness. At the same time, it means deconstructing and resisting all that seeks vengeance on the world or tries to flee from the world as it is. Waiting at the foot of the cross in our context is about being very present *to* the world *in* the world, and to all the hidden and unexpected ways God's presence is glimpsed in the midst of life. It means all these things and more. Each relationship and situation, whether on a personal or global level, is the context where we are invited to wait, to hope at the foot of the cross.

One of the most difficult aspects of our reflections on waiting at the foot of the cross in our context is discerning how to respond to situations where power, force, and mastery victimize human and non-human life, distorting both victim and victimizer. The revelation of God in Jesus on the cross and the method of the *via negativa* suggest that power, mastery, and force are simply negated on the cross by the truer and more costly road of love, compassion, solidarity. Indeed, I believe this is true in our understanding of God revealed in Jesus. As well, it is the deeper truth of how things are made to be in the world—God's intention for the world. However, we live in a complex and often ambiguous world where the pathway of love, compassion, and solidarity is complicated to discern; where openness and receptivity can enable violence to continue unabated; where there are often no easy answers; where force over otherness happens as part of the necessity of the world in which we participate.

There are times when we may be compelled to use force and violence to stop another from using force and violence in a way that would cause more harm. In choosing this path, we discern that it is the lesser of two evils, if you will—that not to act with power against power would be a greater evil. Should one use fists or knives to stop a random attack on a child by a stranger? Is it permissible to use possibly lethal force to prevent an armed militia from entering a refugee camp to rape, loot, and kidnap? When populations are being murdered by their own governments, should other nations intervene with a "strategic" use of force? We must not fool ourselves. We live in the world and are caught up in such necessities. To lesser and greater degrees, being caught up in ways of relating that use force, power, and mastery over others has consequences. These consequences function both externally and internally. Externally, the use of violence and force perpetuates cycles of violence and force. Internally, it blocks the movement and presence of love within us, so that our relationships become disordered. As we become mindful of these ways of relating, we are called back to wait at the foot of the cross, in painful humility to recognize the consequences of our actions (even when such actions are deemed necessary), to make amends where we can, to confess, to repent, and to be open to receive the forgiveness offered there.

To wait for God at the foot of the cross in our context is to live in hope, not as a future outcome of our mastery, but as a relationship that is always becoming. With such hope the future is open and the fullness of possibility in the present comes into view.

Practices of Hope as Waiting for Today

This chapter has already identified many practices of hope as waiting through postures of being in relationship with otherness in trust, openness, receptivity, attentiveness, reverence; in acts of love, solidarity, and compassion in the face of suffering; through acts of resistance against injustice and the oppressive use of force; through discerning a pathway forward in difficult circumstances; through living in transparency to God, self, and others as the temptations to mastery are stripped away. Building upon what has been identified already, in this final section I explore practices of hope as waiting under the headings of Prayerful Living; Joy, Delight, and Laughter; and Nurturing Community. These practices are not exhaustive, but rather suggestive, intended to invite readers to imagine further possibilities for their own lives. Developing regular practices that help to ground us in right relationship with God, with other human and non-human being, and with the self builds both resilience and a greater capacity for hope.

Prayerful Living

Prayer is about keeping open to God. It includes awareness of God's presence in all of life and in all we do. How we pray and what we pray about reflects a great deal about our theology and our understanding of who God is, how God acts, and our assumptions about the relationship between creation and Creator. Prayerful living as a practice of hope as waiting means keeping open the channels of communication with God all the time, remaining open and attentive to God's hidden presence. In our prayer habits we can intentionally practice waiting for God, a waiting that shapes and impacts our way of being attentive to God in the rest of life. Since God is ultimately the source, energy, and focus of our waiting hope, mindfulness of our relationship with God is central. Part of this includes paying attention to God's hidden presence in life, in the beauty (and hidden beauty) of other human and non-human life of which we have spoken of at length. Of the many other aspects to prayerful living, we will explore some here.

First, prayerful living is about seeking complete transparency before God and a willingness to be open and to lay down before God all that is moving within our hearts and souls in any given moment. This includes the good, the ambiguous, and the negative, difficult, even vengeful, currents within us. In the Psalms, the people of Israel express all the range of emotions toward others to God, most notably vengeance and rage towards others.[4] But the Psalms express anger not only toward others but also toward God.[5] In the practice of Israel demonstrated in the Hebrew Scriptures, there is a willingness to trust and expose to God even the

4. For example, see Ps 139:19–21.

5. For example, see Ps 88.

most hateful, difficult, and desperate sides of human life and relationships. We too need to live such transparency before God if we are truly to hope in our context. We must not hide away and try to pretty things up before God, as if we need to protect God from all the dark and difficult currents within us that we do not like. If we do this in our relationship with God, we no doubt do it in our other relationships as well, thereby undermining the possibility for living in true hope and trust. Rather, as we seek to be in relationship with this Other we are called to be open, honest, and transparent, and to trust God enough that we can truly come as we are, edges and all.

Second, prayerful living is a way of being in relationship with all that is and in ongoing dialogue with God in our daily lives, yes; but it is also about maintaining a regular practice of intentional prayer and meditation. Having a regular or daily practice of prayer is important in developing the resilience and patience of hope as waiting. While it is important in prayer to raise our concerns for the world and for ourselves to God, it is equally (and oftentimes more) important in prayer to listen for God, in receptivity and openness. This is an intentional practice of waiting for God. Usually, in order to be receptive, listening, and attentive to God, we need first to have been cleansed of our distractions and preoccupations, our edginess, busy-ness and self-focus. Each person needs to sort out for herself/himself the best ways to pray and to open to God. In the Protestant and Roman Catholic traditions, our prayers are often filled with many words. How can words open us to listen for and wait upon God? Where is the place for silence? For breath? For visualization? For body movement? For stillness? In practicing prayer as waiting, each person can find ways that most enable opening, listening, and attentiveness to God's hidden presence.

Third, prayerful living as a practice of waiting as hope requires resistance to all the ways our prayer life reflects a desire for God to be a god of our own making, rather than the Other with whom we are in relationship. The most common habit in prayer is to want God to take charge and be in control, to master our lives and the life of the world. But the God of the cross is not one who intervenes as power and control to change things how we want them to be. We need to be mindful of our temptations to make God into an extension of our own desire for mastery and control in life. To pray for this or that to happen as if God can jump in and force things to go a different way feeds into the understanding of hope as mastery and the illusion of God being one of power, force, and control and not of love, compassion, and solidarity. It denies and obscures the God revealed in the cross of Jesus. In saying this I am not suggesting that God does not act in the world nor that we should not raise concerns and intercessions for our world to God in prayer. However, how we do this is of utmost importance. God works as the energy and movement of love in life. It is with such energies that situations are transformed and new life can emerge. Discerning ways to pray and language to use in prayer that reflects this reality is essential if we are to practice hope as waiting at the foot of the cross. Not only is this necessary for individuals in their personal prayer practice; it is also particularly important for those in leadership whose prayers are intended to represent a body of believers.

Joy, Delight, and Laughter

It is difficult to consider how joy, delight, and laughter can be practices of hope as waiting at the foot of the cross. The image of waiting at the foot of the cross and laughing while Jesus hangs there is offensive and off-putting. However, there are a number of ways to consider the importance of joy, delight, and laughter as practices of hope especially as we wait at the foot of the cross.

First, joy, delight, and laughter point to the unfathomable absurdity of believing that hidden in this terrible death and ending is resurrection, newness, life abundant. There is an incredible irony in the cross that must not be lost for fear of losing touch with the resurrection life hidden beneath its opposite. Paul declares that we live as fools for Christ, trusting God's impossible possibilities in the midst of life and at its end. There is a frivolous joy in this that runs so completely counter to the ways of the world and to the working of force in the world! When we practice joy, delight, and laughter in life we feed hope and reflect a deep and abiding trust in and celebration of God's ways rather than human ways.

Second, joy, delight, and (especially) laughter enable us to embrace the fragility, fallibility, and finitude of our lives with a lightness of being that points to a deeper trust in God, rather than a worry that everything is all about us. Yes, it is true that all our actions and inactions have consequences and that there is much to resist and to contend with in this world. However, it is also true that we are but dust, living a short time on this earth, dependent, quickly forgotten. When we take ourselves too seriously we lose sight of the bigger picture, along with the possibility of hope that is beyond our limits and control. Laughter, in the face of our foibles and short-comings, our pretensions, and idiosyncrasies, feeds hope as waiting for that which is beyond us.

Third, practicing joy, delight, and laughter in life reflect a way of being in relationship with human and non-human life that celebrates and enjoys the other, without seeking to control and master the other. Such practices include joy and delight in the beauty of the natural world, and in all creatures great and small. They include joy and delight in literature, art, music, and science. They include joy and delight in other people and in the particular and unique ways they are who they are. These practices point to a joyful reverence for God's creation of which we are a part, and they open up space for hope to breathe.

Nurturing Community

The primary emphasis throughout this book so far has been on the relational character of hope. The critique of hope as mastery has grown out of a relational understanding of hope and of what it means to be human. When relationships to others, God, the self, time, and creation are dominated by mastery, control, and power, the possibility for hope is foreclosed—bound to failure. When these relationships are shaped by waiting—trust, receptivity, openness, reverence, indeed love—hope is opened up and nourished. An important part of practicing hope as waiting in our context is the building of community based on these ways of being in relationship. There are several different ways in which the practice of nurturing community is a practice of hope as waiting.

First, it is in community with other people that we find ourselves in ongoing relationships of otherness and where we meet our own temptation to mastery and control over otherness. When others do not act as we act or as we want them to act, we are forced to face our own temptation to mastery and desire to usurp the place of God in that other's life. It is in community with many different people where we are stretched to really wait, trust, and be present and open to otherness, without trying to change others to who we want them to be. This can take hard work and much inner and outer discipline. At the same time, it is here in the context of community where people come together in all our variety and difference, all our vulnerability and fragility, all our beauty and complexity, where hope as waiting is most nourished and most real. It is in community that the freedom to be in relationship as God intended is glimpsed in real time—in moments of celebration and worship, in moments of collective mourning and sadness, in gatherings where people are free to be who they are without fear, where difference is invited and discernment comes through dialogue. Nurturing community is a practice of hope. Not only does it practice hope as waiting in relationships with other people; when different people come together in freedom and oneness—in community—it also builds the capacity for hope in the one and in the whole.

Second, nurturing community across borders and boundaries is a practice of hope as waiting. Acts of solidarity and love across lines of difference feed hope. While I am writing the people of Syria are being bombed and attacked by their own government. The rest of the world does not know a way forward—to use force to what extent? As I ponder what to do and what a practice of hope as waiting might look like in this context, a few things emerge. First, faith–based communities across the world have been praying for the people of Syria. This is a practice of hope as waiting in action feeding that which it manifests while holding up a vision of justice and love and of God's possibility in the midst of human impossibility. Second, through technology and the use of social media (though limited by the Assad regime), the Syrian people have reached out and felt connected with the larger world. This action has fed hope and the sense for some that, even if the worst happens, they will be remembered. All is not in vain. Finally, the solidarity of communities of believers throughout the world with the people of Syria and with particular communities of believers in Syria has been a message of hope: that they are not alone, that they are held in the hearts of people throughout the world, that there is a bigger whole within which they exist. While it may seem small in the face of the force and power wreaking havoc in Syria, these practices of hope as waiting across boundaries of geography, religion, language, and race are not insignificant and can feed greater hope and further actions of courage, resistance, and solidarity.

Third, nurturing community with the larger creation is a practice of hope as waiting. The community of creation is vast, and the opportunities for practicing hope as waiting in relationship with creation are also vast. One of the greatest problems with the modern western understanding of hope as mastery is the relationship it presupposes between humans and the larger creation. In modernity we saw creation as a resource to be managed and mastered to our benefit. Indeed, most governments and many people today still function with this understanding. Nurturing relationships with all God's creation is critical for a robust understanding of hope as waiting. First, the cycles of the seasons of growth, death, and growth again have much to teach us about the patience necessary for hope as waiting. Second, we can learn from the intricacy and diversity of ecosystems about how difference comes together in a much larger whole, where the fullness of possibility of the one is connected to the fullness of possibility of the all. Finally, in developing relationships of reverence in creation, humans find themselves not in relationships of mastery and control, but waiting upon the recognition of beauty, of possibility, and of new life. Indeed, because humans have not nurtured such a relationship with creation, ecological disaster is happening across the globe. Waiting upon and loving creation gives us clarity and passion to resist its destruction and inspires action to honour its otherness. Hope is fed by the recognition of beauty. When our vision is converted by waiting and we are given eyes to see, creation has much to teach us about a robust and resilient hope.

Conclusion

In this chapter we have begun to construct a theology and practice of hope that grows out of the contextual theologies of the cross of both George Grant and Douglas Hall. This chapter represents both a response to and a building upon their work as discussed in the preceding chapters. The bulk of the book has explored Grant's and Hall's analysis of hope as mastery, and has highlighted their intimations of hope as waiting at the foot of the cross. This final chapter seeks to give some more flesh to those bones—to begin to construct ways to think, act, and live in a posture of hope as waiting today.

Needless to say, there is much more that can be said. We find ourselves in the midst of a rapidly changing and often violent world, where fear holds sway and the compulsion to react in power, control, and mastery, or, conversely, in avoidance, resentment, or indifference easily lays hold and in fact is leading to the planet's demise. The call from the cross challenges our knee-jerk reactivity, our fear, and our yearning for finality. The call from the cross urges us to wait, to trust, to pay attention, to love, and to be open to God's hidden possibility in the midst of the uncertainty, darkness, and the shadow of death; God's hidden possibility where only endings appear and where humans have hit their limit. Like no other time before, now is the time for people of faith to wait at the foot of the cross in our world, for it is here that true hope for the world is given. It is here that God's resurrecting love changes everything.

Bibliography

Adams, Michael. "The Continental Divide." *The Walrus*, April–May 2004, 62–71.

Althaus, Paul. *The Theology of Martin Luther*. Translated by Robert C. Schultz. Philadelphia: Fortress, 1966.

Angus, Ian H. *A Border Within: National Identity, Cultural Plurality and Wilderness*. Montreal: McGill-Queen's University Press, 1997.

———. *George Grant's Platonic Rejoinder to Heidegger*. Lewiston: Mellen, 1987.

Anselm of Canterbury. "Proslogion." In *A Scholastic Miscellany: Anselm to Ockham*, edited and translated by Eugene Fairweather, 69–70. Philadelphia: Westminster, 1956.

Athanasiadis, Harris. *George Grant and the Theology of the Cross*. Toronto: University of Toronto Press, 2001.

———. "Political Philosophy and Theology: George Grant, Leo Strauss and the Priority of Love." *Toronto Journal of Theology* 20/1 (2004) 23–32.

———. "Waiting at the Foot of the Cross: The Spirituality of George Grant." *Religious Studies and Theology* 27/2 (2008) 231–45.

Augustine of Hippo. *The City of God*. Translated by G.G. Walsh et al. New York: Image, 1958.

———. *The Confessions of St. Augustine*. Translated by R. Warner. Toronto: New American Library of Canada, 1963.

Barth, Karl. *Dogmatics in Outline*. New York: Harper & Row, 1959.

———. *The Epistle to the Romans*. London: Oxford University Press, 1933.

Baum, Gregory. *Christian Theology after Auschwitz*. London: Council of Christians and Jews, 1976.

———. *Theology of the Americas*. Edited by S. Torres and J. Eagleson. Maryknoll, NY: Orbis, 1976.

Baum, Gregory, and Harold Wells, editors. *The Reconciliation of the Peoples: Challenge to the Churches*. Maryknoll, NY: Orbis, 1997.

Becker, Ernest. *The Denial of Death*. New York: Free, 1973.

Bell, Richard H., editor. *Simone Weil's Philosophy of Culture: Readings toward a Divine Humanity*. Cambridge: Cambridge University Press, 1993.

Bellah, Robert N. *Habits of the Heart*. Berkeley: University of California Press, 1985.

Bernanos, Georges. *The Diary of a Country Priest*. Chicago: Thomas More, 1967.

Bevans, Stephen B. *Models of Contextual Theology*. Maryknoll, NY: Orbis, 1997.

Bonhoeffer, Dietrich. *The Cost of Discipleship*. Translated by R. H. Fuller. London: SCM, 1948.

———. *Letters and Papers from Prison*. Translated by R. H. Fuller and Frank Clark. London: SCM, 1971.

Brueggemann, Walter, editor. *Hope for the World: Mission in a Global Context*. Louisville: Westminster John Knox, 2001.

Buber, Martin. *I and Thou*. Translated by Ronald Gregor Smith. Edinburgh: T. & T. Clark, 1937.

Cayley, David, editor. *George Grant in Conversation*. Toronto: Anansi, 1995.

Cochrane, Charles Norris. *Christianity and Classical Culture*. New York: Oxford University Press, 1957.

Coleridge, Samuel Taylor. *The Selected Poetry and Prose of Samuel Taylor Coleridge*. Edited by Donald A. Stauffer. New York: Random House, 1951.

Christian, William. *George Grant: A Biography*. Toronto: University of Toronto Press, 1984.

Combs, Eugene. *Modernity and Responsibility*. Toronto: University of Toronto Press, 1984.

Cone, James. *God of the Oppressed*. New York: Seabury, 1975.

Cousar, Charles B. *A Theology of the Cross: The Death of Jesus in the Pauline Letters*. Minneapolis: Fortress, 1990.

Davis, Arthur, editor. *George Grant and the Subversion of Modernity*. Toronto: University of Toronto Press, 1996.

Dillenberger, John. *God Hidden and Revealed: The Interpretation of Luther's Deus Absconditus and its Significance for Religious Thought*. Philadelphia: Muhlenberg, 1953.

Dostoevsky, Fyodor. *The Brothers Karamazov*. Translated by D. Magarshack. England: Penguin, 1958.

———. *Crime and Punishment*. Translated by Constance Garnett. New York: Random House, 1950.

———. *Notes from the Underground and the Grand Inquisitor*. Translated by R. E. Matlaw. New York: Dutton, 1960.

Dunn, James D. G. *The Theology of Paul the Apostle*. Grand Rapids: Eerdmans, 1998.

Ebeling, Gerhard. *Luther: An Introduction to His Thought*. Translated by R. A. Wilson. London: Collins, 1970.

Eliade, Mircea. *The Myth of the Eternal Return: or, Cosmos and History*. Princeton: Princeton University Press, 1954.

———. *The Sacred and the Profane: The Nature of Religion*. New York: Harcourt, Brace, & World, 1959.

Ellul, Jacques. *The Technological Society*. New York: Knopf, 1964.

Emberley, Peter, editor. *By Loving Our Own: George Grant and the Legacy of "Lament for a Nation."* Ottawa: Carlton University Press, 1990.

———. "Values and Technology: George Grant and Our Present Possibilities." *Canadian Journal of Political Science* 21/3 (1988) 465–94.

Endo, Shisaku. *A Life of Jesus*. Translated by Richard A. Schuchert. New York: Paulist, 1973.

———. *Silence*. Translated by William Johnston. Tokyo: Tuttle, 1969.

Farley, Wendy. *Tragic Vision and Divine Compassion: A Contemporary Theodicy*. Louisville: Westminster John Knox, 1990.

————. *The Wounding and Healing of Desire: Weaving Heaven and Earth.* Louisville: Westminster John Knox, 2005.

Forde, Gerhard O. *On Being a Theologian of the Cross: Reflections on the Heidelberg Disputation.* Grand Rapids: Eerdmans, 1997.

Gorman, Michael J. *Cruciformity: Paul's Narrative Spirituality of the Cross.* Grand Rapids: Eerdmans, 2001.

Grant, George P. "The Academic Study of Religion in Canada." In *Scholarship in Canada, 1967: Achievement and Outlook,* edited by R. H. Hubbard, 59–68. Toronto: University of Toronto Press, 1968.

————. "Acceptance and Rebellion." In *Collected Works of George Grant,* edited by Arthur Davis, 2:221–99. Toronto: University of Toronto Press, 2002.

————. "Addendum." In *Two Theological Languages by George Grant and Other Essays in Honour of His Work,* edited by Wayne Whillier, 16–19. Queenston: Mellen, 1990.

————. "Adult Education in the Expanding Economy." *Food for Thought* 15/1 (1954) 4–10.

————. "The Beautiful and the Good." In "Lecture Notes on Plato from Notebook E." Unpublished manuscript, 1970s. Printed copy. In the author's possession.

————. "The Beautiful Itself." Lecture on Plato's Symposium. Unpublished manuscript, 1970s. Printed copy. In the author's possession.

————. "Canadian Universities and the Protestant Churches." In *Collected Works of George Grant,* edited by Arthur Davis, 2:22–33. Toronto: University of Toronto Press, 2002.

————. "Carl Gustav Jung." In *Architects of Modern Thought, 5th & 6th Series: 12 Talks for CBC Radio.* Toronto: Canadian Broadcasting Corporation, 1962.

————. "Celine's Trilogy." In *George Grant and the Subversion of Modernity: Art, Philosophy, Politics, Religion and Education,* edited by Arthur Davies, 13–53. Toronto: University of Toronto Press, 1996.

————. "Charles Cochrane." In *Collected Works of George Grant,* edited by Arthur Davis, 2:110–15. Toronto: University of Toronto Press, 2002.

————. *Collected Works of George Grant.* Vol. 1, *1933–1950.* Edited by Arthur Davis and Peter C. Emberley. Toronto: University of Toronto Press, 2000.

————. *Collected Works of George Grant,* Vol. 2, *1951–1959.* Edited by Arthur Davis. Toronto: University of Toronto Press, 2002.

————. "Comments on Hegel and on Religion and Philosophy Notebooks 1, 2 and 4." In *Collected Works of George Grant,* edited by Arthur Davis, 2:519–32. Toronto: University of Toronto Press, 2002.

————. "Confronting Heidegger's Nietzsche: Tribute to James Doull." Unpublished manuscript, date unknown. Printed copy. In the author's possession.

————. "Conversation Between Pilate and Jesus." Unpublished manuscript, 1969. Printed copy. In the author's possession.

————. "Dennis Lee—Poetry and Philosophy." In *Tasks of Passion: Dennis Lee at Mid-Career,* edited by K. Mulhallen, Donna Bennett, and Russell Brown, 229–35. Toronto: Descant, 1982.

————. *English-Speaking Justice.* Toronto: Anansi, 1998.

————. "An Ethic of Community." In *Social Purpose for Canada,* edited by Michael Oliver, 3–26. Toronto: University of Toronto Press, 1961.

————. "Faith and the Multiversity." *The Compass: A Provincial Review* 4 (1978) 3–14.

———. "Five Lectures on Christianity." In "Notebook A." Unpublished manuscript, 1976. Printed copy. In the author's possession.

———. "Fyodor Dostoevsky." In *Architects of Modern Thought*, 71–82. 3rd & 4th Series. Toronto: Canadian Broadcasting Corporation, 1962.

———. "George Grant and Religion: A Conversation Prepared and Edited by William Christian." *Journal of Canadian Studies* 26/1 (1991) 47–53.

———. *George Grant in Process: Essays and Conversations*. Edited by Larry Schmidt. Toronto: Anansi, 1978.

———. *The George Grant Reader*. Edited by Sheila Grant and William Christian. Toronto: University of Toronto Press, 1998.

———. *George Grant Selected Letters*. Edited by William Christian. Toronto: University of Toronto Press, 1996.

———. "Good Friday" (poem). *The United Church Observer* 14/3 (1952) 3.

———. "The Gospels, The Resurrection, Dostoevsky's Christianity." In "5 Lectures on Christianity for 1B6, McMaster (1976?) Notebook A." Unpublished manuscript, [1976?]. Print copy. In the author's possession.

———. "Ideology in Modern Empires." In *Perspectives of Empire: Essays Presented to Gerald S. Graham*, edited by J. E. Flint and G. Williams, 189–97. London: Longman, 1973.

———. "An Interview with George Grant." Edited by Larry Schmidt. *Grail: An Ecumenical Journal* 1/1 (1985) 34–47.

———. "Jean-Paul Sartre." In *Architects of Modern Thought*, 65–74. 5th & 6th Series. Toronto: Canadian Broadcasting Corporation, 1955.

———. "Justice and Technology." In *Theology and Technology: Essays in Christian Analysis and Exegesis*, edited by Carl Mitcham and Jim Grote, 237–46. Lanham, MD: University Press of America, 1984.

———. "Kill the Retarded? Cause for Despair." *The Globe and Mail*, July 30, 1977.

———. "Knowing and Making." *Transactions of the Royal Society of Canada*. 4/12 (1974) 59–67.

———. *Lament for a Nation: The Defeat of Canadian Nationalism*. 1965, 1978. Ottawa: Carlton University Press, 1991.

———. "Lecture Notes from Course on Revelation Theology (Augustine)." In "4F6 (1973–74)." Unpublished manuscript, 1973–1974. Printed copy. In the author's possession.

———. "Lecture Notes on Philosophy and Theology." Unpublished manuscript, 1959. Printed copy. In the author's possession.

———. "The Minds of Men in the Atomic Age." In *Texts and Addresses Delivered at the Twenty-Fourth Annual Couchiching Conference*, 39–45. Toronto: Canadian Institute on Public Affairs and Canadian Broadcasting Corporation, 1955.

———. "The Modern World." Unpublished manuscript, 1953. Printed copy. In the author's possession.

———. "Notebook for class on Simone Weil." Unpublished manuscript, 1976. Printed copy. In the author's possession.

———. "Notes by G. P. G. While Reading Simone Weil's Notebooks I and II." Transcribed by Arthur Wills. Unpublished manuscript, 1957. Printed copy. In the author's possession.

———. "Notes on the Good and Technique." In "Notes towards a book." Unpublished manuscript, 1976. Printed copy. In the author's possession.

————. "Notes on Simone Weil." In "Notebook I," 100–103. Unpublished manuscript, 1956–1957. Printed copy. In the author's possession.

————. "Notes on Simone Weil's La Connaissance Surnaturelle." Unpublished manuscript, 1960s. Printed copy. In the author's possession.

————. "Notes on Simone Weil's Notebooks." Unpublished manuscript, 1958–60. Printed copy. In the author's possession.

————. "Obedience." *The Idler*, July–August 1991, 23–28.

————. "The Owl and the Dynamo: The Vision of George Grant." Interview, CBC-TV Arts, Music, Science, February 13, 1980.

————. "Philosophy." *Royal Commission Studies: A Selection of Essays Prepared for the Royal Commission on National Development in the Arts, Letters and Sciences*. Ottawa: Cloutier, 1951.

————. "Philosophy 7." Unpublished manuscript, 1959. Printed copy. In the author's possession.

————. "Philosophy and Religion." In *The Great Ideas Today 1961*, 336–76. Chicago: Encyclopaedia Britannica, 1961.

————. *Philosophy in the Mass Age*. Edited with an introduction by William Christian. Toronto: University of Toronto Press, 1995.

————. "Plato and Popper." *Canadian Journal of Economics and Political Science* 20/2 (1954) 185–94.

————. Preface to *Heritage: A Romantic Look at Early Canadian Furniture*, by Scott Symons and John de Visser, n.p. Toronto: McClelland & Stewart, 1971.

————. "Realism and Political Protest." *Christian Outlook* 21/2 (1965) 3–6.

————. "Religion." Unpublished manuscript, [1967?]. Printed copy. In the author's possession.

————. "Religion and the Multiversity." Early version, written at McMaster University, of the essay that later appeared as "Faith and the Multiversity" in *Technology and Justice* (1986). Unpublished manuscript, date unknown. Printed copy. In the author's possession.

————. "Religion is a human activity." Unpublished manuscript, [1967?]. Printed copy. In the author's possession.

————. Review of *The Great Code: The Bible and Literature*, by Northrop Frye. *The Globe and Mail*, February 27, 1982, E 17.

————. Review of *Nietzsche's View of Socrates*, by Werner J. Dannhauser. *American Political Science Review* 71/3 (1977) 1127–29.

————. Review of *The Secular City*, by Harvey Cox. *United Church Observer* 28/9 (1966), 16.

————. Review of *Simone Weil—A Life*, by Simone Petrement. *The Globe and Mail*, February 12, 1977, 43.

————. "Revolution and Tradition." In *Tradition and Revolution*, edited by L. Rubinoff, 79–95. Toronto: Macmillan, 1971.

————. "The Rite of Holy Communion." Sermon, McMaster University. Unpublished manuscript, early 1960s. Printed copy. In the author's possession.

————. "Sermon for Student Service, October 6, 1961." Unpublished manuscript, 1961. Printed copy. In the author's possession.

————. "Simone Weil: An Introduction." Unpublished manuscript, 1963. Printed copy. In the author's possession.

————. "Simone Weil: Some of GPG's Favourite Passages (late 1970's)." Unpublished manuscript, 1970s. Printed copy. In the author's possession.

——. "Some Comments on Weil and the Neurotic and Alienated." Unpublished manuscript, early 1960s. Printed copy. In the author's possession.

——. "Speech on Education at Teacher's Institute." Unpublished manuscript, 1954. Printed copy. In the author's possession.

——. *Technology and Empire.* Toronto: Anansi, 1969.

——. *Technology and Justice.* Toronto: Anansi, 1986.

——. *Time as History.* [Transcription of 1969 Massey Lectures, CBC]. Toronto: University of Toronto Press, 1995.

——. "Training for the Ministry." *The United Church Observer* 13/6 (1951) 16.

——. "The Triumph of the Will." In *The Issue Is Life: A Christian Response to Abortion in Canada,* edited by D. O'Leary, 156–66. Burlington: Welch, 1988.

——. "Two Theological Languages." In *Two Theological Languages by George Grant and Other Essays in Honour of His Work,* edited by Wayne Whillier, 6–19. Queenston: Mellen, 1990.

——. "The Uses of Freedom—A Word in Our World." *Queen's Quarterly* 62/4 (1956) 515–27.

——. "The Value of Protest." Unpublished manuscript, 1966. Printed copy. In the author's possession.

——. "Value and Technology." In *Conference Proceedings: Welfare Services in a Changing Technology,* 21–29. Ottawa: Canadian Conference on Social Welfare, 1964.

——. "What is Philosophy." Unpublished manuscript, 1954. Printed copy. In the author's possession.

——. "Why Read Rousseau?" *Speech given in honour of J.H. Aitchison.* Unpublished manuscript, date unknown. Printed copy. In the author's possession.

Grant, George, and Sheila Grant. "Sacrifice and the Sanctity of Life." In *New Life: Addressing Change in the Church,* edited by K. M. Haslett, 78–99. Toronto: Anglican Book Centre, 1989.

Grant, John Webster. *The Churches and the Canadian Experience: A Faith and Order Study of the Christian Tradition.* Toronto: Ryerson, 1963.

Hall, Douglas John. "Accounting for Hope." *Journal for Preachers* 24/4 (2001) 12–18.

——. "Against Religion: The Case for Faith." *The Christian Century,* January 11, 2011, 30–33.

——. *An Awkward Church.* Occasional Paper. Theology and Worship Committee, Presbyterian Church (USA), 1993.

——. "Barmen: Lesson in Theology." *Toronto Journal of Theology* 1/2 (1985) 180–99.

——. *Bound and Free: A Theologian's Journey.* Minneapolis: Fortress, 2005.

——. *The Canada Crisis: A Canadian Perspective.* Toronto: Anglican Book Centre, 1980.

——. *Christian Mission: The Stewardship of Life in the Kingdom of Death.* New York: Friendship Press, 1985.

——. "Confessing Christ in a Post-Christendom Context." *Ecumenical Review* 52/3 (2000) 410–17.

——. *Confessing the Faith: Christian Theology in a North American Context.* Minneapolis: Fortress, 1996.

——. *A Covenant Challenge to Our Broken World.* Edited by Allen O. Miller. Atlanta: Darby, 1982.

——. "The Cross and Contemporary Culture." In *Reinhold Niebuhr and the Issues of our Time,* edited by Richard Harries, 183–201. Grand Rapids: Eerdmans, 1986.

———. "Cross and Context: How My Mind has Changed." *The Christian Century*, September 7, 2010, 35–40.

———. *The Cross in Our Context: Jesus and the Suffering World.* Minneapolis: Fortress, 2003.

———. "Despair as a Pervasive Ailment." In *Hope for the World: Mission in a Global Context*, edited by Walter Brueggemann, 83–93. Louisville: Westminster John Knox, 2001.

———. "Discovering Gospel for Here and Now." *The Living Pulpit* 11/1 (2002) 20–23.

———. *Ecclesia Crucis: The Church of the Cross.* Chicago: Chicago Community Renewal Society, 1980.

———. "Ecclesia Crucis: The Disciple Community and the Future of the Church in North America." In *Theology and the Practice of Responsibility: Essays on Dietrich Bonhoeffer*, edited by Wayne W. Floyd and Charles Marsh, 59–76. Valley Forge, PA: Trinity, 1994.

———. *The End of Christendom and the Future of Christianity.* Valley Forge, PA: Trinity, 1997; reprint, Eugene, OR: Wipf & Stock, 2002.

———. "Faith: Response in Relationship." *The Living Pulpit*, 2000, n.p.

———. "For and Against a Theology of Liberation." *ARC* 12/2 (1980), 39–55.

———. *The Future of the Church: Where Are We Headed?* Toronto: United Church, 1989.

———. *The Future of Religion in Canada.* (Booklet.) New Brunswick, NJ: Mount Allison University, 1988.

———. *God and Human Suffering: An Exercise in the Theology of the Cross.* Minneapolis: Augsburg, 1986.

———. *Has the Church a Future?* Philadelphia: Westminster, 1980.

———. *Hope against Hope: Towards an Indigenous Theology of the Cross.* Geneva: World Student Christian Federation, 1972.

———. "Hope from Old Sources for a New Century." In *Hope For the World: Mission in a Global Context*, edited by Walter Brueggemann, 13–23. Louisville: Westminster John Knox, 2001.

———. "Huron Memories." *Huron: For Alumni and Friends of Huron College*, Fall 2009, 20–22.

———. *Imaging God: Dominion as Stewardship.* Grand Rapids: Eerdmans, 1986.

———. "A Jewish Challenge to Post-Constantinian Christianity." N.d. Online: http://www.doubleclicked.net/ICJS/hall.html.

———. "Justice, Peace and the Integrity of Creation (JPIC): The Message and the Mission." *Ecumenical Review* 41/4 (1989) 492–500.

———. *Lighten Our Darkness: Toward an Indigenous Theology of the Cross.* Philadelphia: Westminster, 1976.

———. *Lighten Our Darkness: Towards an Indigenous Theology of the Cross.* Revised with foreword by David J. Monge. Lima, OH: Academic Renewal, 2001.

———. "Luther and the Peace Movement." *Ecumenist* 22/4 (1984) 58–61.

———. *The Messenger: Friendship, Faith and Finding One's Way.* Eugene, OR: Cascade, 2011.

———. *Mission as a Function of Stewardship.* (Booklet.) Toronto: United Church of Canada, 1980.

———. "On Being Church in English Montreal." *Ecumenist* 15/6 (1977) 85.

———. "On Being Church in Quebec Today." *ARC* 5/1 (1977) 8–10.

————. "On Contextuality in Christian Theology." *Toronto Journal of Theology* 1/1 (1985) 3–16.

————. "Our New Challenge: To Speak Hope from the Wilderness." *United Church Observer* 63/6 (2000) 22–24.

————. "Preaching to People with Cancer: The Eschatology of the Body." *Journal for Preachers* 29/2 (2006) 29–36.

————. *Professing the Faith: Christian Theology in a North American Context.* Minneapolis: Fortress, 1993.

————. *The Reality of the Gospel and the Unreality of the Churches.* Philadelphia: Westminster, 1975.

————. *Reinhold Niebuhr (1892–1971): A Century Appraisal.* Edited with Gary A. Gaudin. Atlanta: Scholars, 1994.

————. *Remembered Voices: Reclaiming the Legacy of "Neo-Orthodoxy."* Louisville: Westminster John Knox, 1998.

————. "The Significance of Grant's Cultural Analysis for Christian Theology in North America." In *George Grant in Process*, edited by Larry Schmidt, 120–29. Toronto: Anansi, 1978.

————. *The Steward: A Biblical Symbol Come of Age.* New York City: Friendship, 1982.

————. *The Steward: A Biblical Symbol Come of Age.* Rev. ed. Grand Rapids: Eerdmans, 1990.

————. "Stewardship as a Missional Discipline." *Journal for Preachers* 22/1 (1998) 19–27.

————. "A Theological Proposal for the Church's Response to its Context." *Currents in Theology and Mission* 22/6 (1995) 417–25.

————. "The Theology of Hope in an Officially Optimistic Society." *Religion in Life* 40/3 (1976) 376–90.

————. "Think, For the Night is Coming." *Living Pulpit* 5/3 (1996) 12–13.

————. "Thinking Biblically about the Trinity." *Living Pulpit* 8/2 (1999) 12–14.

————. *Thinking the Faith: Christian Theology in a North American Context.* Minneapolis: Fortress, 1989.

————. "Towards an Indigenous Theology of the Cross." *Interpretation* 30/3 (1976) 153–68.

————. "Trinitarian Thinking in Our Context." *Trinity Seminary Review* 25/1 (2004) 21–30.

————. "A View from the Edge of Empire: Prophetic Faith and the Crises of Our Time." *ARC* 20 (1992) 21–33.

————. *Waiting for Gospel: An Appeal to the Dispirited Remnants of Protestant Establishment.* Eugene, OR: Cascade, 2012.

————. "We Would See Jesus." *The Living Pulpit*, 2000, n.p.

————. *When You Pray: Thinking Your Way into God's World.* Valley Forge, PA: Judson, 1987.

————. *Why Christian? For Those on the Edge of Faith.* Minneapolis: Fortress, 1998.

————. *This World Must Not Be Abandoned.* (Booklet.) Toronto: Church World and Development Relief, 1981.

Hall, Douglas John, and Rhoda Palfrey Hall. "George Grant (1918–1988), A Tribute." *Grail* 5/2 (1989) 73–80.

Hall, Douglas John, and Rosemary Radford Reuther. *God and the Nations.* Minneapolis: Fortress, 1995.

Hanson, Philip J. "George Grant: A Negative Theologian on Technology." *Research on Technology and Philosophy* 1 (1987) 308–12.

Harries, Richard, editor. *Reinhold Niebuhr and the Issues of Our Time*. Grand Rapids: Eerdmans, 1986.

Hedges, Chris. "What if America Fails? A Metaphor for America." *The Walrus,* November 2012, 25–33.

Hegel, G. W. F. *The Philosophy of History*. Translated by J. Sibree. London: Colonial, 1900.

———. *The Phenomenology of Mind*. Translated by J. B. Baillie. New York: Harper & Row, 1967.

Heschel, Abraham. *The Prophets*. New York: Jewish Publication Society of America, 1962.

Heidegger, Martin. *Basic Writings*. Edited and translated by David F. Krell. 1977; San Francisco: Harper Collins, 1993.

———. *Nietzsche*. Translated by David F. Krell. 4 vols. San Francisco: Harper Collins, 1991.

Hoffman, Bengt R. *Luther and the Mystics*. Minneapolis: Augsburg, 1976.

Jüngel, Eberhard. *The Freedom of a Christian: Luther's Significance for Contemporary Theology*. Translated by R. A. Harrisville. Minneapolis: Augsburg, 1988.

———. *God as the Mystery of the World: On the Foundation of the Theology of the Crucified One in the Dispute between Theism and Atheism*. Translated by D. L. Guder. Grand Rapids: Eerdmans, 1983.

———. *Karl Barth: A Theological Legacy*. Translated by Garret E. Paul. Philadelphia: Westminster, 1986.

Käsemann, Ernst. "The Pauline Theology of the Cross." *Interpretation* 24/2 (1970) 151–77.

Kelsey, David H. "Method, Theological." *The Westminster Dictionary of Christian Theology*, edited by Alan Richardson and John Bowden, 363–68. Philadelphia: Westminster, 1983.

Kierkegaard, Søren. *Attack upon Christianity: 1854–1855*. Translated by Walter Lowrie. Princeton: Princeton University Press, 1968.

———. *The Present Age and of the Difference Between a Genius and an Apostle*. Translated by Alexander Dru with Introduction by Walter Kaufmann. New York: Harper & Row, 1962.

———. *Sickness Unto Death*. Translated by Walter Lowrie. Princeton: Princeton University Press, 1951.

Kroker, Arthur. *Technology and the Canadian Mind: Innis, McLuhan, Grant*. Montreal: New World Perspectives, 1984.

Lasch, Christopher. *The True and Only Heaven: Progress and Its Critics*. New York: Norton, 1990.

Lash, Nicholas. *A Matter of Hope: A Theologian's Reflections on the Thought of Karl Marx*. Notre Dame: University of Notre Dame Press, 1982.

Lewis, Alan E. *Between Cross and Resurrection: A Theology of Holy Saturday*. Grand Rapids: Eerdmans, 2001.

Lind, Christopher J. L. "An Invitation to Canadian Theology." *Toronto Journal of Theology* 1/1 (1985) 17–26.

Lindbeck, George A. *The Church in a Post-Liberal Age*. Edited by James J. Buckley. Grand Rapids: Eerdmans, 2002.

————. *The Nature of Doctrine: Religion and Theology in a Postliberal Age*. Philadelphia: Westminster, 1984.

Little, Janet P. *Simone Weil: Waiting on Truth*. Oxford: Berg, 1988.

Luther, Martin. *Disputation against Scholastic Theology*. Translated by Harold J. Grimm. In *Luther's Works*, edited by Harold J. Grimm, 31:3–16. St. Louis: Concordia, 1958.

————. *Explanations of the Ninety-Five Theses*. Translated by Carl W. Folkener. In *Luther's Works*, edited by Harold J. Grimm. 31:77–252. St. Louis: Concordia, 1958.

————. *Heidelberg Disputation*. Translated by Harold J. Grimm. In *Luther's Works* edited by Harold J. Grimm. 31:35–70. Saint Louis: Concordia, 1958.

————. *First Lectures on the Psalms 1–75*. Vol. 10 of *Luther's Works*. Edited by J. A. Bouman. Translated by Hilton C. Oswald. St. Louis: Concordia, 1974.

————. *First Lectures on the Psalms 76–126*. Vol. 11 of *Luther's Works*. St. Louis: Concordia, 1976.

————. *Lectures on Romans*. Vol. 25 of *Luther's Works*. Edited by Hilton C. Oswald. Translated by Walter G. Tillmanns and Jacob A. O. Preus. St. Louis: Concordia, 1958.

————. *Luther's Works*. Vol. 31, *Career of the Reformer I*. Edited by Harold J. Grimm and Helmut T. Lehmann. St. Louis: Concordia, 1958.

————. *Ninety-Five Theses*. Translated by C. M. Jacobs, revised by Harold J. Grimm. In *Luther's Works* edited by Harold J. Grimm. 31:17–34. St. Louis: Concordia, 1958.

Mandel, E. "George Grant: Language, Nation, the Silence of God." *Canadian Literature* 98 (1983) 10–30.

Mannermaa, Tuomo. *Two Kinds of Love: Martin Luther's Religious World*. Translated, edited, and introduced by Kirsi I. Stjerna, with afterword by Juhani Forsberg. Minneapolis: Fortress, 2010.

Marty, Martin. *Martin Luther*. New York: Viking, 2004.

McCarroll, Pam. "The Whole as Love: George Grant's Theological Vision." *Toronto Journal of Theology* 24/2 (2008) 183–95.

McGrath, Alister E. *Luther's Theology of the Cross: Martin Luther's Theological Breakthrough*. Oxford: Blackwell, 1985.

McKay, Stanley, and Janet Silman. "A First Nations Movement in a Canadian Church." In *The Reconciliation of Peoples: Challenge to the Churches*, 172–83. Edited by Gregory Baum and Harold Wells. Maryknoll, NY: Orbis, 1997.

McQuaig, Linda. *The Cult of Impotence*. Toronto: Penguin, 1998.

Moltmann, Jürgen. *The Church in the Power of the Spirit*. Translated by Margaret Kohl. Minneapolis: Fortress, 1993.

————. *The Crucified God: The Cross of Christ as the Foundation and Criticism of Christian Theology*. Translated by R. A. Wilson and J. Bowden. London: SCM, 1974.

————. *God in Creation: An Ecological Doctrine of Creation*. Translated by Margaret Kohl. Minneapolis: Fortress, 1993.

————. *The Theology of Hope*. Translated by Margaret Kohl. London: SCM, 1965.

————. *The Trinity and the Kingdom of God*. Translated by Margaret Kohl. Minneapolis: Fortress, 1981.

————. *The Way of Jesus Christ*. Translated by Margaret Kohl. Minneapolis: Fortress, 1993.

Mueller-Fahrenholz, Geiko. *The Kingdom and the Power: The Theology of Jürgen Moltmann*. Minneapolis: Fortress, 2001.

Niebuhr, Reinhold. *The Essential Reinhold Niebuhr: Selected Essays and Addresses.* New Haven: Yale University Press, 1986.

———. *Faith and History: A Comparison of Christian and Modern Views of History.* New York: Scribner's Sons, 1951.

———. *The Nature and Destiny of Man.* 2 vols. New York: Scribner's Sons, 1953.

Nietzsche, Friedrich. *Beyond Good and Evil.* Translated by R. J. Hollingdale. Middlesex: Penguin, 1973.

———. *The Genealogy of Morals.* Translated by W. Kaufmann and R. J. Hollingdale. New York: Vintage, 1969.

———. *The Portable Nietzsche.* Edited and translated by W. Kaufmann. New York: Penguin, 1954.

———. *Thus Spoke Zarathustra.* Translated by Marion Cowan. New York: Gateway, 1961.

———. *The Will to Power.* Translated by W. Kaufmann. New York: Vintage, 1968.

Oberman, Heiko A. *Luther: Man between God and the Devil.* Translated by E. Walliser-Schwarzbart. New York: Image, 1989.

Petrement, Simone. *Simone Weil: A Life.* Translated by R. Rosenthal. New York: Pantheon, 1976.

Plato. *The Collected Dialogues of Plato.* Edited by Edith Hamilton and Huntington Cairns. New York: Pantheon, 1961.

———. *The Great Dialogues of Plato.* Edited by Eric H. Warmington and Philip G. Rouse. Translated by W. H. D. Rouse. New York: New American Library, 1956.

———. *The Republic.* Translated by Frances MacDonald Cornford. London: Oxford University Press, 1941.

Polter, Julie. "The Politics of Fear." *Sojourners Magazine,* October 2004, 17–22.

Reimer, A. James. *Mennonites and Classical Theology.* Waterloo: Pandora, 2001.

Rigelhof, T. F. *George Grant: Redefining Canada.* Lanzville, BC: XYZ, 2001.

Rohr, Richard. "Fear Itself." *Sojourners Magazine,* October 2004, 13–17.

Schmidt, Larry. *George Grant in Process: Essays and Conversations.* Toronto: Anansi, 1978.

———. "In Defense of George Grant." *Grail* 7/2 (1991) 10–17.

Schweitzer, Don, and Derek Simon. *Intersecting Voices: Critical Theologies in a Land of Diversity.* Ottawa: Novalis, 2004.

Scott, Graham, editor. *More Than Survival: Viewpoints toward a Theology of Nation.* Toronto: Canec, 1980.

Sherrard, Philip. *The Greek East and the Latin West: A Study in the Christian Tradition.* London: Oxford University Press, 1959.

Smillie, Benjamin G. *Political Theology in the Canadian Context.* Waterloo: Wilfred Laurier University Press, 1977.

Smith, James K. A., and James Olthius, editors. *Radical Orthodoxy and the Reformed Tradition: Creation, Covenant, and Participation.* Grand Rapids: Baker Academic, 2005.

Sobrino, John. *Christology at the Crossroads: A Latin American Approach.* Translated by John Drury. Maryknoll, NY: Orbis, 1978.

Springsted, Eric. *Christus Mediator: Platonic Mediation in the Thought of Simone Weil.* American Academy of Religion. Atlanta: Scholars, 1983.

Thompson, Deanna. *Crossing the Divide: Luther, Feminism, and the Cross.* Minneapolis: Fortress, 2004.

Tillich, Paul. *The Courage to Be*. New Haven: Yale University Press, 1952.

———. *The Dynamics of Faith*. New York: Harper & Row, 1957.

———. *A History of Christian Thought: From Its Judaic and Hellenistic Origins to Existentialism*. New York: Simon & Schuster, 1967.

———. *The Protestant Era*. Translated by James Luther Adams. Chicago: University of Chicago Press, 1948.

———. *Systematic Theology*. Vol. 1. Translated by G. T. Thomson. Chicago: University of Chicago Press, 1951.

———. *Theology of Culture*. Edited by Robert C. Kimball. New York: Oxford University Press, 1959.

Umar Usuf K., ed. *George Grant and the Future of Canada*. Calgary: University of Calgary Press, 1992.

Vandezande, Gerald, editor. *Justice Not Just Us: Faith Perspectives and National Priorities*. Toronto: Public Justice Resource Centre, 1999.

Vanier, Jean. *Eruption to Hope*. Toronto: Griffin House, 1971.

Von Loewenich, Walther. *Luther's Theology of the Cross*. Translated by Herbert J. A. Bouman. Minneapolis: Augsburg, 1976.

Weil, Simone. *Formative Writings. 1929–1941*. Edited and translated by Dorothy Tuck McFarland and Willhelmina Van Ness. London: Routledge, 1987.

———. *Gateway to God*. Edited by David Raper. Glasgow: Collins & Sons, 1974.

———. *Gravity & Grace*. Translated by Emma Crauford. London: Routledge, 1952.

———. *Intimations of Christianity among the Ancient Greeks*. 1957; Reprint, London: Ark, 1987.

———. *Lectures on Philosophy*. Translated by Hugh Price. Introduced by Hugh Winch. Cambridge: Cambridge University Press, 1978.

———. *The Need for Roots*. London: Rutledge, 1952.

———. *The Notebooks of Simone Weil*. Translated by Arthur Wills. 2 vols. London: Routledge, 1956.

———. *On Science, Necessity and the Love of God*. Translated and edited by Richard Rees. London: Oxford University Press, 1968.

———. *Oppression and Liberty*. Translated by Arthur Willis. London: Routledge, 1958.

———. *Seventy Letters*. Translated by Richard Rees. London: Oxford University Press, 1965.

———. *Waiting For God*. Translated by Emma Crauford. New York: Putnam's Sons, 1951.

Wells, Harold. *The Christic Centre: Life-Giving and Liberating*. Maryknoll, NY: Orbis, 2004.

———. "The Theology of the Cross and the Theologies of Liberation." *Toronto Journal of Theology* 17/1 (2001) 146–66.

Wengert, Timothy J. "Peace, Peace . . . Cross, Cross: Reflections on How Martin Luther Relates the Theology of the Cross to Suffering." *Theology Today* 59/2 (2002) 190–205.

Whillier, Wayne, editor. *Two Theological Languages by George Grant and Other Essays in Honour of His Work*. Queenston: Mellen, 1990.

Wiesel, Elie. *Night*. New York: Discus, 1958.

Williams, Delores. *Sisters in the Wilderness: The Challenge of Womanist God-Talk*. Maryknoll, NY: Orbis, 1993.